John Hall, George Stuart

The American Evangelists

John Hall, George Stuart

The American Evangelists

ISBN/EAN: 9783741123146

Manufactured in Europe, USA, Canada, Australia, Japa

Cover: Foto ©Lupo / pixelio.de

Manufactured and distributed by brebook publishing software (www.brebook.com)

John Hall, George Stuart

The American Evangelists

THE
AMERICAN EVANGELISTS,

D. L. MOODY
AND
IRA D. SANKEY,

IN GREAT BRITAIN AND IRELAND.

BY

JOHN HALL, D.D., NEW YORK,

AND

GEORGE H. STUART, PHILADELPHIA.

NEW YORK:
DODD & MEAD, PUBLISHERS,
762 BROADWAY.

PREFATORY NOTE.

THAT the present religious movement in Great Britain, which it has pleased God to further through the American evangelists, is entitled to adequate and permanent record in book-form on this continent, no one can doubt, to whom its extent and character are known.

If any apology is needed for the editors in undertaking this work, it will be found in their personal knowledge of Messrs. Moody and Sankey, deep interest in the scenes of their Christian labors, and acquaintance with the "brethren beloved" who have stood by them, co-operated in their efforts, and borne cheerful testimony to the moral and spiritual results.

In the reports, from whence the following pages have been compiled and arranged, there is much descriptive eulogy of the men whom God has used for spreading His truth. This has been uniformly omitted, in the firm belief that Christian readers, like the evangelists themselves, desire that man should be of little account, and that God should be all in all.

The methods of operation are detailed without the

expression of opinion, favorable or unfavorable. Many forms of Christian work are determined by Christian wisdom, and the conditions of society; and men's views of plans are largely influenced by habits of thought, education, and general church-life. On these topics, and on the place and work of the evangelist our readers are commonly as competent to form a judgment as are the editors; and our care has been to give a clear, colorless, and continuous view of the facts. We do not pronounce, and we do not predict.

The main considerations, we venture to think, are that substantial truth is being held forth, and that the Spirit of God is blessing it, as evidenced by spiritual results. So far as it appears, with the exception of an occasional word respecting the coming of our Lord, there has been no expression of view out of harmony with the truths most surely believed among us; as indeed may be inferred from the cordial approval given to Mr. Moody's teaching by University and Theological Professors in Edinburgh, Glasgow, and Aberdeen; in Trinity College, Dublin, and in Belfast; by more than one Bishop of the Irish Church, and by the most trusted ministers of all evangelical denominations in England, Scotland, and Ireland.

PREFATORY NOTE.

It has always been admitted that the best evidence of facts is their uncontradicted publication by reliable men, at the time and place of occurrence. This evidence we have sought to present, availing ourselves of the published communications of Christian men, such as Drs. Arnot and Blaikie of Edinburgh, Kirkpatrick of Dublin, Rev. R. W. Dale of Manchester, C. H. Spurgeon of London, Dr. Lowe of Liverpool, Lord Radstock, Reginald Radcliffe Esquire, and others in whom the Churches of Christ, on both sides of the Atlantic, justly repose confidence.

Partly from the desire to condense, and partly from the effort to present the facts as they have been reported by eye-witnesses, the narrative is rapid in movement, and sometimes abrupt in its transitions. Quotation-marks might have been employed in places where they do not appear, because, though the substance of communications is given, there is so much necessary abbreviation that it would hardly be just to the writers to make them responsible for the more curt phraseology we have found necessary in a volume of the extent which we desired to produce.

The order followed is of the simplest kind: Who are these men? How did they come to the front, in

America? How did they enter Great Britain? What has been their progress? What did they teach? What are the results? These questions we have sought to answer; and as to the vital matter, the truths set forth, we give several of Mr. Moody's addresses, as condensed in various journals, to speak for themselves. They occupy over sixty pages of this book, and give to it a peculiar interest.

One striking and important feature of Mr. Moody's operations we feel it right to emphasize—the co-operation of the ministers uniformly sought and secured. So rigid is his rule on this point that he declined a visit to Sheffield, until substantial unity was secured in an invitation from the evangelical ministers of the town. On the same principle, meetings are not held at the usual hours of divine service, unless in the judgment of the local ministers* they are desirable. He has always felt that it is mischievous in the highest degree for occasional laborers, however admirable and useful to weaken the hands of the stated ministry, on whose efforts the systematic and permanent instruction of

---

* It may be proper to say, that in England, by the clergy is understood the ministry of the Episcopal Church. This will explain the apparent solecism, "The clergy, and ministers."

the people must, under God, depend. To this wise policy—the same pursued by Nettleton in this country—has been due in a large degree the blessed unity of action, and may we not add, the large spiritual success, vouchsafed. If anything is fitted to mar a spiritual work, it is surely vituperation of its pledged friends and supporters.

That opposition to this movement has appeared is known to all, though its amount has been far below what might have been expected. It has come from three quarters: those to whom all spiritual religion is fanaticism; those who can only conceive of true work within their own ecclesiastical lines; and those who have either looked at it from a distance, or formed their estimate of it from unfavorable critics. The first class learns nothing; the second learns slowly; and to the third good men can only say, "Come and see."

That the interest shown in mass-meetings and by eager crowds where the evangelists have been present should continue, is not to be expected in the nature of things. Only the most superficial will consider the results on this account evanescent. Sunshine, dews, and rains that water the earth, are evanescent in the same sense. The mightiest movements advance, often enough, as does the tide; each successive wave, though refluent in a degree, rising higher on the beach than did its predecessor. This wave, whose progress we are watching, has carried light and love where certainly they had not gone in our time: and, as the very report of what God does in one region has often raised inquiry, hope, and effort in another, we are not without the expectation that the record of progress in our mother-countries may stimulate zeal and effort on this continent, where the children enjoy a no less free Christian life, and where thought and feeling travel no less rapidly.

Humbly beseeching Almighty God, the Father of our Lord Jesus Christ, whose Gospel we count the means in the hands of the Holy Ghost of all true life and progress, to further His work by this lowly instrumentality, we respectfully dedicate this volume to the ministers of the Gospel, to the Sabbath-school teachers, to earnest laborers with tongue, and pen, and purse, who pray and toil that this fair America may be as the garden of the Lord, and her people a "righteous nation that keepeth the truth."

THE EDITORS.

The American Evangelists.

CHAPTER I.

THE INSTRUMENTS EMPLOYED.

MESSRS. MOODY AND SANKEY.*

Mr. D. L. Moody was born in the year 1837 in one of the New England States, in the district which was the scene of the great awakening, under Jonathan Edwards, about a hundred years before. He was brought up a Unitarian, and had not even heard the gospel of the grace of God till he was about seventeen years of age. Going, about that time, to Boston, to be trained for business in the establishment of an uncle, he one day went into the church of the late Dr. Kirk. There, for the first time, he listened to an evangelical sermon. It had the effect of making him uncomfortable, and he resolved not to go back. He felt

---

* Abridged from *The British Evangelist*, edited by Rev. W. Reid M. A., and Rev. W. P. Mackay, M. A

that his heart had been laid bare, and he wondered who had told the preacher about him. Something, however, induced him to go back next Sunday, and the impression was renewed. A Sunday-school teacher, in whose class he had been, having come to see him and ask for him at his place of business, he opened up his mind to him, and he was enabled to enter into peace and joy in believing.

Not very long after this Mr. Moody left Boston and proceeded to Chicago, where he entered into business for himself. Being full of the desire to be useful, he went into a Sunday-school, and asked the superintendent if he would give him a class. In this school there were twelve teachers and sixteen pupils; and the answer to his application was that if he could gather a class for himself he would be allowed to teach them. Mr. Moody went out to the streets and, by personal application, succeeded in bringing in a score of boys. He enjoyed so much the work of bringing in recruits, that instead of teaching the class himself, he handed it over to another teacher, and so on until he had filled the school. Then he began to entertain the notion of having a school of his own. He went to work in a neglected part of the city, where

Roman Catholics and Germans abounded. Mr. Moody saw that, to succeed in such a population, a school must be exceedingly lively and attractive, and as he observed that the Germans made constant use of music in their meetings, he was led to consider whether music might not be employed somewhat prominently in the service of Christ. Not being himself a singer, he got a friend who could sing to help him, and for the first few evenings the time was spent between singing hymns and telling stories to the children, so as to awaken their interest and induce them to return. A hold having in this way been established, the school was divided into classes, and conducted in the usual way.

This school became the basis of wider operations. After a time a lively interest in divine things began to appear among the children. This led to the holding of meetings every night, and to the offering of prayers and delivery of addresses suitable to the circumstances of the children. These meetings began to be attended also by the parents, some of whom shared the blessing. Some of those young persons who were converted at this time remain to the present day the most valuable and active coadjutors in the work with which Mr. Moody is associated in Chicago. In most cases neither the children nor their parents had hitherto been connected with any Christian Church. Mr. Moody began to find himself constrained to supply them with spiritual food. At first he encouraged them to connect themselves with other congregations. But it was found that in these they were next to lost or swallowed up; they felt themselves strangers, sometimes unwelcome strangers, while they lost all the benefit of neighborhood, mutual interest, and combination in the worship of God. Gradually, therefore, Mr. Moody felt shut up to taking charge of them, and supplying them with Christian instruction. Both school and church continued to increase, the school amounting to about a thousand, and suitable buildings were erected through the liberality of friends. Mr. Moody had by this time given up business, so that he might be free to give his whole time and attention to the work. As he felt himself called by the Lord to this step, he resolved to decline all salary or allowance from any quarter, and trust for his maintenance solely to what it might be put into the hearts of God's people to contribute. Being quite destitute of private means, this resolution showed that his faith in a divine call to give himself to Christian work was capable of bearing a great strain. At the same time, while adopting this course for himself, he has never pressed it upon others, unless they should clearly see it to be their duty. And while believing himself called to a kind of supplementary work in the ministry, he is very far from prescribing the same *rôle* to others. On the contrary, he is the steady friend of a regular ministry, being fully persuaded that in "ordaining elders in every city," the apostles meant to set up the permanent platform of the Christian Church.

Mr. Moody had acquired a position of much influence in the United States in connection with Sunday-school and mission work, when the war broke out between North and South. This led to a new turn being given to his labors. There was a large camp in the neighborhood of Chicago, to which he gave much attention, going there night after night and striving to bring the soldiers under the influence of Divine Grace. When the Christian Commission was organized he was president of the Executive branch for Chicago, and nine different times he went to one or other of the scenes of warfare, remaining some weeks and working with all his might. These services with the army were of no little use, not only in producing direct fruit, but also in developing that prompt and urgent method of dealing with men, which is still so conspicuous a feature of his mode of address. With wounded men, hovering between life and death, or with men in march, resting for an evening in some place which they were to leave to-morrow, it was plainly, so far at least as he was concerned, the alternative of "now or never;" and as he could not allow himself or allow them to be satisfied with the "never," he bent his whole energies to the "now."

Mr. Moody's labors in the army were often much blessed. Of all his campaigns of this kind there was none on which he looked back with more pleasure than that in the State of Tennessee, in connection with troops under the command of General Howard. That General being in the fullest sympathy with Mr. Moody, their work together was very earnest and much blessed.

The war being ended, Mr. Moody had more time to develop his work in Chicago. To set others to work in the vineyard had long been one of his chief aims, and by means of the Young Men's Christian

Association, in which he took a great interest, he was highly successful. The hall of the association became one of the stated scenes of his own labors. The association was very unfortunate in the matter of fires—its first building having been burnt down in 1867, and its second in the great fire of Chicago, in 1871. Mr. Moody was accustomed to preach to his own people in the morning, to superintend a Sunday-school of about a thousand in the afternoon, and to preach again in the evening in the hall of the Young Men's Association.

In October, 1871, occurred the terrible fire which destroyed a great part of Chicago. Mr. Moody and his wife and two children were roused in the middle of the night to find the fierce fire approaching their dwelling, and, leaving the house and household gear to their fate (all the property he possessed) had to hurry along to seek shelter in the houses of friends.

In one month after the fire a temporary erection for mission purposes was completed! No small energy must have been required to accomplish this, amid the confusion, the bustle, and the variety of things that had to be attended to. But reared the wooden building was, and it has served the purpose of church and school till now, when a new and substantial building is sufficiently advanced to allow the basement story to be used for public services.

It was shortly before the fire that Mr. Sankey began to work along with Mr. Moody, who, happening on some public occasion to sit near him, was attracted by his beautiful voice. The thought struck him that Mr. Sankey would be a valuable assistant to him in many ways—in the Sunday-school, in the church, and in the training of the Young Men's Christian Association. He accordingly entered into an engagement with him to help him in his work by conducting "The Service of Song." Mr. Moody has always been eager to secure music—and especially good music—as an aid in preaching the Gospel.

When things had settled down after the Chicago fire, Mr. Moody began to think of permanent premises for his school and church. A suitable site was secured, and it was resolved to proceed with the erection of a large and commodious building, which, besides accommodation for the schools, will have a hall or church, containing sittings for 2,500. A little while ago it seemed likely that the whole sum necessary would be provided, but the general collapse in business deprived the enterprise of some of the expected contributions.

The immediate cause of his visit to Great Britain was an invitation by two gentlemen—Mr. Pennefather of London, and Mr. Bainbridge of Newcastle. It was a singular circumstance that both these gentlemen died before or about the time of his arrival. In regard to the spiritual superintendence of the congregation, it is supplied in a large measure by members of the flock, with occasional help from other pastors. Mr. Moody trains his people to be independent in fact, as they are Independent in name. It may be stated, however, that in one respect the congregation is Presbyterian; it is governed by a session, not by the whole membership.

MR. SANKEY.

Mr. Ira D. Sankey was born at Edinburg, in the State of Pennsylvania, U. S., in the year 1840. He possessed the advantage of pious parents, so that, like Timothy, "from a child he knew the Holy Scriptures, which are able to make us wise unto salvation," and in his case the truth of the text was exemplified, "Train up a child in the way he should go, and when he is old he will not depart from it." Although so religiously educated, it was not until the year 1856 that he experienced that saving change of heart, the *new birth*, which can alone constitute us members of Christ. In his earlier years he had not been without the strivings of the Holy Spirit, which at such times as the death of relatives, the conversion of companions, or at seasons of religious revivals, often visit the hearts of the unconverted.

The circumstances under which he was brought to Christ were as follows :—With some young companions he attended a series of special meetings held in a little country chapel, three miles from his father's home, and while sitting in a state of heedlessness and levity, the Spirit of God put it into the heart of an old elder of the church to go and speak to him about his soul. Evening after evening the old man would search him out after the sermon, and plead with him to give his heart and consecrate his life to Jesus. Fear of what his young associates would say kept him long from coming to the Cross of Christ. But at last, after a struggle, lasting seven days, the experienced elder led him to Jesus.

He early displayed a taste for sacred music, and took an active part, after his conversion, in promoting the efficient training of Sunday-school children in the singing of hymns, and as soon as he became a Church member, he was invited to conduct the service of praise. In this department of Christian usefulness, together with superintending the Sabbath-school of his Church, and working in the Young Men's Christian Associations of his State, he developed his present power of rendering sacred song. Before meeting Mr. Moody, much of his time was devoted to conducting "Evenings of Sacred Song," and leading the singing at large Sunday-School Institutes, and Christian Conventions.

It was at a National Convention of Young Men's Christian Associations in Indianapolis, Indiana, that Mr. Moody was struck by his voice; and, as, on further acquaintance, they found each other's views and desires in regard to energetic mission work identical in aim and spirit, they agreed to labor unitedly in evangelistic services.

For two or three years they worked together in conducting meetings at Chicago, as their headquarters, besides occasionally visiting other towns and cities, such as Philadelphia, Pittsburg, and Springfield.

Mr. Sankey is fully persuaded that his mission is to stimulate and encourage the service of singing in religious worship. He is a strong advocate of good hearty congregational singing; and approves of a large *Christian Choir* to lead, but not to monopolize the service of praise.

In regard to the solo singing, Mr. Sankey, in singing alone, does not propose to substitute this for worship or praise, any more than the minister does when he preaches a sermon. But his aim is to speak to men in hymns and "Spiritual songs," admonishing them that Jesus of Nazareth is passing by.

The melodeon and songs of Mr. Sankey have played an important part in the revival. As a means of awakening the people, they have been most effectual. Many who would not have gone to hear the preacher, have been drawn into meetings by reports of the sweet singing; and nothing can exceed the impression produced, after some stirring address by Mr. Moody, by the sweet voice and clear enunciation of Mr. Sankey taking up and enforcing the same theme in song.

CHAPTER II.

INTRODUCTION TO ENGLAND.

IN YORK.

On Sunday morning, June 22d, 1873, Mr. Moody preached in Salem Congregational Chapel to Christian workers; in the afternoon, in the Corn Exchange, to about one thousand persons; and in the evening in Wesley Chapel. Many were impressed and some brought to trust in the Saviour. Every evening the following week, Bible lectures were delivered in various chapels, each service appearing to awaken souls, but especially to quicken believers.

On Sabbath-day, June 29th, Mr. Moody preached in two other chapels, and also twice in the Corn Exchange to audiences numbering about one thousand each. Every week-evening service was preceded by a service of song by Mr. Sankey. Prayer-meetings were held every noon at the rooms of the Young Men's Christian Association, and many there offered themselves and others for the prayers of God's people.

The congregations were from the first increasingly large: all denominations opened their chapels and gave their presence and help, various of the clergy also heartily bidding them "God speed." *

From York they proceeded, during the month of July, to Sunderland, and commenced their labors in the Victoria Hall, a place capable of holding about three thousand souls. The evening meeting was a large one, and very successful.

At the close of the meeting, a large number adjourned to Bethesda Chapel (Rev. A. A. Rees); much prayer was offered up, and many anxious souls were pointed to Jesus, several finding everlasting life through His precious blood. The meetings continued every night for a week, and at all the meetings souls were awakened, and some at all the meetings found peace.

On Sunday (July 27), they were again at the Victoria Hall. In the evening the attendance was enormous, every seat being occupied, and the aisle and the lobbies crowded; upwards of three thousand souls were present. The audience was very deeply impressed. An adjournment was then made (as be-

---
* Reported by Geo. Bennett, Sec. York Y. M. C. A.

fore) to Bethesda Chapel. Here a very touching scene occurred. A young man, who had long backslidden, came up the aisle to his father and mother, who are godly persons. He first put his arms round his father's neck, and kissed him, asking his forgiveness with many tears; then kissing his mother, and asking her forgiveness; afterwards kissing his younger brother. Several other backsliders returned to the Lord, giving hope that their repentance is truly the Lord's work.

Newcastle, built, as its name implies, on the river Tyne, is a thriving, populous town, in which the coal and iron give employment to great multitudes of operatives. It was now approached.

The minister of the John Knox Presbyterian Church, in Newcastle-on-Tyne, among many others, placed his church-building at the disposal of the Evangelists. Good meetings had been held in the Baptist Church edifice here, Mr. Skerry co-operating heartily. We shall allow the minister of the John Knox church to give his impressions of the work up to 9th September, 1873:

"For some time before the meeting commenced, the church was densely crowded in every part, including aisles, stairs, and side rooms, with persons of all sects, from town and country, while many were obliged to go away who could not obtain admittance. I have not witnessed such proofs of the Holy Spirit's saving power for several years. Mr. Sankey was at North Shields, where an interest in spiritual things has been awakened in the hearts of many. Mr. Moody preached. The pure, full-orbed truths of God's Word came in close and certain succession from his lips, and fell with telling power on the hearts of the throng. The impression produced was too deep and true to show itself in violent ebullitions of feeling. The dense mass seemed at every point the subject of intense solemnity and awe.

"A large mass of people waited for the second meeting, and seemed quite unwilling to go away. Many convicted ones were prevailed on afterwards to retire to the vestry, where Christian friends were in readiness to point them to the Lamb of God who taketh away the sin of the world; others received instruction in the pews of the church. All that were addressed personally retired, so far as I could see, rejoicing in God their Saviour.

" This town has not been blessed in the same manner since I knew it, and for many years before that, according to the testimony of older inhabitants who are quite competent to judge. What amount of fruit will remain we must wait to see, but for present things God's people have very abundant reason to thank God and to take courage."

Special addresses to Christians, a sermon in the "Friends' meeting-house," at the request of members who had been deeply impressed; meetings at Gateshead for those whose salvation was a matter of deep concern to their relatives; addresses to the factory workmen in the Tyne Theatre at their own request, formed some of the means employed in this great northern center, and on which the Divine blessing richly rested.

As many as thirty-four meetings were arranged for one week, and the interest in the noon-prayer meeting was unprecedented.

Let the following incident, reported by Mr. Henry Moorhouse, illustrate the feeling among the poor and needy:

A gentleman passing down a street in Gateshead heard some one knocking at the window of a cottage. He stopped and a respectable woman came to the door, and said : " Come in ! " He said he could not then, as he was going to a meeting.

"Oh, sir, for God's sake come in, and tell me something about Jesus, for I am wretched."

"What is the matter?" said my friend.

She said, "I am lost; oh tell me what I must do to be saved. I have been standing at my window all the day to see if a Christian would come along, and if it had only been a beggar who loved the Saviour, I would have called him in."

She had been at a meeting a week before, and had been in a miserable state ever since. A Christian lady called to see her and told her about the love of Jesus. She trusted, and was saved. "I saw her to-day," said the speaker, "as happy and bright as possible."

At so early a date as October, 1873, Mr. Moody had faith enough to lead him to say to the daily prayer-meeting, at which nearly nine hundred Christians of all ranks were present, that they were on the eve of a great work, which might cover Britain, and make itself felt in America. God would bless them, were they willing to let His Spirit work through them, and to place their influence wholly at His disposal. The daily prayer-meeting must be maintained and cherished if directly evangelistic efforts are to be wisely conducted, and be accompanied with a stream of true life. To his own soul the daily prayer-meetings in America had been a source of unspeakable blessing—nay, had done more to refresh and fit him for evangelistic enterprise than all other means of grace put together. The prayer-meetings in his own city had kept his soul on edge from the date of its commencement, fifteen years ago, to the present time. "Why," said our friend, "may the fire not burn as long as I live? When this revival spirit dies, may I die with it!"

The extent of this work around Newcastle is thus described by the Rev. Mr. Skerry, minister of one of the Baptist churches, already mentioned.

"Thus it will be seen that, from the common center of Newcastle, which may almost be regarded as the base of Messrs. Moody and Sankey's spiritual operations, there has spread throughout the neighboring towns and villages this powerful spirit of earnestness, and longing for the glory of God to be seen in the quickening of Christian people and the salvation of sinners—a spirit which we trust will grow to more and more fully developed dimensions, until the whole of Tyneside, with its vast industry, and the whole of the north of England, with its sin and suffering, and with its deep and widespread need, shall have come beneath the reviving touch of the Spirit of God.

"Truly God has been good unto Israel, and we render to Him all praise and thanksgiving for sending to us, by the hands of our honored American brethren, this blessing from on high. For these brethren and their work we also pray most heartily. Wherever their feet may turn, we beseech the God of grace to go before them, and prepare their way, inclining the hearts of Christian workers to sympathize with and help them with their self-imposed and arduous though glorious task, so that in many a town and district the work of the Lord may prosper abundantly, and many precious souls may be won for the dear Lord and Master."

In the might of such blessing as these prayers bring down, the brethren proceeded, after two months of earnest and fruitful work, on which they had entered with little introduction, to other fields, such as Bishop Auckland.

There all the non-conformist ministers and their people had devoted a week to prayer for the blessing of God, on their visit. The Rev. Thomas Boyd, Presbyterian minister of the place, after describing the meetings in the Wesleyan Chapel, says, after the evangelists had gone:

"Such has been the number of cases, and such many of the parties, that had it been told to any Christian friend a fortnight ago, he would not have believed it. Even with all this before us, so wonderful is it, that we almost feel as if we dreamt. God's Spirit still works powerfully. Every night souls are aroused, and, under the guidance of Christian friends, led to Jesus."

At Stockton-on-Tees, in which the early part of November was spent, the result is thus described by an intelligent observer on the spot; and once for all we call attention to the union of prayer and Catholic feeling before and in the work:

"This work has been very great; and in examining, for our own future guidance and the guidance of others, into the apparent causes of success, we are struck with the following: First, *the preparation of united, believing prayer*. Mr. Moody said, that on coming into the first meeting, he and Mr. Sankey felt that they were amongst a praying people; and to this and the next cause, viz. : *the united action of the ministers of the town,* he mainly attributed the fact, that in no place which they had visited had they witnessed such evident results in so short a time. It was very delightful to see, at each of the services, eight or ten of these devoted pastors, most of them in the vigor of young manhood, strong-souled, intelligent men, representing various shades of denominational belief, but merging all differences in mutual affection, and the common desire to aid in the glorious work; and many hearts were constrained by the sight to give thanks for such a ministry in Stockton. Another very important feature was the *absence of noise* in the meetings. The experience of the past few days will, we think, have convinced them that the best and most successful prayer-meetings ever held in Stockton have been the quietest, reminding us of the old lady's description, 'God Almighty was so near that nobody had to shout to Him.'"

The Convention, in some degree an American institution, has been introduced into Great Britain, the first of any moment in connection with this movement having been held at Newcastle-on-Tyne, on Wednesday, November 12th, 1873. The topics discussed were of immediate interest, such as:

EFFECTIVE MEETINGS.

How to reach the Masses, How to Conduct Prayer-meetings, How to Conduct After-meetings, How to Secure the Young for Christ, What are the Hinderances to the Lord's Work?

Fifteen minutes were allowed for the introducer of each subject, and to other speakers five minutes each, Mr. Moody keeping time by means of a small table-bell.

On prayer-meetings the Rev. Mr. Haigh said: "Special objects should be stated, with appropriate Scripture promises, and special requests ought to be sent in to the president. On Sunday evenings the one subject ought to be the salvation of souls. Prayer should generally be short. A woman once said to a man who was circumlocuting in prayer, 'Ax Him summat, man!' The best means of putting down a man who prays too long is to speak to him privately. In all meetings there ought to be moments of silent prayer. Singing in a meeting ought to be subordinate to prayer, and partake of a petitionary character. Mr. Spurgeon had said, 'The prayer-meeting stood in the same relation to the church as the engine did to the factory. If it decline, all our efforts will be abortive.'"

Mr. Moody gave a few words of advice. Get the people close together. Bury all stiffness. When the leader comes in with formal dignity, and is very stiff, no one can pray. There should be good ventilation. A change is good; a word of talk is good.

The Rev. W. R. Skerry recommended young people's prayer-meetings, and in reference to prayers of excessive length, said: " As regards long prayers, a man once said to a person who prayed very long—and it is sometimes true—' Brother, if you prayed more at home, you would have less to say when you come here.' "

Nowhere in England can there be found a more practical, stolid, and unromantic people than the men of Northumberland and Yorkshire. The judgment they formed of the leader at these meetings is concisely put:

" Mr. Moody's tact in conducting is marvelous. Common sense stamps all his earnestness and all his plans, and this wins in a remarkable manner the confidence of all who come in contact with him. Whatever else may be said of him, no one can call him a fanatic; and this gives to his steady, invincible, untiring self-sacrifice such irresistible power. By bodily vigor, and mental and spiritual endowments, he seems to be peculiarly a vessel unto honor meet for the Master's use."

The border-town of Carlisle is next approached. The evangelists are nearing Scotland. The place where, in former days, Englishman and Scotsman used to meet in desperate feud, becomes the scene of victories of another kind. The truth is the weapon, and the Victor is Jesus Christ. This none would more readily own than the instruments He employed.

Carlisle was reached on Saturday, 15th November (1873), and the following week spent there. All denominations were represented by their ministers. Let a local laborer report the result, as he follows the American brethren, with a prayer, to Edinburgh:

"This is the Lord's doing: it is marvelous in our eyes. As in other places, the meetings have been crowded to excess; the United Presbyterian Church, of which Mr. Christie is the pastor, proved altogether inadequate to accommodate the throngs, and the large Wesleyan Chapel close at hand was also thrown open, both buildings being completely filled. The power of God was present in a most marked degree; the solemn and magnificent songs, seeming now to bring Jesus of Nazareth right down into the streets of our own city, or, again, to take us right up to the gates of heaven, prepared the way for the word of life from the lips of Mr. Moody; that word was with power, and many were the anxious souls pressing forward to know the way of life. Jesus has become precious to many; souls have been born of God, and tears of contrition have given place to tears of joy.

"This much as to the blessing bestowed on the unconverted; but what shall be said as to that which has rested upon the Christians? It has been a time of drawing together such as we have not known anything of before. Ministers of the different denominations have thrown themselves heart and soul into the work, and the close of the week finds us recognizing, not in theory but in fact, that we are all one in Christ Jesus, and banded together, that by our union in Him we may honor His blessed name."

So the American strangers had their way opened up in England, and the report under God prepared the people of Scotland to hope and expect great things.

CHAPTER III.

EDINBURGH.

The Rev. John Kelman, of Free St. John's Church, Leith, was induced to visit Newcastle, and became so convinced of the reality and extent of the work of grace there, that, on his return home, he largely spread the good tidings among his brethren in the ministry, and devoted Christian laymen. An earnest invitation was given to Messrs. Moody and Sankey to visit Edinburgh and Leith, which was accepted.

This led to the proposal of a conference of those gentlemen interested in the anticipated visit of the American brethren to Edinburgh. A meeting was accordingly held in the Craigie Hall, at which a number of leading ministers and Christian laymen assembled, and gave decided and full expression of their opinion of the great importance of the proposed services; and thus practically gave a cordial and earnest anticipatory welcome to the American brethren.

Following up the proceedings of this conference,

a prayer meeting was held in the Craigie Hall every Monday, and, as the time approached for the expected visit, it was transferred to the Upper Queen Street Hall, and held daily at 3 P. M. These meetings were characterized by the remarkable fervor, unction, and faith of the supplications poured forth from hearts intensely earnest for the bestowal of the blessing desired. The brief hour of each meeting was felt to be a hallowed season, and from what was experienced at these meetings, a strong impression was formed that a great blessing was about to descend upon Edinburgh.

On Saturday, the 22d of November, 1873, Messrs. Moody and Sankey arrived in Edinburgh. On the evening of the following day (Sabbath), a meeting was held in the Music Hall for the purpose of hearing Mr. Moody preach, and Mr. Sankey sing, the gospel. The large hall, capable of holding over two thousand persons, was densely crowded, and thousands could not gain admission. Various city ministers and laymen took part in the exercises through which were interspersed Mr. Sankey's sacred songs, conducting the entire services of the meeting with much unction and power. This introductory meeting con cluded the evening services, there being no after meeting for inquirers held on this occasion. Mr. Moody was hoarse and sick; but the meeting was well sustained by ministers and laymen, and by Mr. Sankey's singing.

Next day, the daily prayer-meeting was transferred from the Upper Queen Street Hall to the Lower, which is capable of containing about twelve hundred people, and the hour was changed to twelve o'clock, noon. Messrs. Moody and Sankey were accompanied to the platform by the leading ministers and laymen, several of whom aided in conducting the services. This was the commencement of the noon-day prayer meeting, which, as will be shown in the sequel, has assumed such large proportions, and which has been so fraught with richest blessing.

In the evening, meetings were commenced in the Barclay Church (Rev. Mr. Wilson's) at seven o'clock, by Messrs. Moody and Sankey. The latter accompanied his sacred gospel songs with the American organ, which in no respect prevented the distinct hearing of the gospel message, so strikingly communicated with clear and perfect articulation, to the thousand listening ears.

At the conclusion of the first meeting, a second was held for special prayer, and a large congregation remained in their seats. During this time and afterwards, anxious inquirers, of whom there were many, were dealt with in the several halls of the church by Mr. Moody, the minister of the church, and by other ministers and qualified persons.

During the currency of the week, the work greatly deepened and extended. On the following Sabbath evening three meetings were held, the first in the Barclay Church, the second in Viewforth Church, and the third in Fountainbridge Church. Every part of these churches was crowded long before the time fixed for the meetings, and thousands could not gain admittance. At all the meetings many were awakened, and in the next day's noon prayer-meeting, prayer was asked for several special cases; two, for instance, who had been awakened in the regular forenoon's service in the Barclay Church, and another who had been awakened in the Fountainbridge Church evening meeting. Thanksgiving was also requested to be given for those who had found the Saviour.

During the progress of the week's meetings, the

ministers and others engaged in the work were, through astonishment and joy, as men that dreamed. Many avowed their joy at the inquiry meetings; others felt it without any open declaration. An elder, for example, met a man and his wife who had never been at the inquiry meetings returning to their home with their countenances radiant with gladness.

The impression made on the Christian mind of Edinburgh is thus stated by the Rev. John Kelman, after three weeks' labor in the city :

" The part of the service toward which all the others tend, and in which the power culminates, is the address by Mr. Moody, in which, in simple, vigorous, and telling language, he holds up before men the truth as it is in Jesus, and makes most earnest and powerful appeals to heart and conscience. Mr. Moody is strikingly free from all pretense and parade; he speaks as one who thoroughly believes what he says, and who is in downright earnest in delivering his message. His descriptions are characterized by remarkable vividness and graphic power. He has a great wealth of illustration, and his illustrations are always apposite, bring out into the clearest light the point which he intends to illustrate, and fix it forever in the memories of many. There is very little excitement. There is no extravagance. But the effect of the services is seen in the manifest impression produced on the audience generally, in the anxious inquirers (varying in number from about forty to upwards of seventy, as on Friday last), who remain behind for spiritual conversation and prayer after every meeting, and also in the hundreds of persons, in all grades of the social scale, scattered through Edinburgh and neighborhood, who are more or less awakened to realize the importance of eternal things, are burdened with a sense of sin, and longing to obtain salvation. Not a few also profess to have been brought out of darkness into marvelous light, to have been made partakers of a new life of faith in Jesus Christ, and to be going on their way rejoicing."

The daily prayer-meeting having been a remarkable feature of the work in Edinburgh, it may be proper to notice its history and character:

"On the day on which the first meeting was held, more than five hundred persons were present. The attendance steadily increased, till there was some difficulty as to fixing on a suitable place. The Rev. A. Whyte, of Free St. George's, being applied to, kindly offered his church for the prayer-meeting. Ultimately, on account of its central situation, it was resolved to hold the meeting in the Free Assembly Hall. The attendance there was usually upwards of a thousand daily.

"The first half of the hour is employed with singing part of a psalm or hymn, reading (in a summarized form) the requests for prayer, prayer, and a few remarks by Mr. Moody on some passage of Scripture. During the second half, the meeting is open, any person present being at liberty to engage in prayer, read a short passage of Scripture, make a statement about the work of God, or request the singing of any particular psalm or hymn. This meeting is felt to be of the most delightful and refreshing character; and when one o'clock strikes, every person is surprised, and can scarcely believe that the hour is ended.

"Christians, who had looked on with a desire to see what would come of the movement, found their difficulties melting away by contact with the work, and cordially identified themselves with it. Denominational differences were lost sight of, and oneness in Christ was realized and rejoiced in." Even then, Mr. Kelman, in the faith that expects an answer, and of which we had an example in Mr. Moody's address in

Newcastle, could write—"It seems as if a winter of wonderful blessing were lying before Edinburgh and Leith."

It is not needful to say that Scottish Christians attach little weight to mere feeling without intelligence, and in this they were in hearty sympathy with the evangelists, by whom instruction was considered a main and all-important branch of their work. There was no public meeting on the Monday evening following the close of the first week's services in the Barclay Church; but, instead of this, a meeting for the converts who had, during the previous week, professed to have closed with Christ, and those who were anxious, was held on that evening in the Free Assembly Hall. The Monday evenings thereafter were always devoted to such meetings.

Some apprehension was felt as to the hymns and instrument of Mr. Sankey producing an unfavorable impression. The Rev. Dr. Thomson published his views after a week's labor in his church, the Broughton Place United Presbyterian.

"The service of song conducted by Mr. Sankey, in which music is used as the handmaid of a gospel ministry, has already been described in your columns.

I have never found it objected to, except by those who have not witnessed it. Those who have come and heard, have departed with their prejudices vanquished, and their hearts impressed. We might quote in commendation of this somewhat novel manner of preaching the gospel, the words of good George Herbert:

> 'A verse may win him who the gospel flies,
> And turn delight into a sacrifice.'

"There is nothing of novelty in the doctrine which Mr. Moody proclaims. It is the old gospel—old, yet always fresh and young too, as the living fountain or the morning sun—in which the substitution of Christ is placed in the center, and presented with admirable distinctness and decision. It is spoken with most impressive directness, not as by a man half convinced, and who seems always to feel that a skeptic is looking over his shoulder, but with a deep conviction of the truth of what he says, as if, like our own Andrew Fuller, he could 'venture his eternity on it,' and with a tremendous earnestness, as if he felt that 'if he did not speak, the very stones would cry out.' The illustrations and anecdotes, drawn principally from his strangely-varied life, are so wisely chosen, so graphically told, and so well applied, as never to fail in hitting the mark."

There was the greatest variety among the inquirers. There were present from the old man of seventy-five to the youth of eleven, soldiers from the Castle, students from the University, the backsliding, the intemperate, the skeptical, the rich and the poor, the educated and the uneducated.

"There was," adds Dr. Thomson, "a considerable number of skeptics among the inquirers, but their speculative doubts and difficulties very soon became of no account, when they came to have a proper view of their sins. Some have already come to tell me of their renunciation of unbelief, and their discipleship to Christ. One has publicly announced that he can no longer live in the ice-house of cold negations, and has asked Mr. Moody to publish the address which brought light to his heart, and to circulate it far and wide over the land."

The movement in the capital of Scotland had now assumed the most impressive proportions. The people crowded to meetings in such numbers that admission had occasionally to be secured by ticket. The "working-classes" crowded the churches, and

AN ALL-DAY MEETING. 45

young men alone sometimes filled the Free Assembly Hall. Christian young men eager to receive direction in Christian work, children to be simply spoken to of the way of life, and eager and interested general audiences proved how thorough a hold divine truth had acquired over the feelings and consciences of the people.

With the view of extending the movement, an all-day meeting was arranged for the 17th December (1873), at which special subjects were assigned for different hours, the discussion of which was introduced in an address of about a quarter of an hour; full liberty being given to any one in the audience to express his thoughts. Prayers were also offered by various brethren, and Mr. Sankey led the service of praise. Mr. Moody presided.

"We are struck," says the Rev. Mr. Taylor, "with the solemn stillness. One of the Edinburgh ministers is closing some remarks on the subject of praise, and is followed by Mr. Moody. We listen to a rapid speaker, with a marked American intonation; it requires a moment or two to habituate our ear to his utterance; but that attained, we forget all peculiarities, in the clearness, earnestness, directness, and telling character of his statements. 'Get full of the word of God' is the conclusion of what he says, 'and you can't help praising Him.' He tells of a young pastor, newly placed over a church, who, finding his prayer-meetings ill-attended and lifeless, surprised his people one Sabbath, by announcing that there would be no prayer-meeting that week, but a meeting for praise. Curiosity brought out a large gathering of his church; he told them that as they were so reluctant to pray, he wished every one now to look back on his past life, and see if he did not remember something to thank God for, and just to rise up and thank God for it. The result was, that one after another rose up, thanking God for this and that mercy, till the hour was over before they were aware, and they went away declaring it to be the best meeting they had ever had; and not only so, but this proved to be the beginning of a revival among them. Then followed Mr. Moody's coadjutor, Mr. Sankey.

"After a few words of exhortation not to abuse praise in our churches, by employing it merely to fill up time, but to utter real praise, Mr. Sankey explained briefly the principle of his singing, as intended to be a real 'teaching.' And as he proceeded to sing, we felt that it was real teaching. Not merely was there his wonderful voice, which made every word distinctly heard in the remotest corner of the hall, and to which the organ accompaniment was felt to be merely subsidiary, but it was the scriptural *thought* borne into the mind upon the wave of song, and kept there until we were obliged to look at it, and feel it in its importance and its preciousness."

A month's labors in the city had inspired confidence, overcome any prejudice that existed against any part of the evangelists' methods, the hymns in which—and with an instrument, too—less familiar to Scottish than to American ears—might especially have been expected to provoke criticism. The number of meetings was increased. We find such men as the Rev. Dr. Blaikie, of the Free Church College (remembered by his visit as a Delegate to America a few years ago), bearing public testimony to the general movement, and to particular parts of it.

"Among the most direct and touching fruits," says Dr. Blaikie, " of saving impressions in the case of any one, affectionate interest in the welfare of other members of the family is one of the surest and most uniform. A working man of fifty years of age, for example, is impressed and brought to peace in believing, and immediately he comes to the minister and cries out, with streaming eyes, 'Oh! pray for my two sons!' A father and his son are seen at another meeting with arms round each other's necks. In many cases the work of conversion seems to go through whole families. That peculiar joyfulness and expectation which marks young converts, is often the means of leading others to the fountain, and two, three, four, and even more members of the same family share the blessing. There have been some very remarkable conversions of skeptics. Dr. Andrew Thomson told of one who, having been awakened on the previous week, had gone for the first time to church on the previous Sunday. He had hardly been in a place of worship for years, and a week before he would have scouted the idea. He was so happy in the morning that he returned in the afternoon. The blessing seemed to come down upon him. We have heard of the case of another skeptic who had carried his unbelief to the verge of blasphemy, and who has now come to the foot of the Cross."

In St. Stephen's congregation the Rev. Dr. Nicholson presided; and every evening there were around the pulpit ministers of all denominations, from all parts of the country, while among the audience there were members of the nobility, professors from the university, and distinguished lawyers from the Parliament House. Many came to criticise and seek grounds for opposition, who went away to approve and pray.

An Edinburgh newspaper (*The Daily Review*), representing the general religious feeling of the city, thus describes the condition of things:

"There is a general feeling, and it has prevailed for some time, that we need, and that we may expect, a blessing of unusual magnitude. Never, probably, was Scotland so stirred; never was there so much expectation. May it be graciously granted that the blessing shall be even above all that we can ask or think!

"Requests for the services of Messrs. Moody and Sankey are pouring in from all quarters. Requisitions, signed not only by ministers, but by provosts, councilors, and leading citizens, are received daily from towns, large and small. The anxiety for a visit seems to be of a remarkably serious and earnest kind. It is not to gratify curiosity, but to promote spiritual and eternal good, that their presence is sought. Even remote rural parishes in Scotland are meeting to pray for a blessing on their labors, and the belief prevails that what is now going on in Edinburgh will radiate over the country."

The work now began to extend; Leith was visited. Seafaring men were reached, and in lonely ships at sea, the good influence was extended.

On Sabbath, 21st December, at 9 A. M., Mr. Moody addressed a meeting of Sabbath-school and Bible-class teachers in the Free Assembly Hall. Having read five or six portions of Scripture, to show that when Christ was on earth He was the light of the world, and when He went, He left His followers to reflect that light, he spoke at length of the duty of Christians to do this, the eyes of the world being upon them. He then passed on to press the importance of parents and teachers early putting the question to their children, "Are you a Christian?" and seeking not only to point out to them the way to the Saviour, but to take them by the hand and lead them to Him. He showed that the work of Sunday-school teachers among children would be most blessed, if the teachers first sought to gain their confidence, and convince them it was not merely from a sense of duty but from love to them, that they sought to win them to Christ.

Edinburgh always contains a great body of students, and a meeting for them was held in the Free Assembly Hall. So great was the eagerness to obtain admittance, that the doors were besieged by an immense crowd, even after it had become apparent that the hall was already filled. To mitigate the disappointment of those who found it impossible to get into the hall, Mr. Moody, before he addressed the meeting inside, went out and spoke for some time to the immense gathering in the quadrangle. While he was engaged, Dr. Rainy, Mr. Whyte, the successor of Dr. Candlish, Professor Charteris, and Mr. Sankey conducted service inside. Around the platform there were professors from nearly all the faculties in the University, and from the Free Church and College, and nearly two thousand students.

Meantime numerous requests had been received from all parts of the country for visits. From Berwick-on-Tweed, the Rev. Dr. Cairns appeared as a deputation. Mr. Moody suggested that deputations should be sent out from Edinburgh to visit the various towns from which the applications had come, and assist in conducting religious meetings. Several ministers and laymen stated their readiness to go. Dr. Cairns took part in the exercises of the meeting.

We cannot better close this chapter than with the words of Dr. Charles Brown, one of the oldest and most highly respected ministers in Edinburgh. "I have watched," said he, "all the religious movements of the last forty years, and I have never seen anything that, in extent and depth of interest, approached to the present movement. I have often prayed for such a blessing, and always longed for it; and though my prayer had remained unanswered for many years, I am so enriched with gladness at the sights around me, that I could say with Simeon, 'Now, Lord, lettest Thou Thy servant depart in peace, according to Thy word, for mine eyes have seen Thy salvation, which Thou hast prepared before the face of all people.'"

The Grassmarket, a spacious square in the center of the old town of Edinburgh, was the scene in by-gone days of those martyr executions which stained the reigns of Charles the Second and James the Second

THE GRASSMARKET.   53

of England. On the south side of this square is the Corn Exchange, an immense building, capable of holding six thousand persons. In this place a meeting was held on Sabbath evening, the 28th December, for men only, admission by ticket. The immense hall was filled with above five thousand men. Mr. Moody put it to them if they would like to have another meeting of the same kind, in the same place, next evening. Nearly all hands were raised. Meantime, in the Free Assembly Hall, the general audience had been dismissed, and the inquiry meeting was going on in the center of the hall, when the doorkeeper came up to Dr. Bonar, who was engaged, along with others, in dealing with the inquirers, and said that Mr. Moody had brought up the whole Grassmarket with him.

The intelligence was embarrassing, for there were too few to deal with the inquirers already in the hall. It was arranged, however, that these inquirers, with the friends dealing with them, should remove to the galleries, and leave the body of the hall for the "Grassmarket." This was done, and in streamed hundreds of men—many of them young men—it was believed to the number of six or seven hundred.

These could not be conversed with separately, and Mr. Moody accordingly addressed them; asked those who were anxious to find Christ to stand up, when a great body of them stood up. He then desired those of them who wished to give themselves to Christ to kneel down, when they all, and every one else in every part of the hall, knelt down. Over these bended, and, may it not be added, broken-hearted suppliants, Mr. Wilson of the Barclay Church, and afterwards Mr. Moody, prayed, or rather led *their* prayer in giving themselves to Christ. This must have been a sight for angels to rejoice in.

These men would have remained till midnight, but it was deemed expedient to dismiss them at half-past ten o'clock. So the work went on—on Monday evening another meeting in the Corn Exchange, attended by three thousand persons of the poorer classes; on Sabbath evening another immense meeting in the Corn Exchange, and a service in the Free Assembly Hall for women only, admission by ticket, in reporting which next day at the noon hour of prayer, Dr. Bonar said, " that in all his life he never preached to such an audience."

During the last week of December a call to prayer

was sent to every minister in Scotland, suggesting the week of prayer from 4th to 11th January as a favorable opportunity for combined action. This call bore the following, among other honored names:

J. H. Balfour, Professor of Botany; W. G. Blaikie, D.D., Professor, New College; Horatius Bonar, D.D., Chalmers Memorial Church; Chas. J. Brown, D.D., Free New North Church; H. Calderwood, Professor of Moral Philosophy; A. H. Charteris, D.D., Professor of Biblical Literature; Thos. J. Crawford, D.D., Professor of Divinity in the University of Edinburgh; Alexander Duff, D.D.; William Grant, Bristo Place Baptist Chapel; William Hanna, D.D., Robert McDonald, D.D.; Hamilton M. MacGill, D.D., Secretary of Mission Board, United Presbyterian Church; James MacGregor, D.D., Professor, New College; W. Scott Moncrieff, St. Thomas' Episcopal Church; Robert Rainy, D.D., Professor, New College; Wm. Reid, United Presbyterian Church, Lothian Road; A. Moody Stuart, Free St. Luke's; Andrew Thomson, D.D., Broughton Place United Presbyterian Church.

Such were the men who declared that "God's power was wonderfully at work," and who urged dependence not on any human agency, but on God, and earnest crying over all Scotland for His blessing.

The last night of the year was observed by special service in the Free Assembly Hall. Mr. Moody announced that "anything that is worship will be in order, and when I am speaking, if any one has an illustration to give, or would like to sing a hymn or offer prayer, let him do so." This gave constant variety to the meeting, so that the interest never flagged, and every one who stole a glance at the clock wondered to see how time passed. Prayer was offered at intervals. Mr. Moody surpassed himself in marvelous fluency and fertility of discourse, as he reviewed the seven "I wills" of Christ. Soon after eleven the Bible study ceased, and the remainder of the year was given to prayer.

The intense interest and solemnity of the meeting increased as midnight neared. Five minutes before twelve all sound was hushed. The distant shouts of the revelers outside could be heard. Kneeling, or with bowed heads, the whole great meeting, with one accord, prayed in silence, and while they did so the city clocks successively struck the hour. The hushed silence continued five minutes more. Mr. Moody then gave out the last two verses of the hymn, "Jesus, Lover of my Soul," and all stood and sang, "Thou, O Christ, art all I want, more than all in Thee I find," etc. After a brief prayer the benediction was pronounced, and all began, like one family, to wish each other a Happy New Year—"a year of grace, a year of usefulness." There probably never was a New Year brought in in Edinburgh with more solemn gladness and hope of spiritual good.

The question, "What is the meaning of all this?" was now being asked over Scotland. Dr. Horatius Bonar replied in a letter, of which we give the concluding portion, his name being a guarantee for a clear spiritual estimate of the movement:

"I must say that I have not seen nor heard any impropriety nor extravagance. I have heard sound doctrine, sober, though sometimes fervent and tearful speech, the utterance of full hearts yearning over the wretched, and beseeching men to be reconciled to God. That I should accord with every statement and fall entirely in with every part of their proceeding, need not be expected. Yet I will say that I have not witnessed anything sensational or repulsive. During the spiritual movement which took place in

Scotland about thirty years ago, in most of which I had part, I saw more of what was extreme, both in statement and proceeding than I have done of late. There was far more of excitement then than there is now. The former movements depended far more upon vehement appeals, and were carried along more by the sympathetic current of human feeling than the present. When the present movement began, I feared lest there should be a repetition of some of the scenes which I had witnessed in other days, and I did not hesitate to express my fear to brethren. My fears have not been realized. I have been as regular in my attendance at the meetings as I could, and though I will not say that there was nothing which I might not have wished different, yet I have been struck with the exceeding calmness at all times—the absence of excitement—the peaceful solemnity pervading these immense gatherings of two or three thousand people, day by day—the strange stillness that at times so overawed us; and I felt greatly relieved at the absence of those audible manifestations of feeling common in former days. Rowland Hill was once asked the question, 'When do you intend to stop?' 'Not till we have carried all before us.' So say our brethren from Chicago. We say Amen. This needy world says Amen. Human wickedness and evil say Amen. Heaven and earth say Amen. The work is great and the time is short. But the strength is not of man but of God."

The "Week of Prayer" had been emphasized by the call to Scotland, and at the meeting on Friday, 2d January, the Assembly Hall was filled to overflowing—passages, doorways, and platform all crowded. The feature of the meeting was a series of directions for conducting prayer-meetings given by Mr. Moody. He began by saying that there was probably more talent in Scotland than in any other place of the same size, but it was in a great measure buried talent. He did not refer to the ministers so much as to the people, who did not draw out their talents for the good of the Church. This was an important matter. If he drew out the energies of ten men, and got them to work, it was much better than doing ten men's work himself. Hence the importance of some of the rules he was about to give them. Such as that the people must sit close together, for if scattered, the meeting would be cold and disjointed. The hall or room must be well ventilated, heated, and lighted; they should have good singing; when a meeting was special, the prayers and remarks ought to be special; requests and thanksgivings should be brought before the meeting; the leader must take no further part in the meeting than to give the key-note; the subject should be known beforehand, that the people's thoughts may be directed to it; not to scold the people who had come because others had kept away; if discouraged not to let the people see it;. variety should be given to the meetings; no formal address; the meetings short and the people sent away hungry, but not weary, else they would not come back; they should avoid discussions, and put down discussion among the audience; leave the meeting open a part of the time, and be invariably punctual. Under such sensible regulations the meetings proceeded with the deepest interest, and crowds so great that on at least one occasion the prayer-meeting overflowed into the corners of the quadrangle of the Free Church College.

Take a specimen of a single meeting. Lord Cavan said he had been particularly struck by the number of requests made on the previous day for prayer. He himself met with eight or nine young men, and he humbly believed that by the grace of God they were all drawn to Him, and sealed by the Holy Spirit of promise. Rev. Mr. Grant, of Tain, thanked God for the effect which even the reports of this movement had had in communities far-distant from Edinburgh. The Rev. Mr. Wilson (Tolbooth Church) said the meetings in his church had grown in interest as the week of prayer wore on. He thought it would be well for the ministers to open their vestries for inquirers after each of the ordinary services in their churches. They had hesitated in his church, but the people had taken it into their own hands, and at the close of the services in the Tolbooth, on Sabbath, several persons had come to his vestry inquiring the way to salvation. He thought the previous day the most remarkable in the history of Edinburgh. The Rev. Mr. Talon (Episcopal) said he had never been present at such refreshing meetings. New life had been given to him by them, the days of youth had been renewed, and, to the glory of Christ, he had to say that for twenty years he had not preached with the fullness and freeness he did on Sunday, and he did not believe that there had been seen in his preaching such effects as were produced on Sunday. Rev.

Mr. Wemyss (Congregational Church) spoke of many hopeful cases in his district.

"Some said," remarked Mr. Moody, "of these meetings that they merely influenced people by exciting them and working on their feelings till they became anxious. Now, he had never said less than he had spoken at the previous night's meeting, and at that of Sunday night, and yet there was a perfect host of inquirers on those occasions. He had asked those who wished to see him to retire with him to a private room, intending, when he had spoken to them, to come into the hall and invite out more; but this he did not need to do, for more than one hundred inquirers came forward spontaneously. He had to close the door on about fifty, being unable to see them. A great many who had not been at the meetings at all had had conviction brought home to their hearts, God having answered the prayers of others on their behalf.

The Rev. Mr. Robertson, of Newington, stated some facts in regard to the special services held by Messrs. Moody and Sankey in his church during last week. He shrank from premature announcement of results, but it was not too much to say that the Lord had been working with these evangelists. In Newington the indifferent were being awakened, the undecided brought to a blessed decision, and the tempest-tossed carried into a haven of rest. He did not speak of the inquiry meetings merely, or of the number who had gone into them, but he spoke of many coming and calling upon him and others privately afterwards, or waiting for them at the corners of streets, and asking to be helped out of their difficulties, or to be confirmed and strengthened in their faith. He could tell, too, of many Christians being stirred to newness of life and exertion. What had struck him very much was, that many who had been taken up with an empty profession had been seeing the great gulf between the mere form of godliness and its living power. There had been old men on the brink of the grave coming and receiving salvation as a little child, and there had been not a few little children, both boys and girls, perhaps chiefly boys, who were seeking rest, and not able to get it until they had found it in the Saviour; and then going away rejoicing, having found the pearl of great price.

The Rev. J. M'Ewan (Canongate Free Church) said that they, "the ministers, were, with a few of the laymen, so much occupied by the converts that came in, that they had not an opportunity of taking impressions of what was going on; but the missionaries in the district, who were in the habit of meeting and talking with the people, told him that there was a striking impression made upon the population. They were to meet to-day, to see what could be done in the way of following up the blessing."

So the week of prayer closed on Sabbath, the 11th January. A week, the like of which, according to the testimony of the wisest and most sober of its Christian citizens, never before passed in Edinburgh.

A Convention on Wednesday, the 14th January, in the Free Assembly Hall, fittingly followed. Mr. Moody presided.

Ministers and others from all parts of the country were present, for the purpose of consulting together and obtaining the advantage of the experience of the two American brethren, in regard to the best methods of conducting various departments of Christian work. The hall was greatly crowded, and so eager were those outside to obtain an entrance, that it was found necessary to lock the quadrangle gate. Dr. Bonar struck the key-note of the conference, in a short

FINAL MEETINGS. 65

address on personal effort, and was followed by representative men from various parts of the country, lay, clerical, legal, military, and literary. The meeting continued with unflagging interest from eleven o'clock in the forenoon till nearly four o'clock in the afternoon. Several of the ministers present stated that already they were conducting their prayer meetings on the model of those held in the Free Assembly Hall.

Before the separation of the Convention, Mr. Moody asked the prayers of the assembly for Berwick-on-Tweed, amongst other towns in Scotland. He shortly described the meeting held there, and stated his belief that an important spiritual movement had been commenced in that town. He believed that God was going to give a great blessing to Scotland, if they were ready to receive it. The meeting was then closed with praise and the pronouncing of the benediction.

The evangelists' last meeting was at the usual union prayer-meeting in the Free Church Assembly Hall, and a conference with ministers and elders in the Free Assembly Hall in the afternoon, on the subject of the duties of the eldership; and a union prayer-meeting in the evening. Mr. Moody stated that he had received many letters from young converts, and a great many had come to see him with the question— What can I do for Christ? It was a sure sign of conversion to be anxious to work for the Master. This disposition should be encouraged and cultivated. Mr. Moody went on to urge upon young Christians not to neglect their work at home, but to adorn the doctrine of Jesus Christ. He prayed, as he left them, that the young converts might stand firm, that God might keep them from the world.

And so the brethren left the city of Edinburgh on Wednesday, the 21st January, and proceeded to Dundee, the next scene of their arduous evangelistic labors, in which were spent two busy and most useful weeks, with the same results as in Edinburgh.

Meantime a flying visit had been made to Berwick-upon-Tweed for a single day. Professor Cairns thus describes the result:

"I feel constrained to add my testimony to the profound impression which has, by the blessing of God, been made on the town. I cannot attempt to describe the appearance of Wallace Green Church at the evening meeting on Tuesday, when the overwhelming meeting in the Corn Exchange was dismissed, and those who gathered for prayer, with the anxious inquirers, crowded in to fill up every corner of the spacious church. The shadow of eternity seemed cast over the great congregation. Many were observed to be in tears; and as the inquirers, with hurried and trembling step, passed into the vestry (though others found a more private entrance), the deepest awe and sympathy pervaded the meeting. This continued for a full hour, and such a gathering I hardly ever expect again to see in this world. It is believed that nearly fifty in all were conversed with in the Corn Exchange, in the afternoon, and in the church in the evening. Last night (Wednesday) a considerable addition was made to this number, after the addresses of Mr. Leitch, of Newcastle, and Mr. Chedburn of this town. I would close by earnestly commending to all brethren in the ministry a movement which, so far as I know it, is so full of blessing, and so remarkably free from irregularity, or counteracting elements of any kind."

GLASGOW.

Glasgow is too near to Edinburgh to remain unaffected by any movement that is felt in the capital. Desire and expectation were strong in this great commercial center. It teems with working people, shrewd, keen, but in too many instances intemperate, careless, and ignorant of the way of life, and this around very admirable and effective churches and ministers.

Messrs. Moody and Sankey began their work in the City Hall, by addressing and leading in sacred song a crowded meeting of three thousand Sabbath-school teachers, and other religious workers, at nine o'clock on Sunday, February 8th. The meeting in the evening of that day in the City Hall was densely crowded, and the overflow filled many of the neighboring churches. The entire daily press of Glasgow next morning gave favorable notices of the meetings.

Said the *Glasgow Herald:* "Mr. Sankey has a good voice, and the words of the hymns are enunciated with great distinctness. Mr. Moody's manner is abrupt and hurried; but though his style is perhaps more forcible than pathetic, the anecdotes he tells illustrative of the plan of redemption are often touching and effective. He speaks as a man fully assured of his own salvation, and who wishes others to enter on the immediate possession of like confidence—by laying hold of the promises of acceptance and eternal life insured to all who place their reliance on the atonement of Christ."

The noon prayer-meeting, held in the Wellington Street U. P. Church, was quite crowded, and on Monday, 9th, there was a large meeting at noon, and about two thousand persons heard the gospel in the Barony and Free Barony Churches in the evening. Wellington Street U. P. Church was filled to over-flowing next day. Mr. Moody in a short address on the 9th of Daniel, struck the key-note: "what was wanted was power from on high." He had been told that there were in Glasgow seventy thousand young men between the ages of fifteen and twenty-five. When he heard it, his heart sank within him, and he said, "Who is sufficient for these things?" Then he thought of this prayer of Daniel, and considered if fathers and mothers and God's people would unite in prayer on behalf of these young men, how easy it would be for God to turn their hearts. Daniel sought to be heard "for the Lord's sake." Mr. Moody said that before he was converted he did not understand what was meant by praying "for Jesus' sake." He never prayed for Jesus' sake, but for his own sake.

The meeting was thrown open, and, among others, Dr. A. A. Bonar urged to expectant faith: "Can the arm of God, which shook Egypt, not shake Glasgow? Will that arm which divided the Red Sea not do wonders here? Is the power of the cross vanished? Is the merit of the sacrifice gone? Is there no more room, or is the great Substitute weary of taking the sinner's place? We are a little company, but the Spirit of the times of Pentecost is still among us. Let us pray, and never doubt, and the arm of the Lord will still be seen mighty to save."

Incidents made their own impression. In the the Barony Established Church the previous evening, while Mr. Moody was speaking, a deeply solemn feeling prevailed. Inquirers were asked to retire into the vestry, but all seemed disposed to follow Mr. Moody to the Free Barony Church. In a short time the house was empty, with the exception of one young man, who stood leaning against the door of one of the pews, in deep distress. Mr. Topping and a friend approached and spoke to him. Mr. Moody's remarks on Rom. iii. 23, "all have sinned," had impressed him. His distress was great. The Rev. Mr. Topping and a friend explained to him the grace of the Lamb of God, and he left professing to see the way of salvation. The ministers having entered into the work in concert, no difficulty was experienced in procuring suitable buildings in Glasgow.

The meetings moved from church to church: able assistance was derived from the local clergy, the Earl of Cavan, the missionaries of the city, and admirable elders who entered into the conferences with great earnestness. A spectator, writing to a friend in London, gives the impression made by the evening meetings after a week's labors. "The evening meetings in the Established and Free Barony Churches have been most solemn, every night this week crammed to overflowing, and such a number always staying behind to be spoken with. Thursday night at half past eight, in the City Hall, was a meeting only for men. You never saw such a sight; and Messrs. Moody and Sankey say it is the best they have had in this country. A great many stayed, and Mr. Moody jumped down amongst them off the platform. In a moment he was surrounded by a whole set of rough fellows. One seized his hand, and those who could not get near bent their ears to try to catch his words. It was most affecting; and a great work was done, I believe, as thanks were given at the noon meeting yesterday for answers to prayer for that meeting."

The noon-day prayer-meeting here also became a power. The laborers came together to pray, caught the common spirit, and diffused information. In illustration of the state of feeling the Rev. Mr. Riddall remarked that in the midst of a contested election two of the largest churches in the city were filled with people daily. Mr. J. Campbell White read a letter from Sabbath-school teachers in Dundee. It stated that at the close of the usual Sabbath School service a meeting for prayer was held. It was attended by upwards of two hundred boys and girls, nearly every one of whom was bathed in tears, and upwards of seventy were completely broken down, sobbing as if their hearts would break. The Rev. Mr. M'Murtrie, Edinburgh, reported regarding the progress of the work in that city, stating that there was no going back there, and that the meetings were as largely attended as ever. A gentleman read a letter from a village near Perth, showing the awakening that was taking place there. So the movement was diffusing itself over the surrounding towns and villages.

It was decided to address the young directly. The meeting on Saturday, Feb. 14, was for children, of whom there was a large gathering, accompanied by their parents or friends, the place being crowded in every part, while Ewing Place Congregational Church was also well filled with an audience of adults. Messrs. Moody and Sankey went first to the Wellington Street Church, and then to the other. Mr. Moody addressed the children on the subject of faith, impressing on them how God honored faith, and granted the desires of those who had confidence in Him, illustrating this principally by the case of the little maid who waited on the wife of the Syrian captain, who was cured of his leprosy. Sabbath-school teachers had their meeting, and Mr. Moody gave an address for the purpose of stimulating them and encouraging them in their work. A meeting for women only was held, Mr. Moody taking for his theme the freeness of the Gospel message, enforcing and illustrating his subject with characteristic energy and point. Mr. Sankey also gave a short address in the afternooon. In the evening meeting, which was for men only, Mr. Moody delivered an address on the same subject as that chosen in the afternoon. At each of the meetings Mr. Sankey sang several solos, accompanying himself on the harmonium.

But instead of a detailed account of the meetings, let a general view of the work be given, as it struck intelligent observers on the spot, when about three weeks had been spent by the evangelists in Glasgow. Thus writes the editor of the *British Evangelist*, early in March :

"The meetings here go on with ever-increasing spiritual momentum and ever-widening usefulness. The noon meetings and Bible lectures have been very profitable to believers. In John Street United Presbyterian Church very large numbers have remained for conversation ; and in Ewing Place Chapel, which has been nightly crowded with young men, most interesting inquiry meetings have afterwards been held, sometimes extending beyond eleven o'clock.

"In the City Hall, on Sabbath morning, the meeting was for young men, specially got up by the

Young Men's Christian Association. In the afternoon, at five o'clock, and in the evening, crowded meetings were held in the same place. About ten thousand would hear in that one place the gospel of their salvation; and hundreds were impressed with the importance of being saved.

"As the Monday meetings are mainly for the purpose of reporting progress, and the Rev. Mr. Taylor (Kelvinside Free Church) wished to tell that the Lord was granting His Spirit not only in the Eastern and Central districts of Glasgow, but in the Western district, where he lived and labored. On Sunday, special services had been commenced in his church; and the blessing which was being enjoyed in other parts of the city was attending the work in Hillhead. These services, following on weeks of united prayer meetings in the district, were conducted chiefly by Mr. Brownlow North.

"Rev. Dr. Wallace said he should never forget the meeting of the Young Men's Christian Association in the City Hall on Sunday morning. It was the most wonderful meeting he had ever witnessed; the hall crowded from floor to ceiling, a sea of anxious faces! It was also most delightful, as he looked along his own congregation, to see here and there young men who had been amongst those one hundred and one who had come forward in Ewing Place Chapel last Tuesday evening, and confessed Christ publicly. Had he been told a few weeks ago what was to take place in the city during the last week as to the young men, he feared he could scarcely have believed it possible. He had been in warehouses where he had seen young men take out their pocket Bibles from their pockets and say, 'Sir, this is my book for the time.' And with what delight he had seen passages pencilled and leaves folded down! This spirit was pervading all classes of the community. He could give many particular instances; but there were some who had felt the influence, who trembled under deep emotion, but who, grasping his hand, had said, 'Let us keep in the background yet, till we see if it be real.'

"The Rev. Mr. Howie (Govan), told how, on Sunday night, and during the week, he had spoken to a number of young men, some of them merchants, some students of divinity, and some students of medicine. If this work went on, he could not tell what might be the influence in the future of the history of our great city.

"YOUNG CONVERTS."

"It was reported that in a house in the neighborhood of the Saltmarket, a prayer meeting was held by a number of mothers who could not attend the public meetings. They prayed for the conversion of the locality.

"Mr. Moody declared that one minister was worth a hundred laymen, because of his influence in the pulpit. He announced that it had been resolved to hold a meeting next Wednesday in Mr. Stewart's church for fathers, on Thursday for mothers, and on Friday for sisters. Through the efforts of the latter, it might be possible to reach the girls in the city warehouses. The meeting of fathers in Edinburgh had been signally blessed, and he anticipated a like result for all the meetings in Glasgow."

How the awakened were dealt with may be seen from the following from the same paper:

"About two hundred young converts met Mr. Moody, and about seventy (chiefly youths and maidens) testified before each other that they had been converted to God. At the same time about two hundred inquirers assembled in the rooms below to to be conversed with, and many of them passed into the joyful liberty of the gospel of Christ. We sat beside four (two of them being from Paisley), and three of the four went away rejoicing, but the fourth was held back by her trouble about a dead husband and a hard heart; and when nearly at the edge of decision, stood back a dozen times. We then went to the young men's meeting at Ewing Place, and as we entered were struck with the impressive sight of a thousand young men, the great majority of whom were evidently on the Lord's side. After prayer and a brief address from a young man, Mr. Moody, who had just come from the other meeting, spoke a little about confessing Christ. This young men's meeting has been going on for a fortnight, with meetings for inquirers at its close, and night after night many young men have been brought to Christ."

How the young men were dealt with may be learned from a statement of the Rev. Mr. Riddel, who, speaking of the meeting held the previous evening, said that, of the twenty-three young men who entered the inquiry-room with him, only one seemed to go away with a cloud of darkness resting on his spirit. There are young men coming in numbers to the Lord. If we are faithful, the Lord will own it.

WORKING.

A young man was sent to me from the country with a certificate of church membership. I said, "That is all right so far as the visible church is concerned, but what about connection with the Lord Jesus. Are you united to Him?" "No, sir, I am not; that question was never put to me. I have often felt I had no right to be at the Lord's Table, but did not see how I could stay back, for I was a Sabbath-school teacher." The Lord opened his eyes to see that it was all done for him in Jesus—he came and said, "Salvation is mine now."

The manner in which the hymn is introduced is well illustrated in this meeting. Mr. Sankey said, "Now is the time for *working*. I saw on a tombstone at Stirling yesterday this word deeply carved in the stone—'*Waiting*.' There will be time for waiting by and by, but now is the time for *working*." He then sang—

> Hark, the voice of Jesus crying
> Who will go and work to-day?
> Fields are white, and harvest waiting,
> Who will bear the sheaves away?
> Loud and long the Master calleth,
> Rich reward He offers thee;
> Who will answer, gladly saying,
> Here am I, send me, send me?

"Why," said Dr. Wallace, "just now everybody seems anxious to be spoken to. People look at you on the street with anxiety depicted on their countenances. The other afternoon, coming down from the services in the College Church, a young man looked at me with so much anxiety apparent in his face, that I spoke to him. I found the young man, who was a student, in a state of distress about his soul; and I spoke some comforting words to him, for which he seemed very grateful. Many, many more than we think, are waiting to be spoken to. What Sir Garnet Wolseley said to his officers when attacked in the bush near Coomassie, when they could not see the enemy, was applicable to every man in Glasgow at the present time—'You have your orders—advance, and let every man do what he can.' 'She hath done what she could.'"

So young men were appealed to in the crowded city, and the Lord gave the blessing. No wonder that gratitude mingled with penitent cries, and that praises went up with prayers.

"There is something far better than gold. God thinks so little of gold, that, in the New Jerusalem, it is used for paving the streets," said Mr. Moody, "and every Christian man will understand it. Even the joy of winning souls, and of seeing souls won to Christ, is better joy than the world's best."

The "thanksgivings" at the various meetings are worthy of notice. The leper who has been blessed must return to give glory to God. Here is an average sample of those sent in to the Daily Prayer-meeting—

"Thanksgiving asked for the conversion of a young gentleman, brought to the Lord on a visit to Glasgow. He is now rejoicing in the Lord, and has written home to tell the good news; for a young man led out of difficulty in answer to prayer; a sister's thanks for the conversion of a brother; for large blessing on Broughton; for a wonderful blessing on the work at Musselburgh; for the conversion of a daughter; for the return of a prodigal, in answer to prayer; for good received at meetings in London; for the conversion of a Sabbath class; for the conversion of three girls, who, since the first Week of Prayer, have given themselves to the Lord; for two souls brought to the Lord, one of them a sister long prayed for; for a young woman in Dundee, often prayed for as bordering on despair, but now trusting in Jesus; for a mother prayed for last Tuesday as desirous of coming to Christ, who believes that now she has closed with Him; for a sister prayed for at these meetings, who is now happy in Jesus; for prayer answered in the reconciliation of a family professing to be Christians; from one who found Jesus last night in the College Church; a minister desires praise for a recent awakening in his congregation."

Help came from brethren, such as Mr. George Wilson, of the Tolbooth Church, Edinburgh; Mr. Maclaren, from Manchester, and Mr. Arnot, from Edinburgh. At the daily prayer-meeting, it became an every-day thing to see the pulpit, the pulpit-stairs, and the three front seats, filled with ministers from town and country. There were a hundred ministers oftentimes, and Mr. Moody took the utmost pains to avail himself of their co-operation, in view of the vast influence they exert on their people when they are themselves filled with the Holy Ghost. Whitefield used to say, in regard to this, that "every minister's name was *Legion.*"

An eye was being kept, all this time, on the places in England that had been visited. Men in whom the churches have confidence reported. The Rev. Dr.

Cairns, for example, at the Noon-meeting, at which he presided, said:

"I have been requested to say a few words about the awakening which, by God's grace, has lately taken place in Berwick-on-Tweed, the town where I have so long labored as a minister. I am happy to state that this work continues and is bearing fruit unto holiness, of which the end shall be eternal life. There are, in all the Churches of Christ there, movements, awakenings more or less, prayer-meetings, in addition to the noon-day prayer-meetings; and tokens of interest are not wanting, as, for example, in the coming forward of young persons who have been awakened to seek admission to the Communion of the Church. It was only the other day that I intimated the Communion, and already as many persons have come forward seeking admission to the Table as I have admitted almost at any time in the course of my ministry; and I doubt not that the number, before the Sacrament season comes round, will be very considerably increased. This is what we desire and hope for. Oh, how delightful it is to speak to these young persons! There is not that difficulty in obtaining answers to the questions that we propose; there is not that reserve and reluctance on speaking of personal religion and Christian experience that ministers at such a time so often have to lament. In other words, there is evidence that this work of God is deep and genuine in that place. We have now ceased to hold evening meetings in our Corn Exchange, which holds about fifteen hundred people. We met there for more than twenty days in succession, and each day it was crowded. We have ceased to hold these special meetings, but only to direct our energies into the districts where the population is composed of fishermen and other classes who could not conveniently attend the town meetings. Last week I spoke at five district meetings on successive evenings, and other brethren who have entered heartily into this work have been doing the same. There have been some inquirers at these meetings, although not quite so numerous as at the beginning in Berwick-on-Tweed; but we trust that good will be done in this way."

The reproducing and self-extending power of deep religious feeling found many illustrations in Glasgow. Every night at nine o'clock the young men met, and the work among them made steady progress, Mr. Moody coming in, as usual, near the close of the hour, and making some remarks on the importance of "*confessing Christ with the mouth.* Through neglect of this, many are left in something like darkness, and have little joy. We ought to speak for Christ; at the same time we must beware of spiritual pride. Heart utterances are what we want, not flowing eloquence. Whenever the devil whispers 'That was a good address,' you are in danger."

After a hymn, for example, an opportunity is given to those recently brought to Christ to tell "how great things the Lord had done for them, and how He had compassion on them." A young man begins by saying, "I was one of the one hundred and one." He meant by this expression to refer to the memorable Tuesday night, when a breathing of the Holy Spirit passed through the assembly, and one hundred and one young men came to the front seats, asking to be prayed for and guided into the truth. The speaker added, "I had been wishing to be saved for many years. When those who were sure that they were Christians were asked to stand up, I felt that I could not honestly do so, though I was a member of the Church, a Sabbath-school teacher, and was one of ten who had sent in a request for our warehouse, for prayer on our behalf. I kept my seat. Mr. Moody then asked all that were Christians to leave the three front pews. I occupied one of these, and when the others went out I kept my place. Thinking that I had, perhaps, misunderstood him, Mr. Moody kindly said to me, 'Are you not a Christian?' I said, 'I am not.' But that very night I found Christ."

A young student next spoke: "I also was one of the one hundred and one of that night. Though taking part in Christian work, I felt my need of what I had not found. That night, at the meeting for conversation, five of the young men in succession spoke to me; and each, unknown to the other, quoted to me John v. 24, 'Verily, verily I say unto you, He that heareth my word, and believeth on Him that sent Me, *hath* everlasting life." I was at length enabled to apprehend the truth, and I now thank the Lord for saving me, and pray that all here may be brought to Christ."

Another spoke: "I had been seeking Christ a long time. That night, when I was going away without relief, Mr. Moody came up, and took me kindly by the hand. He looked at me—I might say he put his two eyes right through mine—and asked me if I would take Christ now. I could not speak, but my heart said, Yes."

One very intelligent young man told briefly, but very clearly, what his state had been till he was awakened, and how miserable he had been, not able to see that salvation was for him. Getting a ray of light, he went home, read John iii. 36, "He that believeth on the Son hath everlasting life," and sought on his knees to be led to the truth. "And," he added, "God heard me. I believed then; I believe now; I am a ransomed soul." Scottish youth are not at all demonstrative in regard to their feelings; it is not usual for them to tell out what is passing in their hearts on the subject of their state towards God; until they have faith, they are slow to speak about their feelings.

The Rev. A. A. Bonar, an honored Christian minister in Scotland, who describes these incidents, adds: "I am writing to you about Glasgow specially; but you may like to get notice about God's work in less known localities. Requests for prayer come to hand from all quarters—*e. g.*, one came to me, asking my congregation to pray for a work of God in the district of John O'Groat's house; and another from Christian friends who live near Cape Wrath. Preaching on Wednesday at Auchterarder, I found unmistakable traces of God's goings in that quarter; and passing on in the evening to Dollar, found an assembly of above one thousand souls, eager to hear the word; and at the close, beside others, about fifty of the boys and young of the Dollar Institute waited for conversation and inquiry. At the Stirling noon-day prayer-meeting, next day, there was a large attendance. There have been not a few awakened there of late, and the interest is deepening. The ministers of all denominations take part most cordially. There,.too, I heard of work going on not only in such places as Alva and Dunfermline, but in obscure parishes. Souls are coming from great distances to ask the way of life at the lips of those who can tell it, and these souls awakened to this concern by no direct means, but evidently by the Holy Spirit who is breathing over the land. It is such a time as we have never had in Scotland before. The same old gospel is preached to all men as aforetime, Christ who was made sin for us, Christ the Substitute, Christ's blood, Christ's righteousness, Christ crucified, the power of God, and the wisdom of God unto salvation; but now the gospel is preached "with the Holy Ghost sent down from heaven." And amid all this the enemy is restrained, so that we are solemnly reminded of Rev. vii. 1-3, the time before the coming of the Lord, when the four angels are charged to let no storm burst, not to allow the wind even to ruffle the sea's smooth surface or move a leaf of any tree, till the seal of the living God has been put on his elect. Is not this sealing going on daily among us? Are not the four angels looking on? Surely it is time to seek the Lord, that He may rain righteousness upon us."

Is it strange that a thrilling interest marked meetings replete with incidents like the following?

Thanks were given for a person who had been blessed while the hymn "Jesus of Nazareth passeth by," was being sung; and several other cases were reported in which the same hymn had been blessed. A Christian working-man said, that "in the building-yard where he worked, this week there had been two boys and three men brought to Christ." "I give thanks for six," was on a paper handed in at the prayer-meeting; while a disciple, who had for many years been pleading for the conversion of near and dear relatives, asked the meeting to join him in thanksgiving for a daughter saved, a nephew and several nieces. A letter said: "We cannot leave Glasgow without telling you that the brother whom we told you of as having come here to attend the meetings, left for London this evening, we firmly believe, resting in Jesus."

A lady asked prayer for her own conversion, stating, "I have come from Switzerland on purpose to be present at the meetings. I have been well brought up, but am not a Christian."

A person about twenty miles out of town wrote: "Dear sir, would you kindly forward four tickets to admit to the morning meeting, on Sabbath first, to the City Hall. I have never had the pleasure of being present at any of these precious meetings that have been held in Glasgow, though a constant reader of the reports given in the various newspapers; but I will be in Glasgow on Sabbath first, along with three friends. Going in the spirit of anxious inquirers, we pray God that it may be our blessed privilege to come home having found that Christ is indeed precious to each of us."

Another day, at noon, four young men from a mining district in Ayrshire were found waiting at the close of the meeting to speak to Mr. Moody, if possible. He had gone out; but they sat down in the inquiry-room with one of the ministers who was still there. "Are you all of one mind? Are you all in Christ?" was the question put to them. "Three of us are Christ's, but our friend here (pointing to the fourth) is not." The minister entered into conversation with the unsaved but anxious one, and found out his state of mind. He showed him that Christ was offering to be his substitute, and to appear in the presence of God for him, and asked, "Will you believe in Him as He so offers Himself to you?" In a moment the lad's countenance changed, and half springing from his seat, he struck the Bible with his hand, exclaiming, "I see it all!" The scale had fallen from his eyes, and he, with his three friends, who had been to him like the friends of the palsied man, left the room to return home by the train, rejoicing.

One other case. A young man attracted Mr. Moody's attention at an inquiry-meeting, an intelligent young man, who had long been anxious. Mr. Moody discovered that one thing had hindered his full decision, viz., want of courage to tell his wife all that was passing through his mind. But last Sabbath afternoon he was enabled to go home and frankly tell all he felt. It turned out that she too was in deep anxiety, only waiting to have the ice broken. The result has been complete deliverance of soul to that young man, who is able now to help others in the way.

From the *Signs of the Times*, in which careful accounts of the awakening appeared from week to week, we extract the programme of meetings for the week March 23-30, from a glance at which an idea may be obtained of the energy with which the work was carried forward:

"Young Men's Meetings (Special Week).

"East U. P. Church, Partick, 8 P. M. (Mr. Sankey present), on Tuesday and Thursday.

"Ewing Place Congregational Church, 8:30 P. M. (Mr. Sankey present); on Tuesday and Thursday.

"Eglinton Street Congregational Church, 8 P. M. (Mr. Sankey present), Wednesday and Friday.

"Sydney Place U. P. Church, 8:30 P. M. (Mr. Sankey present), Wednesday and Friday.

"Free St. Mary's, Govan, 6:30 P. M. (Mr. Sankey present); Eglinton Street U. P. Church, 8 P. M.; Burnbank U. P. Church, 7 P. M.; London Road U. P. Church, 7:30 P. M.

"Mr. Moody will address men who desire to become Christians in East Campbell Street U. P. Church (Rev. Dr. Wallace's), on Tuesday, Wednesday, Thursday, and Friday evenings. Admission by ticket. "Afternoon Bible Lectures by Mr. Moody on Wednesday, Thursday, and Friday, 25th, 26th, and 27th, in Pollok Street Church."

The attention of the Christian people had now been fairly aroused. Mr. Spurgeon, with a view to Glasgow, preached a sermon to young men which was instantly put into circulation, and at the same time gave a cordial invitation to the Evangelists to his Tabernacle in London. Of this sermon 25,000 copies were promptly distributed in Glasgow.

Some idea may be formed of the Scriptural style of address employed in these meetings from the following concise abstract of Mr. Moody's address in St. Silas' Episcopal Church, on Tuesday, March 17, on " Grace." The church is seated for one thousand, but with forms and filling up of the side aisles, there would be thirteen hundred present. After Mr. Sankey had led " Come, Thou Fount " with the choir, the Incumbent, Dr. Hutton, engaged in prayer. The passages of Scripture on which Mr. Moody founded his discourse were John i. 14–17; Rom. v. 15; 1 Cor. i. 3, 4; 1 Peter v. 10, and others. He began by showing grace to be a free gift. "People," he said, "are trying to work for it; if you work for it you are not in a position to receive it. Don't attempt to add anything to the finished work of Christ." Mr. Moody went on to show the contrast between law and grace by reading Deuteronomy xxi. 18–21. The law says "Stone him, smite him;" Christ says, "Kiss him, forgive him." The law says, "Take shoes off;" the father to the prodigal says, "Put them on." Three thousand lost life in one day at the giving of the law, and three thousand found it in one day at Pentecost. Moses, the lawgiver, turned water into blood; Christ, water into wine. He concluded by showing that the Christian must not be satisfied with the gift of grace once, but seek for more grace daily. "God is able to make all grace to abound."

Mr. Sankey sang very touchingly, "Christ hath redeemed us once for all,"—a hymn which has already been the means of bringing peace to souls where it has been sung. At the end of the meeting he sang his hymn on grace, entitled, "More to follow." Rev. Mr. Howie, Free Church, Govan, concluded with a most fervent prayer which seemed to carry the hearts of all present. Dr. Wallace (Established Church) pronounced the benediction.

As a rule the results were the largest and the most promising where prayer had gone before, and instruction was well sustained. Take one case in illustration : Mr. Howie's church, where every Sunday, for two months or so, the pastor had an after-meeting, every one of which has been marked with results which will be recorded in the annals of eternity. So the way was well prepared for Messrs. Moody and Sankey to commence their labors. There, as elsewhere, they have the same old story of their work, churches and halls crowded to overflowing day after day and night after night: many coming, as can be seen, out of sheer curiosity: but with more than one of such the Lord has graciously met in an unexpected hour and manner like. A young lady of talent and education was thus unexpectedly met by the Lord in November in Edinburgh. Immediately on her conversion she began to testify for God. The result is, that she lost her situation as a governess in a family of station. "But I do not mind that," she said; "how could I help speaking to the little ones of Jesus?"

In this district Rev. Mr. Howie reported that "the number of applications for tickets for the meetings to be held there was quite overwhelming, and they had to make selections in the distribution. When Christians applied for them they received them only on the condition that they would give them to unconverted people."

There is a certain degree of uniformity in the methods of operation and in the results, after the attention of the community in Glasgow had been thoroughly aroused; no good purpose, therefore, is served by reciting the details of meetings, and numbers in attendance, and at the inquiry-meetings. It was felt that the inquirers should be visited and followed with instruction, by their own chosen ministers. We are not, therefore, susprised to find that Dr. Jeffrey, minister of London Road Church, sent, after meetings in his church, upwards of eighty letters to ministers of all denominations in the city telling the names of anxious inquirers in their congregations, "that the fruits of awakening may not be lost."

Other places had, besides, been indirectly and incidentally benefited. Bible readings in the south side of the city, had been greatly blessed, especially to the richer portion of the community. Let the reports of the Rev. Andrew A. Bonar, D. D., give an idea of the diligence and activity of the Christian laborers, and the degree of blessing vouchsafed. We necessarily abbreviate:

"The work goes on. The Lord Jesus, sitting at the right hand of God, is 'confirming the word by signs following.' We hear of conversions coming under the notice of workers for the Lord in all parts of the town. At the close of the evening meetings in John Street United Presbyterian Church and the Wesleyan Methodist Church, the number of inquirers was large; but so well was all arranged for conversing with them, that though there must have been above a hundred at one time, yet all was order and stillness, the different workers in separate seats, and some in separate rooms, dealing with the anxious. No idlers were permitted to look on, and there was time for helping individuals to get at a clear understanding of their own difficulties and hindrances, which in many cases is the main thing needed, in order to their right apprehension of the Gospel."

The manner in which divine truth came to human souls, is illustrated in such incidents as the following:

A young lady remarked to a minister one night, "I understand everything that is said and done. I believe all that you can tell me. You cannot tell me anything but what I believe, and yet I don't feel it."

"But God has said, believe and be saved, not feel and be saved."

"But I do not realize it, and do not feel it at all."

"But it is upon the testimony of God that you must take it. God's word is true, whether you feel it or do not feel it."

"Do you mean to say that I am just to rest on that, without feeling it?"

"*I* do not say so. It is God that says so."

"Then it is upon God's testimony that, believing, I am to conclude that *I* am saved?"

"Certainly; just because God says it."

"I think I see it now. It is just upon God's testimony. I see it now." And as she rose she said, "*I see it now. The burden is all away.*"

"What has taken it away?"

"The testimony of God concerning His Son."

"What makes you so sure?"

"That which is written in this Book," she said, holding up her Bible as she left the room.

REST IN CHRIST.

A lady found a girl in whom she was interested deeply anxious. She brought her to the hall when she could get no peace, and there, in the corridor, was Mr. Sankey, speaking to eight or nine gathered round him. He was dwelling upon "He that believeth *hath everlasting life*," dwelling specially upon the word "*hath*." The young woman listened intently, and at last grasped it, saying, "I have got it. That word 'hath' has done it all." And she went away rejoicing in Christ.

Another was asked if she could not take her stand upon that word, "Christ died for the ungodly," and went away unable to sleep that night for joy.

Many times has the simple question, "Are you saved?" been greatly blessed. One invalid, who, in her sick room, had heard of conversions but could not understand what it meant, was asked the kind question, "Are you a child of God?" which planted a fresh thorn in her pillow. She could not rest, but tossed in agony till, early in the morning, the words came into her mind, "Come unto *Me*, and I will give you rest," and she rested there.

It must not be supposed that, even from the very first, the blessing was in any way limited to the sphere of

Mr. Moody's personal influence. Meetings were thronged to hear the ordinary preaching of the word. A Gospel sermon could hardly be preached without great results. All Christian workers, and specially faithful ministers, found their work doubled in the most blessed way. In their places surrounding the chair each day at noon; scattered here and there at evangelistic meetings every evening; called on continually to speak to inquirers,—one felt that, unless special strength were given, they could not meet the demands on them.

We have said little yet of the work among Christians, yet perhaps to Him who searches hearts, this part of the revival looks as stupendous as the other. It has not been uncommon to find backsliding Christians sitting among the anxious, weeping more bitterly than all;—not for a soul lost, but for a Saviour dishonored; asking if they might still hope that the grieved Spirit would return, and that their lost peace and first love might be restored. To many who have for years been believers, it seems as if the fullness of Christ has opened up a mine of untold riches, which they never dreamt of. Those who lived on the border line, so that neither they nor their friends could tell clearly what they were, have stepped boldly out on to the Lord's ground, and many who passed for Christians, both with themselves and others, have exchanged a false hope for a true one.

Employers showed a lively interest in the men whom they employed. Take an illustration.

On March 30th Messrs. Moody and Sankey were present at the daily prayer-meeting in the ship-building yard of Alex. Stephen and Sons, Linthouse, Glasgow. There was a large attendance of the workingmen, the numbers being variously estimated from one thousand five hundred to two thousand, and all the partners of the firm were also present. All listened with eager interest as Mr. Sankey opened the meeting by singing "Jesus of Nazareth passeth by." Rev. Robert Howie led the prayers of the meeting; and another solo, singularly appropriate, "The Lifeboat," was sung by Mr. Sankey. Mr. Moody then delivered a most solemn and stirring address from the words—"I bring you glad tidings of great joy;" and there seemed to be a deep impression produced. At the close he expressed the delight he experienced in addressing such an interesting audience, and intimated that arrangements would be made by the

Central Evangelistic Committee for sending similar aid from time to time to those seeking thus to honor the Saviour, and obtain blessings for themselves and others. Mr. Stephen, speaking in the name of both employers and employees, expressed thanks to Messrs. Moody and Sankey for their kindness in thus complying with the request sent to them last week, and exhorted all present to show their gratitude by accepting of Christ.

The outlying villages around Glasgow began to feel the influence of the word, and communications from a distance stimulated the laborers.

Mr. Edgar, of the Reformed Presbyterian Church, Landressy street, told of nearly a hundred inquirers in connection with Mr. Moody's meeting there.

Mr. William Sloan, as one of a deputation sent to Belfast, detailed interesting facts regarding a remarkable meeting there, at the close of which five hundred young men waited for prayer.

The Women's meetings in Free Cunningham Church, and the Mill-girls' in Mr. McMunn's Church, Great Hamilton street (conducted by ladies), were very remarkable for the number who remained to be conversed with every evening, and of these one and another have come "out of darkness into marvelous light."

There was no excitement at any of these gatherings; there was quiet, calm solemnity. Strange, indeed, this absence of excitement in such assemblies, considering the great and undeniable results; but all the more did it hereby prove itself to be the work of the Spirit, who comes into the soul as the quiet breath of life. The meetings every evening from Monday, March 29th, in Wellington Palace, a new hall in Commercial road, which accommodates about two thousand or two thousand five hundred persons, were thronged to the door by an audience drawn from the south-east part of the city. Even on nights when Mr. Moody was not there, there was quite a crowded attendance, and ministers of all denominations were present. Each night not fewer than a hundred inquirers waited. Nor was it otherwise at the Townhead Established Church, where the minister, Mr. Turnbull, had thrown himself into the work with all his heart.

Referring to another part of the city and another class, Dr. Elder Cumming, of Sandyford Established Church, declared that he had never known anything like this movement during the twenty years of his ministry. He was able to reckon up something like forty cases of people converted to the Lord during the last two months, some of them among the poor and some of them in the higher ranks of society, but both classes alike rejoicing in the treasure they had found. A minister from the country, Mr. McAulay, of the Free Church, Old Kilpatrick, said on the same occasion "that he had watched the meetings from the view-point of a conservative theology, and rejoiced to discover that nothing was proclaimed but the old truth—man lost, and Christ all-sufficient to save."

The Bible-readings on the south side of the river, in the Congregationalist Chapel, Eglinton street (Mr. David Russell's), continued to be thronged to the door.

In the county of Aberdeen, at Kennethmont, Rothiemay, New Marnoch, there was a shaking among the dry bones, and at Drumblade a great number had been remarkably awakened. "Scores of anxious souls," says one, "were there, ministers, elders, and others directing them to Jesus. I was never made so happy as one night when I found faces suffused with tears, looking into my face, and crying—'O how shall I, how can I, be saved?'" At Pitcaple, in another part of the county, the awakening was every way as remarkable.

During what is called Fast-day week in Glasgow, when religious persons are engaged in the services connected with the communion, and the irreligious take a holiday, Messrs. Moody and Sankey left the city for a few days, and visited Helensburgh, Paisley, and Greenock.

The ground was already prepared, and many were looking forward to their visit with the highest expectations. A general stir in the community, crowds occupying the places of meeting long before the hours advertised, eager and hushed audiences completely swayed by the speaking and singing, the deepest solemnity in the thronged inquiry-rooms—these were the features everywhere. Cordiality and unanimity prevailed among the ministers of the Gospel and Christians of different denominations.

At Helensburgh the first meeting was held in the West Free Church at half-past three o'clock. An hour and a half before the time announced the church was filled to overflowing, and by the time the service commenced the passages and every available space were occupied. Mr. Moody delivered his lecture on "The Blood," and Mr. Sankey sang several hymns. The crowd was equally great in the evening in the United Presbyterian Church. The subject was "The Gospel." After the first meeting believers and inquirers were asked to remain, when about six or seven hundred occupied the whole body of the church. Mr. Moody addressed the anxious, showing that simple trust alone was needed. He then invited those who wished to be spoken with individually to retire into the session-house. About fifty went. It was a most solemn meeting, many being in the deepest distress.

Paisley and Greenock were visited; a Sabbath being given to the latter important place.

The Rev. A. Henderson, United Presbyterian minister, gives the following account of the work in Paisley:

"During the week of prayer in the beginning of the year we had a series of daily meetings in Free St. George's Church, which were attended by numbers that steadily increased till the close. A deep impression was produced, and earnest desires were expressed that Messrs. Moody and Sankey might visit the town.

THE FIELD PREPARED. 107

"Shortly after the close of the week of prayer a meeting of ministers of various denominations was called in the usual way, by circular signed by the senior minister of the town. Almost all denominations were represented at the meeting, and it was unanimously agreed to send a requisition to Messrs. Moody and Sankey, asking them to visit Paisley. This requisition was signed by more than two-thirds of the evangelical ministers of the town. It was agreed at the same time that a daily prayer-meeting should be commenced. That meeting has been regularly held since the end of February in Oakshaw United Presbyterian Church. United evangelistic meetings have been also held on Monday and Thursday evenings. These meetings have occasionally been addressed by those who had taken a part in the movement in Edinburgh and Glasgow. After some of these meetings a few inquirers remained to be conversed with, and some were brought to peace in believing.

"On Wednesday of this week, Mr. Moody came among us. The mid-day prayer-meeting held in Mr. France's church was crowded. Long before the hour announced, the Abbey was filled to hear one of his

Bible lectures, and in the evening the Free High Church was crammed in every corner. More than two thousand people must have been present. Mr. Moody spoke from John iii., on the necessity of the new birth. A very deep impression was made, and about forty inquirers were individually conversed with, many of whom departed rejoicing. On Thursday Mr. Sankey came. The Free High Church was again crowded an hour before the time of meeting. Free St. George's was also opened, and filled to overflowing. A number of inquirers were spoken to in the latter place, and about sixty remained in the Free High Church. Mr. Moody returned yesterday. He addressed the mid-day prayer-meeting, gave a Bible reading in the Free High Church at four o'clock on 'Heaven,' and addressed the meeting in the same place in the evening. An hour before the time the large building was crowded in every part; not an inch of standing room was left. About two hundred inquirers remained. The scene was most impressive. The whole area of the church was occupied by groups of men and women, many of whom were weeping most bitterly, while ministers and Christian friends were engaged in speaking to them of Christ. At the close, Mr.

Moody gathered the inquirers together, and asked all who could say now that they could cast themselves on Christ to stand up and sing 'Just as I am,' when the great majority stood up. It was a sight to be remembered for a lifetime. The cloud of blessing has burst over us at last. The prayers of God's children have been answered, and their hearts refreshed. Brethren of all denominations have come together and have wrought together for a common end."

Of the result, of the Sabbath given to Greenock, the Rev. E. Maclean, Baptist minister, gives the following account:

"The movement in Greenock, which is now felt to be touching and impressing all classes, may be said, under God, to be the outgrowth of daily prayer-meetings and special evangelistic efforts which have been maintained for more than three months.

"Arrangements were made for Messrs. Moody and Sankey visiting the town, and for a visit to the neighboring town of Paisley at the same time; so we had these friends with us alternately. On Wednesday, the 8th of April, Mr. Sankey visited us, and took part in our daily prayer-meeting at noon, in the Town Hall, where between two and three thousand people were assembled. In connection with this service there was a profound impression produced by the singing of the hymn 'Nothing but Leaves.' In the evening there was again a crowded attendance at the Town Hall and St. Michael Street United Presbyterian Church, which was open for the overflow, at both of which places Mr. Sankey was present during the evening.

"On Thursday Mr. Moody attended three meetings. The daily prayer-meeting was crowded; and, after prayer and praise, Mr. Moody spoke from Luke v. 18, in his usual graphic way. In the afternoon, he gave his Bible lecture on 'Heaven.' The solemnity and attention displayed seemed to show that the truth set forth was finding its way to many a heart. In the evening Mr. Moody followed up his address on 'Heaven' by an address on 'Regeneration,' specially addressed to the unconverted, in which he showed that, 'Except a man be born again, he cannot see the kingdom of God.' After the public meeting there were a second and third meeting, at which a large number of inquirers remained.

"On Friday Mr. Sankey was present at the largest forenoon meeting we have yet had; and again in the evening, when Revs. Messrs. Smith, Maclean, Symington, Young, and Jarvie addressed the assembly, numbering over three thousand persons.

"On Saturday the daily meeting was reserved specially for children, and the hall was again densely crowded with children, their parents and friends. Mr. Sankey sang 'Jesus loves Me,' 'Room among the Angels,' 'Hold the Fort,' etc. Altogether during the last few days it may be calculated that from four to five thousand have been hearing the Gospel daily. Nearly all the ministers of the town have taken part in one way or another during the course of the meetings."

By the middle of April, Glasgow Christians felt that they had had time to form an opinion regarding the agencies employed and the results. Rev. James Wells, Free Barony Church, Glasgow, himself a most laborious and successful missionary pastor in a difficult field, says: "I shall give you the impressions of an eye-witness regarding some of the most noteworthy features of the work of grace in Glasgow. Perhaps the most hopeful sign is, that one is hearing continually of cases of awakening and conversion in out-of-the-way corners, and in connection with ordinary agencies. Surprising tokens of the Spirit's power are now found in Sabbath-schools, Bible classes, and mission meetings. The stream in the extraordinary channels is overflowing along the ordinary home channels. Two facts help to account for this. All the efforts of Messrs. Moody and Sankey have been in the closest alliance with, and thoroughly loyal to, existing agencies; and the work may now be said to have been accepted as genuine by the catholic consent of the Evangelical Churches.

"It seems to be generally admitted that the young men have had the largest share of the blessing. Their case from the very first was specially laid upon the hearts and consciences of the praying people. Our spiritual dead among the young men were carried forth like the dead son of the widow of Nain. A widowed Church carried them forth with affectionate sorrow; but not in despair, as Jesus of Nazareth was passing by, and His fame was in the land. At His bidding she stood still, expecting His aid; and many of our spiritual dead heard His life-giving word, and were restored as the crown and joy of the Church. I do not think that I have ever seen better religious meetings than some of those young men's meetings."

The Rev. Dr. Wallace, of East Campbell Street United Presbyterian Church, Glasgow, an experienced pastor, and well entitled to speak on such a topic, writes:

"'The Lord hath done great things for us, whereof we are glad.' This is the spirit in which we regard the present blessed awakening, which God in His mercy has granted us during this precious time of visitation. Truly God has fulfilled His own promise: 'Call unto me, and I will answer thee, and show thee great and mighty things which thou knowest not.' Had we been told at the commencement of this year of the scenes which we have lately witnessed,—crowded prayer-meetings at noon, nighly prayer-meetings for young men, hundreds of anxious inquirers manifesting intense interest in the concerns of their souls; in short, had we been told that ere the spring time would come and pass away there would be such a fresh outburst of spiritual life, we should have felt inclined to say, as the prime minister of Israel did when Elisha prophesied that there would be plenty of food sold at the market price in the gate of Samaria within twenty-four hours, when the famine was sore in the land, 'Behold, if the Lord would make windows in heaven, might this thing be?' *It has been;* 'times of refreshing' have come, and unto God be all the glory and all the praise! It is with a grateful heart that we place on record some of 'the things which we have seen and heard.'"

Mr. Brownlow North, a gentleman of property and eminent Christian zeal, who was many years ago formally set apart to the work of an evangelist by the Free Church, had come to Glasgow. Of his efforts, one of the Glasgow pastors gives this account:

"Mr. Brownlow North gave six addresses; and these were evidently much blessed to not a few. At several of these gatherings, which were thrown open, like the noonday meeting, for prayer and remarks, several young men stood up, and sweetly and humbly testified to the '*blessing which they had got.*' This has become a very significant phrase in these days. All our prayer-meetings have been thrown open, and with the very best results. Unction, brevity, variety are indispensable to a successful 'sweet hour of prayer.' Never have I had so many applicants for admission to the Lord's table for the first time as at this season; but the spirit in which they express themselves is something still more satisfactory than mere numbers. God in mercy grant that the tide of blessing may deepen and spread throughout the whole land!"

Of the state of feeling in Dundee, Rev. A. H. Reid, of M'Cheyne Church, writes:

"With much gratitude and thankfulness to our redeeming God, we are able to report that the good work still goes on silently and unostentatiously. The Spirit is among us, not so much as the rushing, mighty wind, bearing down with violence all obstacles: nor even so much, perhaps, as the 'floods upon the dry ground,' but rather as the gentle summer rain, or the silently falling dew, 'that tarrieth not for man, nor waiteth for the sons of men.' Never was there less of everything approaching to excitement or extravagance; so much so, that outside observers, who are not coming into personal contact with inquirers and converts, can form no adequate idea of the depth and extent of the good that has been done.

"A minister in the east end reported the other day at a meeting of his presbytery, 'We are in the midst of a gracious revival, *without the very least excitement.*' Many others could give similar testimony. Since our beloved brethren, Moody and Sankey, left us, evangelistic services have been held, generally for a week at a time, in many of the churches. These meetings have been addressed by ministers and laymen, both from a distance and from the locality. The results in many instances have been most encouraging; and were it prudent to do so, many sheets might be filled with records of individual cases of conversion. Suffice it to say, that old sinners grown hoary in sin, together with young men and young women in the bloom of opening life, as well as many little children, have felt the sharp arrows of the King in their hearts, and yielded to His scepter. Most of the cases of anxiety exhibited a considerable measure of deep conviction of sin, especially the sin of unbelief, and a desire to be saved not merely from *hell*, as the consequence of sin, but from sin itself in its dominion and power.

"These special efforts have now for the most part given place again to the ordinary means of grace,— weekly prayer-meetings, Bible and young communicants' classes, pastoral visitation, etc. It is believed that the work will continue to go on in these ordinary channels. The influence of the movement on ministers, and on their ordinary ministrations, is very marked. There is a power and liberty and joyfulness in declaring the old, old story of the cross, as well as an eager attention and expectancy in listening to it, not felt before. In some cases, Saturday evening and Sabbath morning prayer-meetings for young men and young women (meeting separately) have been commenced, with an encouraging attendance, for the special purpose of pleading for a blessing in connection with the Sabbath services. The consequence is, that Christians come up to the sanctuary with their mouths wide open, and they are filled abundantly by the Lord Himself. The attendance at the weekly prayer-meetings is in all cases (where the minister is favorable to the work) increased; in some cases it has been doubled, and even tripled. Many of the ministers have been inviting anxious ones to meet them in their vestries or houses, and not a few have taken advantage of the invitation to open up their difficulties.

"One of the most striking evidences of the presence of the Spirit is the facility with which anxious ones are brought to see the simplicity of God's way of salvation, and to trust Christ as their Saviour. The very same truths which before seemed powerless to impart peace have, in many instances, only to be stated in order to be received. Often have we seen the smile of peace brightening up the countenance which, but a moment before, was sad and sorrowful on account of sin, at the very time when we were setting before the soul the *trustworthiness* of the Saviour, the free offer of salvation to *all*, and the privilege and duty of an immediate acceptance of Christ. As we remarked, 'It seems just now *so easy to be saved.*'

"Another token of God's presence is the readiness of multitudes of all classes to converse on spiritual matters. God's people especially have been drawn nearer to each other, and find their hearts refreshed in speaking to one another of the 'things touching the King.' Bible readings in private houses have been commenced, where Christians meet together for the study of God's Word. One of the most encouraging aspects of the work is the taste which has been created for the 'pure milk of the Word.' Many who were believers before testify that, under the fresh baptism of the Spirit which they have received, the Bible has become to them a new book altogether. The number of applicants for admission to the Lord's table is very large. In one congregation in town there are between fifty and sixty."

A Convention in Glasgow was intended to wind up the series of meetings held by Messrs. Moody and Sankey for preaching the gospel. It was "a really successful gathering of thousands of Christian workers from all parts of the land and many parts of the world. There never was a meeting equal to it in our country for the numbers assembled, the variety of churches represented, and the earnest, practical tone and tendency displayed in the addresses. There were seven thousand tickets issued, and we think there were at least five thousand at one time in the 'palace.' They came and went at all the different six hours. There were many there who, by their appearance while Mr. Sankey sang or Mr. Moody spoke, gave one the impression that they were listening to them for the first time; for they seemed to be enrapt in fixed astonishment at the singing of the one and the speaking of the other."

Mr. Moody answered many "miscellaneous practical questions in a brief, practical way." As to a chairman at gospel meetings, Mr. Moody said: "I have noticed during the few months I have been here, that a great many meetings in Scotland have been just spoiled by some one taking the chair;

and after a man has preached a most powerful sermon, the chairman got up and made some observations and offered some resolutions, and took the mind of the audience right away from the sermon. The man to close the meeting is the one who began it."

"I do not see any objection to women working among their own sex. One woman in Mr. Spurgeon's church had six hundred women gathered together from the lanes and alleys of London, and it was a question whether she did not do more for these women than Mr. Spurgeon."

"As to children, I would say, put up some decent buildings. Your rooms in Scotland are dirty, dark, and dingy; and to sit on the hard seats in some of them is enough to make any one sick. I would have the seats low, so that the children's feet might touch the floor. I would have a lot of buildings erected for them: and there ought to be a hundred such buildings in Glasgow—good, cheerful, pleasant buildings. Out of these mission schools, churches would grow.

"As to young converts, what did the Master say to the man whom he dispossessed of the legion of devils? 'Go home to thy friends, and tell them how great things the Lord hath done for thee, and hath had compassion on thee. And he departed and began to publish in Decapolis (a region embracing ten cities), how great things Jesus had done for him, and all men did marvel.' That man went and told his friends in the whole town. If I get good news, I should not confine it to my wife and children, I should spread it. If I have been serving the devil publicly, why not confess Christ publicly? We want a little more of that confession in the churches in Glasgow and Scotland. Some say they are afraid about it, and that these young converts should be taught before they teach. But the spirit of the gospel is get and give. Let these young friends go out and do the best they can. I believe if hundreds of young converts were setting to work they would do immense good. They must be guided; if they make a mistake they should be told of it privately. Their mistakes should not be published abroad. Of course they will make some mistakes. Since I have been a Christian I have made mistakes enough to keep me humble. If they did not make mistakes they might soon get full of spiritual pride. Some men make only one mistake, and that is that they are so afraid of making a mistake that they never do anything.'

"As to the benefit of thoroughly educated ministers, I never saw a man that had too much education. But there is another side to that; if a man goes and sets up education in the place of Christ he will have a good deal to answer for. There was a great cry that some men had got zeal without knowledge. But I would rather have zeal without knowledge than knowledge without zeal. Regularly trained ministers have their place, and it would be very foolish for us to quarrel with one another on that point. It would have been very foolish for Paul to have said to Peter: 'Here, Peter, you are an unlearned fisherman of Galilee: you have got zeal, but you have not got education. I have got a polished education; I am the man to preach.' God used them both."

"As to the outlying masses, if this convention should go on fire with love for Christ, we should soon reach them. The spirit of Christianity is not to open churches and say, 'Come in and be saved,' but to go out and seek the lost. The spirit of the Son of God is to seek and save those who are lost. If they will not come to your nice churches, you should get some tents and go where the masses are. If I went to one of your lakes to fish and caught nothing, I should go to some other one where the fish were. Instead of preaching to empty pews, I would rather go out to the streets where the crowd is. Never mind the talk of your dinner parties but go out and work for Christ.

"As to a Bible lecture on the Sabbath in place of one of our sermons, I do not see anything to hinder it. I would suggest to some of our friends present just to try it. Ministers have got into the habit of using the Bible merely as a text-book, and then going over all Christendom after the sermon. Why do this? One word that God says is worth a hundred of yours. It reminds me of a minister who, on going to church, lost his sermon, and who said to his congregation, 'I have lost my sermon, but I will read you two or three chapters of Job, and they are worth two of it.'"

The question of Total Abstinence is not on the same basis in Great Britain that it has reached here, but Mr. Moody spoke plainly: "I would rather have my right hand cut off than touch the stuff before my children. The friends that have been lost are so many as should rouse us to be as one man in sweeping the drink from our tables. If you want me to sign the pledge, I will take any pledge you may bring; I never touch drink, and never intend to do so. Now for the other side! Some temperance men make a grand mistake, and that is—*they lug in the question every time they get the chance.* Everything in its own place! If I go to a prayer-meeting I do not want to hear temperance or the higher Christian life. There is a man who comes to our noon-day meetings; no matter what the subject is, he gets up and talks every day on the higher life. A friend, in going out of the meeting one day, said to me, 'I like a fiddle with a thousand strings, not with this one of higher life played on every day.' And so it is with temperance."

As to the young men—"What is the work of the Young Men's Christian Association? To look after these young men—not to get up lectures to them, not to have skeptics and infidels lecturing and dealing out to them, I was going to say, damnable stuff. They are infidels now if unsaved—give them the good, pure, gospel. They don't want lectures. They want Christ and let them have Christ. The world is perishing for the want of Christ, and *what the young men of Glasgow or any other city want is* THE SON OF GOD, not lectures and theology. That is all; and that is the only thing that will save them from a drunkard's grave."

Such was the style in which practical themes were discussed by Mr. Moody; and the Convention maintained the same practical and earnest tone throughout. It included hundreds of representative men from every part of Scotland, and of every class and every denomination. Country gentlemen, large employers, lawyers, college professors, and strangers from England, Ireland, and the Continent. Dr. Buchanan of Glasgow, of whom Scottish Christians are justly proud, fittingly opened the meeting with the One Hundredth Psalm and prayer, and Dr. Charteris, Principal Fairbairn, who has since entered into rest, and many others took part. The closing scene of the day meeting (an evening meeting was called for and numbered five thousand persons,) was peculiarly impressive. Instead of further details, an estimate of the whole effort will interest the reader.

At three o'clock all were ready for the last part of that day's programme. Dr. Andrew A. Bonar and Mr. Sankey, with his choir, sang "I am trusting, Lord, in Thee."

Before commencing his lecture on "Works," Mr.

Moody prayed again. He solemnly asked that "this the last hour that we should ever all spend together on earth, might be very memorable, and that the influence of this convention might be felt on the shores of eternity. It is so easy for Thee, O God, to give blessing!" His lecture was addressed to Christians, telling what the *saved were to do*, not how to *save themselves*. As he drew to the close he said, "Napoleon I. once after a victory struck a medal with these words on it, 'I was there!' I shall soon leave Scotland, but I shall look to what has passed there for ever. I shall remember our meeting here, and the 16th day of April, 1874, and rejoice to say, 'I was there.' But shall any of us stand before the throne with 'nothing but leaves?' It is hard to draw to a close. We must say good night; but we shall meet in the morning."

Mr. Somerville prayed, and after singing, "There's a land that is fairer than day," the benediction was pronounced, and this most memorable conference separated, every one blessing the Lord for that day's wonderful enjoyment.

"The right tone was struck at once and maintained throughout, and the impression increased without interruption from the beginning to the close. Invitations had been issued first to ministers and office-bearers, and then to the general public. There were about two thousand ministers and office-bearers present, and the audience altogether numbered about five thousand. It was scarcely an exaggeration when Dr. Cairns said it was a meeting unparalleled in the history of Scottish, perhaps of British, Christianity.

" The external arrangements conduced greatly to the success. The meeting took place in the Kibble Crystal Palace, a very large and beautiful circular building in the Botanic Gardens. A platform for the accommodation of those who were to take a leading part in the proceedings was erected opposite the entrance on the far-off side of the circle. The seats nearest the platform were occupied by ministers and office-bearers, while the outer circle of seats was occupied by the general public. Here and there in the building were large hothouse plants, and in front of the platform there was a beautiful bed of flowers. The weather was fine.

" The first result of the meeting was the impression produced on those present, of which the principal elements probably were a fresher and larger conception of the dimensions and character of the work God has already done, an overmastering feeling of the nearness of the divine love and power, operative and available for further operations, and a sense of the duty of vigorously planning and laboring for the consolidation and promotion of the work in all directions. But the impulses generated in the convention will no doubt spread and multiply themselves; those who took part in it will communicate their impressions to others, and new vigor and enlightenment may be looked for in all evangelistic operations in the West." The Convention was the close of the evangelists' labors in Glasgow.

The *Times of Blessing*, a weekly journal devoted to the spread of good tidings, thus speaks on April 30, 1874: "The work continues to spread and deepen on all hands. Edinburgh and Glasgow are of course the great centers, and probably the movement is most intense in and around them. At Leith, Dalkeith, Portobello, Linlithgow, Musselburgh, Kirkcaldy, Dunfermline, Bathgate, West Calder, and at Greenock, Paisley, Chryston, Douglas, and many other places within their immediate influence, it has been strongly felt. But it is by no means confined to the central districts. The news of what has been doing in them has spread everywhere, and awakened interest and expectation in the remotest places. The result of this has been united prayer on the part of God's people, and the putting forth of special efforts, which success seems everywhere to follow. From the Orkney and Shetland Islands requests for prayer have been sent to Edinburgh, not unaccompanied with thanksgivings for blessings received; and the hymns which have been in so many places the precursors of revival are already popular in these islands. Elgin is the center of a work extending over all the southern coast of the Moray Firth. Similarly, Aberdeen is the focus of an extensive movement. The impulse given by the visit of Messrs. Moody and Sankey to Dundee has continued to propagate itself both in that town and elsewhere in Forfar and Fife. All through the central counties special meetings have been held, and the anticipated results, while nowhere entirely wanting, have in many cases been of the most extraordinary kind. In the southeastern counties the visits of Messrs. Moody and Sankey to Melrose and Berwick, as well as the constant news from Edinburgh, excited a spirit of awakening everywhere. Reports of blessing received at several places in Argyllshire were given in at the Free Synod of that county, and every day brings the most cheering news from new places in the west."

The Rev. W. Arnot, now well known in this country, expressed, at this stage of the movement, his deliberate opinion in the valuable monthly of which he is the editor, the point of view at which he looks at it being its promotion of true Catholicity.

"For some years past, until May of last year, a distressing internal war has raged among us in regard to union. Although a flood had passed over the land these differences could not have been more completely swept away. Men have been lifted up nearer to Christ, and they have, to their surprise, found themselves much closer to one another. The tone of the conference was tender, and humble, and devout, and brotherly in a degree far exceeding anything within the experience of the eldest of us. There was not a jarring note. The meeting threw light for me on the Lord's meaning when he said, 'Except ye receive the kingdom as a little child, ye shall not enter it.' When great warrior men are melted down by the Spirit into little babes, they seem to get into the kingdom more easily than when they march against each other with their armor on. The meeting was too short. The mind of the brethren seemed to be—

'I have been there, and still would go ;
'Tis like a little heaven below.'

"A similar spirit is spreading in many parts of Scotland. Some who, in the various country towns and villages, 'wait for the consolation of Israel,' come over to Edinburgh, and attend the noon meeting for a day or two. When these return they communicate with their friends. An evangelistic union meeting is arranged; a demand reaches Edinburgh for one or more to come over and help; and so this new fiery cross is carried from mountain ridge to mountain ridge, summoning the clans to the standard of the Prince of peace. Great labor falls on those who are able-bodied as well as spiritually qualified; but if the work is severe, the joy is like the joy of harvest, and they do not feel the burden."

Of the Convention the Rev. A. Somerville, who has since been suffered to carry much blessing to India, thus wrote:

"Such a day I have never seen! I almost fear to put my thoughts in writing, lest I should seem to exaggerate. It is only by degrees, and as I come in contact with individuals, since the meeting, that I find that the feelings of others correspond with my own. I can only say that it was to some of us as one of 'the days of heaven upon the earth.' It is impossible, by means of any printed report of what was spoken, to convey an idea of the power, sweetness— aye, blessedness, which pervaded the vast assembly. We may reproduce the utterances on paper; these are like the visible body, but who can reproduce the soul that animated the words? The persons who were fortunate enough to be present from first to last were those most thrilled with sensibility; and this simply from the fact that the longer the time the deeper did the intensity of emotion become.

" The Spirit of the Lord seemed to descend, and to set in tuneful vibration the heart-strings of thousands. An indescribable consciousness of heavenly things being near, and of our susceptibilities being in harmony with these, held us as in a delicious dream, while yet all our mental faculties were in full strain.

"It is not to be supposed, however, that there was merely indulgence in sentiment, or that our experience resembled enjoyment from listening to the concord of musical sounds. No; the speeches throughout the day were manly, unaffected, practical, and thoroughly to the point."

If it be supposed that clergymen are predisposed to regard a religious movement with confidence, the same cannot be said of the legal mind, accustomed as it is to weigh evidence. We subjoin, therefore, the testimony of the Hon. Lord Ardmillan, one of the judges, and well known in literary circles, who, in the course of a public address, said:

"No candid and intelligent observer can doubt that there has been, and still is, a great work of God in the midst of us—a work of awakening, of compunction, of revival, and of conversion. A great blessing has followed the labors of our friends from America and those who have aided them, and it is, we hope, spreading and deepening. But the work is *not of man*—it is of grace, and, therefore, of God; and men, even the most earnest and able, are but instruments in God's hands. None accept this truth more unreservedly than Mr. Moody and Mr. Sankey, whose ministrations have been so greatly blessed, and I think it is a hopeful characteristic of this movement, of which I speak from personal observation at many meetings, that there has been so little self-exaltation, and so much sobriety."

There was good reason for Christian laborers to rejoice, not only in what they saw, but in what they felt. "*The servants that drew the water knew.* At Cana neither the mother of our Lord, nor guests, nor bridegroom, saw the miracle. No eyes but Christ's and the servants' saw it. The servants drew, the servants filled, the servants bare that water, that wine."

In Scotland, wrote Mrs. Barbour, on the 7th of May (1874): "Our pastors have ever been deemed worthy of double honor; but now the Chief Shepherd is sealing this ordinance in the sight of all men with His royal stamp. It is no stranger who watches the sheep and lambs as they pass from the outer into the inner fold, although such strangers were received, coming in the Master's name, as the Master Himself. It is the same faithful men who have dispensed the word of truth for the last twenty, thirty, and forty years among us who speak the word that sets the captive free."

Rev. Mr. Talon (Episcopalian) bore testimony thus: "Can we ever tell what we owe to having been brought within these walls? I, for one, shall never forget the first look I got of the vast multitude from yonder door. As I looked down, and could not get admission, I yet heard a few words, from whom I know not, but I turned away and wept. And since then I have never come but to be blest. Coming in flurried with care, peace has calmed my spirit. Coming in sad, how inspiring have been the glad songs of praise! Coming in discouraged, the tidings of His power and presence manifested in so many parts of the land, have made me take courage. I have been blessed in my soul, blessed in my family, blessed in my flock; and so will all who come hither, looking only to Jesus. It might not occur to us to give the same reason which Paul gave for the gospel's being the power of God unto salvation. We might have said it was from his *mercy* being revealed. Paul says it is from the revelation of God's *righteousness*. And this is free to all—puts all on a level down in the dust. One has said that God seeks his jewels in the dust."

We must, for the present, take leave of these stirring scenes in Glasgow, to follow the steps of the evangelists to other and less conspicuous fields of labor. But before doing so it is with pleasure we place on record a testimony which connects this work and our own land in a very pleasing manner.

THE MODERATOR OF THE REFORMED PRESBYTERIAN SYNOD ON THE AWAKENING.

The Moderator, in bringing the business of the Synod to a close, said :

"The remarkable religious awakening that has taken place in our chief cities, and over much of our country, was most fitly the first subject that came before us. The details given by eye-witnesses among us of its blessed results sent into all our hearts a thrill of gratitude to God. Praise, that in too many districts of Scotland has been little esteemed and slovenly performed, has been felt by multitudes to have had quite a new character given to it, and the abundant calls to its performance in the Word of God have received a fullness of meaning that many of us had not previously realized. And one lesson taught by this remarkable awakening to us who are in the ministry of the gospel is to have faith in the divinely-appointed means, and to prepare for, and to act in, the preaching of Christ crucified, in the full confidence that it is the mode by which men, whether Jews or Greeks, are to be brought to see in Christ the power of God and the wisdom of God. It would be unpardonable, in speaking of this movement, not to own that while there has been a preparedness in many hearts for its coming among us, it has, under God, been largely fostered and spread over our country by the remarkable labors, unweary, untiring, and in full faith in the Divine power to change the hearts of men, of the American evangelists, Messrs. Moody and Sankey. These gentlemen in leaving our shores will carry with them the gratitude of many thousands of the best of our countrymen. And it is not too much to say that they have given a new delightful association to pious Scotchmen with the name of America, and have tended to rivet the bonds of peace and love between the United States and this kingdom— bonds which we pray the Prince of Peace will never suffer to be broken."

CHAPTER IV.

THE WORK IN THE COUNTRY TOWNS OF SCOTLAND.

BEFORE following the American laborers to the less important towns of Scotland, it will be proper to take note of the public declarations made concerning their work after it had been studied in the two great centers of Edinburgh and Glasgow. The Presbyterian system of church administration brings ministers and elders together and affords opportunity for free expression of opinion. The meetings of Synods and Assemblies came just at this time, and official reports and addresses made therein had great weight over the country.

The Free Church moderator devoted one third of his opening address to the awakening. He said:—
"At the very time when the proposal of an incorporating union with brethren of other churches seemed to be relegated to a far distant future—when an answer to the many prayers that 'we all might be one, even as the Father and the Son are one,' seemed

to be withheld—when pseudo-philosophers, with profane levity, were proposing a prayer gauge, to test the efficacy of prayer—the Lord manifested Himself as a faithful and a jealous God—jealous for His own glory and faithful to His promises—as the hearer and answerer of prayer, by pouring out a blessed and copious effusion of His Holy Spirit upon our land, whereby many have been converted and saved, and a most solemn impression has been produced upon the minds of men of all ranks and degrees. The result of this blessed visitation has been the healing of breaches among beloved brethren, and the producing such union of heart and co-operation among the godly and earnest-minded laborers in all our churches as warrant the hope of union on a broader basis than we had dreamt of.

"It has pleased God to make use of two strangers from the other side of the Atlantic as the instruments through whom the spiritual awakening which has gladdened, and still is gladdening, many parts of Scotland, broke forth; and readily and heartily, I am sure, we are ready to render all due honor to beloved brethren whom the Lord Himself has honored —but, at the same time, we must not lose sight of the fact, that by these conferences in our assemblies on the state of religion, by the deputations sent down to visit the various Presbyteries with the same object in view, and by increasing prayer and spiritual effort on the part of the ministers, elders, deacons, and other godly laymen, the ground had already been prepared, the good seed had been copiously sown, and all that was wanting was that 'God should give the increase.' Blessed be the Lord our God, for He hath given the increase, and many of you, beloved brethren, who for many a year 'went forth weeping, bearing your precious seed, have at last returned rejoicing, bringing your sheaves with you.'

"Rev. fathers and brethren, there is still another aspect in which it seems to me we should regard the blessed work of the Holy Spirit, in awakening and reviving the Churches of our land at this time, and that is in the light of 'baptism with fire' ere times of trouble come, ere we are called 'to contend earnestly for the faith once delivered to the saints.' In looking back upon the history of the Church of Christ, we can trace many instances in which such 'times of refreshing from the presence of the Lord' were the preludes to seasons of warfare and distress, of storm and tempest, when men's hearts were ready to fail them through fear, and many made shipwreck of their faith. Surely this is one aspect in which we may regard the outpouring of the Holy Ghost on the day of Pentecost, for scarcely had its blessed effects been felt, than persecution of the infant Church began. The outpouring of the Spirit and remarkable awakening that accompanied the great Reformation of the sixteenth century was at once the prelude to centuries of persecution and martyrdom, and the preparation of God's people for resisting unto blood, striving against sin."

The United Presbyterian Synod includes and represents a large and zealous body of Scottish Christians, whose labors have effected much in the land. The moderator made reference to the awakening in the following terms:—"There is no part of the Synod's proceedings that has been so interesting alike to yourselves and the Christian public, as the conference on the great religious revival and on evangelistic work. While some brethren were perplexed by honest difficulties which explanation removed, and while on the part of none of us was there any disposition shown to give a blind and unqualified approval to everything that had been done or spoken, there was soon manifested a universal readiness to acknowledge in the present awakening a blessed reality, and to recognize in it with adoring gratitude the work of the Holy Spirit. There was a tone of glad and solemn interest, an eagerness for information and for practical suggestions, and an earnest desire that the blessing might spread like a lustral fire over the land. The hearts of the brethren beat warmly and in unison. The comprehensive and thorough nature of the measures recommended by the Synod—in the sending of deputations to presbyteries, the issuing of a pastoral address, and the exhortation to every minister and session to seek revival in themselves and in their flocks, and then to make their churches the center of an earnest evangelism to the regions around them— proves how much the Synod has become of one heart and one soul in this mighty movement. If the injunctions of the Synod are carried out with prayerful and persevering energy, in all our congregations, from Shetland to the Mull of Galloway, and from Berwick to Brighton, it will be a blessed year for our Church; many a full net will be brought to land, and long before another Synod meets, the cry will have gone up from many a congregation, 'And now, O Lord, we thank and praise Thy glorious name.'" At the conclusion of the address, allusion is again made to the subject :—" No doubt many of us will go away with the recollection of the solemn death-roll which was read at the commencement of our meetings sounding in our ears, and with the sad feeling that not a few of us shall be missed when the time of our next great annual gathering returns; and therefore the call is loud to all of us to ' work, work in the living present.' But I trust there is another feeling in our minds, that we have been refreshed, as the pious Jews may be imagined to have been refreshed after a great passover-meeting in Jerusalem, and that we go back to our manses and our homes with the consciousness that there is a cloud of blessing hanging over our land, and with the purpose that by importunate prayer and corresponding effort we shall endeavor to attract to ourselves, our congregations, and our neighborhoods, a large portion of the descending showers. If this is the spirit with which we separate, it requires no prophet to foretell that many a time throughout the land during the coming months shall those words be spoken. 'Jesus Christ being by the right hand of God exalted, and having received of the Father the promise of the Holy Ghost, hath shed forth this which ye now see and hear.'"

For zeal, good sense, sanctified imagination, and power to interest, no man is more valued in Scotland than the Rev. W. Arnot, of the Free High Church, in Edinburgh. As a delegate to the English Presbyterian Church, he gave a most characteristic account of Scottish religious life, as it had been affected by recent events. The report is condensed:

"The country has been greatly moved," he said, "during this last winter and spring. Questions regarding Christ's love, in coming to save us, regarding His kingdom in the world, and our own union with Him, have been forced up, and have risen higher in the common conversation of the streets and companies, than the question of what must I eat and what must I drink. There has been a strange change in this respect, and yet no change of principle.

"We have always been in Scotland, and especially in Edinburgh, a Christianly educated people, and, on the whole, a well-behaved and sober people. I will tell you what I once heard from a railway guard, which illustrates my meaning. We were hindered at a station in Fife. The hour was past for the train to start, and nobody could think what was the reason of the delay. A gentleman said, 'Guard, what is the reason you are not starting? Is there no water?' 'Plenty o' water,' he replied, 'but it's no bilin.' So we had had a religious education, and a certain stateliness of ecclesiastical form amongst us in Scotland, but the water was cold, and it did not give forth much power; and the difference now is, that there has come warmth into it. The love of Christ seems to have got hold of multitudes of human hearts, and is constraining them.

"Let me notice one or two points in which there has been great advancement. One is, that in preaching, both in public and in private conversation in our inquiry-meetings, there is a great deal more practical application of the truth to each individual soul. I read, when Philip met the Ethiopian in the desert, in the short report of the sermon on that occasion, two things, 'He preached unto him Jesus.' We had one of these things as fully in Scotland, I think, before, as to-day. We 'preached Jesus.' But we failed on the other side—'*to him*, Jesus.' God has greatly blessed the efforts of the American evangelists on that point.

And nobody takes it ill when you speak personally to him about sin, and his interest in Christ. Everybody seems rather to expect that we will so speak to them.

"Formerly we seemed to have fired away our shot, and did it not give a crack when it went away? and we thought, 'Have not we done it well?' But did it hit the mark? We did not think so much of that, but now equal attention is paid to both. That is one grand mark of our movement.

"We did not change our creed at all. I hold by that still. But there is one notion that seems to have been changed and overturned. Formerly, for the most part, in Scotland, we were of the persuasion that Christ came to receive saints, but now we have become convinced that 'this Man receiveth sinners.'

"Of the leading characteristics of the movement, one was joy. Many people, who were dull enough, with Christianity in their hearts, but with no outlet for it in their lives, were now finding ways of doing good. This was specially shown in the preaching of the gospel to the poor. Then there was a great use made of sacred song. Many of the Christian ladies now employed the interval between the hours of public worship on Sunday, in going to the hospitals and similar institutions in Edinburgh, and singing hymns to the poor patients, and there was no joy like that of seeing the faces of these people when the gospel was sung to them. In one of these institutions there was a poor old woman, who had been there eleven years, and during that time had never spoken one word. Not that she was dumb in the ordinary sense, but she was stricken with a sort of paralysis. After one of these singings, the matron heard her saying something to herself. She went near and listened, and she was saying—

'Depths of mercy, can there be
Mercy yet in store for me?'

"A little girl was stricken with fever, and taken to the children's hospital, where she died. In her delirium, she said, and continued saying, 'Take me to the meeting, and set me in the front seat that I may hear the ladies sing!'

"Another remarkable effect was that the enemy is almost silent. There was, here and there, a spirit of criticism, such as the 'Comic Gospel' of the *Saturday Review*, but generally the press is either silent or speaking of the work and reporting it respectfully.

The Lord hath done this thing for us, whereof we are glad."

In the Established Church Assembly, the notices of the awakening from the lips of the Rev. Dr. Charteris, and of the Rev. Marshall Lang, successor to Dr. Norman Macleod, were explicit and cordial. They both adverted to a danger apprehended from the outset, and of which some notice had been taken in the official reports on Christian life and work. Dr. Charteris said " that, in regard to the remarkable events of the past few months the committee turned with special expectation to the returns from Edinburgh and Glasgow, in which cities so remarkable an interest in Divine things had been recently manifested. An Edinburgh minister, a member of the Committee, had stated that the experience of nearly five months, since his report was written, had been the happiest and most blessed that he had had in his ministry. The only evil pointed out in those reports was the tendency to Plymouthism. The attraction which Plymouthism offered to young converts was its claim to being a pure Church. In the ardor of their first faith and love those young converts looked for some Church without the stains which came from long contact with the world, and they often found in the small sect in question a claim to spotlessness which drew them towards it in a wonderful degree. If it could be shown distinctly that the older denominations, if not, indeed, of spotless purity, could claim to be ruled by the spirit of the loving Redeemer, and to afford means of usefulness to all, they would rob that deceptive heresy of its chiefest charm, and keep within their own congregations those whom they were always most loath to lose ; for it was the very salt of their flocks of which Plymouthism sought to rob them. Every one was aware of the extraordinary revivals in religion which had been manifested in Glasgow and Edinburgh during the past winter and spring, and the committee were bound to state that all the returns which had been sent in, giving the results of personal observation of that movement, spoke favorably of it, with one single exception."

Rev. Dr. Lang said that he knew from the experience of the past five weeks that Plymouthism was not an imaginary danger, and the only way of checking it was just by welcoming and utilizing all the enthusiasm that was kindled in the hearts of the young men of the Church. Concerning the spiritual and religious movement that has lately been made in the land, he knew that he was touching a subject of considerable delicacy, but he could not read the answers without feeling satisfied that there was a very distinct and memorable movement during the past year. He had had the privilege of taking part from the very beginning in the work which God had so highly honored, and with which were associated the names of the two American brethren who had come amongst them. He would ask the house to think respectfully of that work. It was very difficult for any one who had not been in direct personal relations with it to estimate or understand it. "This I can say, that, having been connected with the work in Glasgow from the very first day of it to the end, I can feel that there have been—and on the floor of the house I am not ashamed to say it—many tokens that God has indeed been blessing the work. I could tell of much in proof of this. I know that Glasgow has been in many of its homes more joyous for the last two or three months, and that in many an old wilderness and solitary place there are now the peaceable and blessed fruits of righteousness. I don't know how you have felt, fathers and brethren, but I have felt during the past year as if there were an increased quickening of the whole spiritual forces of our land, a readiness to receive the gospel, a longing to come into closer communion with the truth as it is in Jesus."

Concurrently with these testimonies in Scotland, the Scottish Deputation to the American Churches, reaching Chicago, visited Mr. Moody's Tabernacle there, and made their report to the churches at home, removing every shade of doubt as to the estimation in which the American prophets were held "in their own country."

"We were much interested," wrote the Rev. J. H. Wilson, "in coming to the field of Mr. Moody's labors. We have met with many of the best Christian people of the place, ministers and laymen, and we have heard but one opinion expressed,—of entire confidence and affectionate regard. All speak of his wonderful energy and zeal and devotedness, and of the great results that have attended his labors. They long to have him back again, and are following him during his absence with their prayers. Only the basement story of his tabernacle is erected as yet. It consists of a large hall, and an admirable suite of rooms for classes, etc. I conducted the ordinary

Sabbath forenoon service, which was attended by a large congregation. In the afternoon we returned to his Sabbath-school, at which nine hundred or a thousand Sabbath scholars, old and young, were present. We met many of Mr. Moody's friends and fellow-workers, who are earnest and zealous like himself. If the building were completed, I have no doubt it will be a great center for evangelistic work in the city. There is much work for our brother to do here; and when he has done his work in our land, he cannot be back a day too soon. He is claimed by the whole Christian community here, just as he is in Scotland, and the door seems open for him everywhere. All over the country we have met with many most attractive Christian people. If America is true to herself, she will occupy a foremost place in the evangelization of the world."

In the meantime the smaller towns were being visited, with results which, without burdening the memory of the reader with order and details, we shall state as they were reported at the time by highly esteemed brethren, whose words commanded the confidence of the community.

KILMARNOCK. 153

At Neilston, a town of four thousand six hundred inhabitants, nine miles from Glasgow, a meeting was held in the evening in the parish church, which was crowded in every part. A remarkable instance of the spirit of unity this revival has produced was afforded in the fact that while the established church minister presided, two others, the Rev. Mr. Ferguson, of the Free Church, and Rev. Mr. Clarke, of the United Presbyterian Church, Barrhead, took part in the service. This is much the same as if in England a Baptist and Methodist minister were to take part in a Church of England service simultaneously with the rector. Souls were quickened and converted. At the after meeting, which was held in the Free Church, upwards of three hundred met together as inquirers after the way of salvation; and some were enabled to express the belief that they there passed from death to life. A choir of ladies from Glasgow assisted Mr. Sankey in the singing.

In the Free Church Assembly at Edinburgh on May 26th, Sheriff Campbell said that the news from Ayrshire was very encouraging. The town of Kilmarnock, for which they had been praying much, had been visited by Messrs. Moody and Sankey, who did not take any part in the ordinary worship; but they had evangelistic meetings, and the result of these, and other meetings from the overflow of these congregations, was that they had upwards of two hundred inquirers in the inquiry-room. He was there amongst them and he never saw more promising cases of conversion. Those whom he spoke to were from fifteen to twenty-five years of age, and some older. All, as far as he could see, were persons who were most deeply impressed, and all that he spoke to before they parted said that they had given themselves to Christ.

At Saltcoats arrangements were made for holding three services, the first in the parish church (Rev. D. E. M'Nab's) at four o'clock, afternoon; also in the same place at seven o'clock, evening; and in the North Church at the same hour.

At the afternoon service, admission to which was by ticket, the church was comfortably filled an hour before the time for opening the meeting. Large numbers of persons continued to arrive, who made their way into the building and through the passages, evidently satisfied to obtain even standing room. Every inch of space in the sacred edifice was packed long prior to four o'clock, and probably there never was assembled so large a congregation in any church in Saltcoats. A considerable number were unable to obtain admission. A large number of persons had come from the towns and villages in the district to attend the services.

The inhabitants of Irvine, which contains a population of eight thousand, having heard of the presence of the American evangelists in their neighborhood, hastened to send a deputation to them in Saltcoats on Monday, to solicit the holding of at least one service by them in the parish church at Irvine. With this entreaty Messrs. Moody and Sankey complied. They arrived on their visit, which may well be described as a flying one, in time for meeting at twelve, noon. There was a large attendance in the church, although a more unfortunate day could not have been chosen, as the streets were full of conveyances, and furniture, and excited individuals, it being Term day, or Flitting day, for the change of residences.

Ayr, a town of nineteen thousand inhabitants, forty miles from Glasgow, was next reached. The meeting was at four P. M., in the Old Church, a fine old commodious building, which was filled an hour beforehand by a great audience of about two thousand people, comprising many of the leading persons of the neighborhood. Many were unable to gain admission from want of room. A number of ministers of all denominations were present, some having come a distance of thirty miles. It is remarkable how the co-operation of the clergy has been everywhere given to these evangelists. The interval of waiting between three and four P. M., was occupied by the reading of portions of Scripture, and by prayer by some of the ministers. A very efficient choir sang extremely well some of Mr. Sankey's hymns. The large audience manifested marked anxiety to see the expected visitors from America, by keeping their vision concentrated on the vestry door, but kept their seats and maintained a proper demeanor.

After entering the church, accompanied by many clergymen, Mr. Moody gave out the One Hundredth Psalm, which was sung congregationally. He then prayed; and the hymn "Once for all" was then sung by Mr. Sankey, with great feeling and expression—the words being heard clearly in the most distant part of the church. Mr. Moody's discourse followed.

Of the visit to Kilmarnock, the Rev. Mr. Leitch

writes, "Their coming was eagerly looked for, and many a prayer was offered that they might come in the fullness of the blessing of the gospel. They held three meetings during the day—all apart from the ordinary church services. In the morning, at half-past eight, a special meeting was held for office-bearers and other church workers in the Low Church. Admission was by ticket, and 1,750 were present. Mr. Sankey, accompanied by a number of ladies, led the service of song: his singing was fraught with great power, and produced deep impression. Mr. Moody spoke on the words 'Occupy till I come,' directing particular attention to the 'feeding of the lambs.' Seldom has any audience been more impressed: for more than an hour he held them spell-bound as he discoursed on Christian work. Many a heart and conscience must have been stirred as he exhorted his hearers to work for the Master. When it is remembered that the large audience was composed of workers not only from Kilmarnock, but from districts miles distant from town, it will at once be seen that the influence of such a meeting will be far-reaching and widespread."

At Irvine next day the church was full, though it

was term day, and though the intimation of their coming was given but a few hours before. As the brethren were on their way to Ayr, they could not tarry for an after-meeting, but the ministers of the town arranged to have a united meeting in the evening.

Of Ayr, the Rev. John Miller, Newton-on-Ayr, reports: "In the month of February we were favored with a visit from Sheriff Campbell and Mr. Brown Douglas of Edinburgh; and to the solemn accounts which they gave of the work in the city, not a little of the impulse given to the cause is due. Subsequent visits by Mr. Mossman and a deputation from the young men's committee in Edinburgh, together with occasional addresses by the Sheriff, produced blessed and widespread results.

"On Tuesday, 26th May (1874), Messrs. Moody and Sankey visited the town. Great interest had been excited, and from all the districts round multitudes came in hope of hearing them. The Old Church— the largest in town—was selected, and long before the hour of meeting was densely packed. About eighteen hundred people must have been present. Shortly after the hour Mr. Moody arrived, and gave an intensely interesting address. From beginning to end the deepest solemnity pervaded the meeting, while not a few were melted to tears. An effect no less striking was produced by Mr. Sankey's singing; and as we left the building, it was with the full conviction that the Lord had been with us of a truth.

"In the evening, at seven o'clock, the same building was crowded again—Mr. Moody delivering a still more powerful address. For the overflow, Cathcart Street United Presbyterian Church was opened, and an address of a telling nature delivered by Rev. Mr. Sloan of Aberdeen. All who wished to be spoken to about spiritual things were requested to go to the Free Church, and the meeting was closed. Great care was taken to allow no one to enter save as an anxious inquirer, and it was found that upwards of one hundred and fifty had come in.

"One marked feature of the work is the number of Christian families into which the blessing has come. Of course this was looked for, but the extent to which it prevails has far surpassed all expectation. In some families there are four who profess to have received a blessing, in several three, in others two, and so on; while in a few, every member of the household professes to have found the Saviour. 'Oh, sir,' said one to me the other day, 'this is a changed house *now*. We used to think that if we went to church and read our Bibles, and taught the little girl to say her prayers, it was all right. But oh, sir, all that is changed now.'"

The historic town of Stirling, picturesque, active, and for many years identified with a useful Tract enterprise, conducted by Mr. P. Drummond, was next approached. How natural is the state of things here described :

"The Erskine United Presbyterian Church was crowded long before the advertised time of commencement. As is frequently the case at the first meeting in a place, curiosity rather than a serious interest predominated. This can hardly be blamed on the part of those who have heard and read so much of the American evangelists, and are at first anxious to ascertain what manner of persons they are. There was an observable change from the commencement of the meeting. The gates were locked after the church was filled, and the overflow directed to Mr. Goldie's (Free South) Church. While Mr. Sankey sang some of his most impressive hymns, ' Almost persuaded,' and the new 'There were ninety-and nine,' there was the hushed attention which showed not mere artistic gratification, but deep heart feeling. Mr. Moody preached an hour on 'Ye must be born again,' and riveted the audience. The service was conducted in the other church by Rev. Mr. Parkhurst, from Chicago, then traveling in Europe. There was a fair after meeting at nine o'clock in the smaller church. Many of the inquirers seemed clearly to make their peace with God."

The noon prayer-meeting in Dr. Beith's church, presided over by Mr. Parkhurst, and Mr. Moody's Bible-reading to an immense audience in the Erskine Church at three o'clock on Thursday, closed the services in Stirling.

Perth, Aberdeen, and Inverness are the northern capitals of Scotland, and their influence is widely felt. More time therefore was given to them than the less important towns just noticed, and in which good work was already in progress. The preparation and expectation in Perth had been earnest and decided.

Noon-day prayer-meetings and evangelistic meetings had been commenced, and continued for twenty weeks, and God gave many drops of blessing during that time. There was a cheering work amongst the children. Professor Martin, from Aberdeen, had held meetings for five weeks, and in these meetings many little ones gave their hearts to Jesus.

It was resolved to make, for one month, a strenuous effort to win the older people to Christ by holding evangelistic services every night in the week, Saturday excepted. During that month Messrs. Moody and Sankey appeared.

A meeting on Friday evening, addressed by the Rev. J. J. Black, LL. D., of Inverness Free High Church and Mr. Robertson, of Newington, prepared the way. Mr. Moody had been called to Edinburgh by the sickness of his child, but Mr. Sankey was present.

On Sunday morning a meeting was held for "Christian Workers and those disposed to work," when the City Hall was crowded. Mr. Sankey sang "Go work in my vineyard," that large congregation listening with glistening eyes, and hearts kindled anew in love to Jesus and a desire to work more diligently for Him who suffered so much for us.

In the evening there were meetings in the open

air on the South Inch (at which between four thousand and five thousand people were present) and in the City Hall, with overflow-meetings in two churches.

There followed the noon-day meetings in the City Hall, Bible reading in the Free West Church, and evening meeting in the North United Presbyterian Church. The number of inquirers was very great, and very many obtained peace. "It has been" says a writer in *the Christian*, "a quiet strong tide of blessing; it is as if God had sent His servants to unlock the flood-gates of His grace, and the water of life has swept out in deep and steady currents, leaving no place for the breaking waves of excitement and mere feeling. Especially this is to be noticed in the Bible-readings, when from day to day the large church in which Mr. Moody lectures is crowded with people reverently and simply studying God's Word."

Mrs. Barbour, of whose account of the movement in Edinburgh we have availed ourselves, thus writes of the meetings in Perth: "It was on Sabbath morning that Mr. Moody and Mr. Sankey began work together at 9 A. M., in the City Hall. The many memories that came crowding in of former years of blessing corresponded with the looks upon the faces of the eager, earnest, half-restless multitude. There was a rim left beyond the crowd during the first ten minutes; and to those corners of the hall where the hearing is not so good when ordinary speakers occupy the platform, groups, hot and tired from a long morning's walk, were noiselessly moving. Some had left their homes at eight, seven, six, five, and even at four to be there. Although the mass of the faces were strangers to us, individuals gathered in during each special visitation of God's love to Perth, were easily recognized. Not a few, with the marks of age and toil, and new joy upon their faces, belonged to the ever memorable epoch of 1840, when William Burns was so wondrously used among us. From far and near they assembled that morning. Fruits of Robert McCheyne's ministry were there. The spirit of Mr. Milne, of St. Leonard's, breathed still so freshly in his flock, and in the town, that we cannot put his name yet among those that have passed away. Sturdy men, unflinching in service, the seals of faithful evangelists, were there. And the whole scene, how it recalled Reginald Radcliffe, as though we had but to look half round to find him! Best of all, the dear ministers of Perth, newly baptized with power, stood there ready to forward the work, and bind the sheaves."

The Rev. Mr. Parkhurst, of the M. E. Church, and the Rev. Mr. Spencer, also from Illinois, were able to give efficient aid here. The weather was unfavorable to open air meetings, which in Perth had been attended with much blessing in former years, particularly in 1860; but "The blesssed Spirit of Promise, who is drawing to himself *all* hope, *all* confidence, as the alone able to glorify Jesus, was powerfully working in some hearts. The cloud, as of a man's hand, was in the sky of that sweet summer's eve, and as the many melted and humbled servants of the King withdrew from the places of inquiry, they silently adored the Mighty One, and saw Him already going forth conquering and to conquer.

"At night Mr. Moody preached on 'Son, remember.' Many a conscience was pierced; many a lingerer arrested; many a believer's soul stirred to the lowest depths, as we were made to lean over the precipice and look down to the pit of despair. You felt as if you would rather not hear the speaker or any one else preach for long, lest by any means the lines drawn on the heart by God's Spirit should be effaced from the tablet within."

The inquiry meeting had become so well-marked a feature of the movement that Mr. Moody made it the subject of an address in which its aims and uses were set forth. "I am more and more convinced every day," said he, "that one of the hindrances to a greater work of grace in our churches is the barrier that seems in such a degree to exist between the pastor and people, and the consequent stiffness and formality which prevent the people from coming to the pastor with their troubles or to seek spiritual advice.

"I believe the preaching would be much more practical and effective if the minister understood more of the difficulties of those to whom he ministers, and I have found no greater help in discovering the wants of the people than in the inquiry meeting, right after the preaching of the word. Jesus encouraged His disciples to ask Him questions, saying to them 'Have ye understood all these things?' (Matt. xiii. 51.) I feel confident that if the pastor invited his people to come freely to him with their questions, setting aside a special time for them to come, they would feel more free to accept than if left to come at any time, though they might, of course, be invited to do that also.

"A few years ago I lost my way in London, and was glad to have a 'shoeblack' direct me aright. Many now are on the wrong road, and they know it, and yet are ashamed to go to any one to ask the right way. May they not be made to feel that their pastor, with other Christian friends who have walked in Wisdom's ways and found them ways of pleasantness, are ready to point to them also the way?

"If Christ encouraged the people to come to Him and inquire of his kingdom, should they not now be encouraged to come and speak *of* Him? On the day of Pentecost we read of a great cry being made by many who had been pricked by the words preached through the power of the Holy Ghost, 'Men and brethren, what shall we do?' The three thousand added to the Church that day show the result of the inquiry. The thought has risen in our minds, what would some of those who oppose the inquiry meeting do should one hundred make the same inquiry now?

"Can we doubt that God sent Philip into the desert that he might meet the eunuch and explain to him that he whom Isaiah had named 'the sheep led to the slaughter' was this same Jesus who had been crucified? We read that he 'began at the same Scripture and preached unto him Jesus.' We can imagine many other ways in which the eunuch might have been reached—even by sending an angel from heaven; but God allows Philip the honor of pointing this inquirer to the finished work of Christ. Would an inquirer now, with the same 53d chapter of Isaiah, find the way made plain if applying for help to some of those boasting of the 'broad' platform on which they stand, and yet being called by *His* name.

"I am frequently asked, 'How often should we have inquiry meetings, and should they be on ordinary occasions?' I see no reason why they should not. I believe we should expect conversions every time we preach the gospel; but the *preaching of the gospel* I would distinguish from the *preaching of the word to Christians* for their edification and establishment in the truth. But when Christ has been preached and offered freely, should we not expect *some* to accept, and therefore give the opportunity to those who would hear more to come and ask?

"The question also, *who* should be admitted into a general inquiry meeting to talk to the anxious has often been asked. I believe if the church has been properly instructed, one half of them ought to be able to point an inquiring one to Jesus. A man or woman whose heart is warm with love to the Saviour, and can give a reason for their hope, ought to be encouraged to go and speak to others. I know of no kind of work which quickens a church so much as work among inquirers."

The closing labors at Perth are thus described: "Messrs. Moody and Sankey have gone from us, and we must turn now from the glad, calm, mountain-heights, to bear to those who are yet in the valley the tidings of the water of life, of which we have been drinking so deeply in the past ten days. In the dust of the conflict we shall look on this time even as David looked back to the 'water of the well of Bethlehem.' God grant that, even as he poured forth that blood-bought water, an offering unto the Lord, we may with willing hands hold forth the cup of living water, blood-bought too for us.

"Mr. Moody's Bible-readings came to an end on Friday, the 5th, but two days of busy work yet remained before he left us for Dundee. On Sunday, the 7th, there was another meeting for Christian workers, at which the City Hall was again crowded. Much precious counsel Mr. Moody gave—counsel which came straight from an enthusiastic and devoted heart, yet never failed to be practical and clear.

"At eleven o'clock he preached at the usual forenoon service in the Free West Church, taking for his subject, 'The love of God;' and in the evening there was the meeting on the South Inch, for which all day long, prayer had been going up to the throne of grace. The evening was one of rare beauty; and when Mr. Sankey's voice was heard leading the well-known tune of the One Hundredth Psalm, it was 'with cheerful voice' that the people followed, while the mountains around and the trees overhead seemed also to join in the song—

> 'For why? The Lord our God is good;
> His mercy is for ever sure;
> His truth at all times firmly stood,
> And shall from age to age endure.'

"It is difficult to compute the numbers of a crowd standing so closely packed as this gathering was, but not fewer than seven thousand must have been within the range of Mr. Moody's voice; while on the outskirts, where even *his* voice could not reach, the words of sacred song may have carried conviction and comfort to many. Between six and seven o'clock the meeting was dismissed, and the people slowly dispersed, many of them to attend one of the other meetings which were still to be held that evening.

"At the children's meeting there was an unusually large attendance. Many of the little ones who had given their hearts to Jesus during the week had brought their companions to seek Him.

"Mr. Parkhurst also had a good meeting in the City Hall, and at the North United Presbyterian Church, where Mr. Moody spoke, and whither many had gone voluntarily declaring themselves unconverted. Very many found peace that night.

"On Monday we had the usual noon prayer-meeting, at which Mr. Moody and Mr. Sankey were both present; and in the evening a meeting for young converts, and the usual evangelistic meeting, at which Mr. Parkhurst for the last time presided. Mr. Sankey was also present for a short time, according to his usual plan before going to the meeting at which Mr. Moody was speaking. His parting message to that assembly was breathed in the low, sad tones of 'Nothing but Leaves.' His last song to the young converts was in the stirring notes of 'Only an Armor-bearer.' Mr. Moody had spoken solemnly and earnestly of the dangers which lay before them in their upward journey, but, withal, so soul-stirringly of the glory to follow, that this song was felt to be the expression of many a young heart's devotion, and there were many whose spirits sang with Mr. Sankey's lips—

> 'Heard ye the battle cry? "Forward!" the call.
> See, see the faltering ones! Backward they fall.
> Surely my Captain will remember me,
> Though but an armor-bearer I may be.'

"Before closing Mr. Moody suggested that there should be a young converts' meeting every Monday evening, as there is already in many places. Once more they were commended to His care 'who is able to keep us from falling,' and then came the inquiry meeting, which that night seemed to be a specially solemn and sacred time.

"Now God's servants have gone from us, but the fruit of their labor remains. They have been as scythes in the Master's hand, to mow down, in swift and steady strokes, 'the bearded grain and the flowers that grow between.' May God grant that mowers and reapers may be raised up in our midst, and that what has been already mown may be gathered in and cared for! He is able to make this but the first-fruits of the harvest; He is able to make even 'the gleaning of the grapes of Ephraim better than the vintage of Abi-ezer.'"

From Perth a second visit was made to Dundee, of which Mr. McPherson gives the following details in the *Christian* of June 18th, 1874:

"This second visit has been much appreciated, and has given a fresh impulse to the work. It has also served to make it abundantly evident that the work of grace has been going on quietly and steadily in this town and neighborhood during recent months. The ordinary channels of worship and work are full of the river of God—in some cases, indeed, full to overflowing. The pulse of Christian life in this city is beating more strongly and healthfully than it has done for many a day. It is now plain enough that the blessing will be largely permanent and abundantly productive. A thousand earnest souls are longing and praying for greater and still greater things. The impetus given to Christian work in all its departments can scarcely be overestimated. This is especially true in regard to work among the young. During the last three months many of the little ones have been carried away by scarlatina. Many death-bed scenes, full of interest and instruction, have been witnessed. I have often of late heard the children in their last moments speak of the things of God with an intelligence and a simplicity of faith which has been both a lesson and a reproof to older Christians. Beyond measure affecting is it to hear the little ones sing their sweet gospel hymns with their dying breath. 'Oh, mother, how I wish you were going with me!' said a little girl the other day as she lay dying. 'I cannot go with you, dear,' replied the mother; 'Jesus wants you to go alone to Him.' 'Going to Jesus,' repeated the child twice, as if pondering the full significance of the word. Then, after a pause, she said she was satisfied, adding, 'Mother, you will come by and by.' She then sang, 'Jesus loves even me,' and died.

"The young doves are flying to their windows. There is sorrow in many a home here; but I have never before seen so much joy and praise in the midst of bereavement and trouble. As the little saved children go in at the gates singing, fathers and mothers are catching glimpses of the glory, and wishing they were in too."

There is necessarily much uniformity in the modes of operation in the various cities. Mr. Moody's plan usually included a meeting at the very outset for the "Christian workers" and all who were willing to be employed. Then followed vivid presentations of vital truth on such Scripture words as "There is no difference," "The Two Adams," or "Sinners' Excuses," and direct and faithful dealing with men's souls.

Thus it was at Aberdeen. The labors of the evangelists commenced on Sabbath, the 14th, by a nine o'clock meeting for Christian workers, admission by ticket. There were three thousand issued, and the Music Hall was quite filled, every available place being occupied, either sitting or standing. The singing of the Hundredth Psalm opened the proceedings, after which the Rev. T. Gardiner, Old Aberdeen Free Church, engaged in prayer. Mr. Moody then rose, and, after reading a short portion of Scripture, spoke for about three quarters of an hour from the text, "Here am I; send me." Mr. Sankey, assisted by a most efficient choir of male and female voices, effectively rendered several hymns, among which the principal were, "Hark, the Voice of Jesus Calling," "Go, work in my Vineyard," and "Nothing but Leaves." The meeting was a most solemn one, and the audience was most attentive.

The evening meeting, at 5 P. M., was on the Links, in the natural amphitheatre of the Broadhill, where a platform had been erected for choir and speakers. It was here that the deep interest in these gentlemen— arising, of course, from mixed feelings of curiosity and desire to know more of that better way of which they speak—showed itself. One may be allowed to say that the town was moved to come, and see, and hear. Some ten thousand were in position before and around the platform long before the hour of meeting; and yet from before five till past six there were continuous streams of men, women, and children, from the city, Footdee, Woodside, Old Aberdeen, and as far as Dyce, flowing to the one point on the Broadhill. There could not have been fewer than twenty to twenty-two thousand on the Links that evening. Mr. Moody spoke from the words, "The wages of sin is death," and was listened to with rapt attention, while the hymns were distinctly heard over the vast crowds in the stillness of a quiet summer evening.

The next meeting was announced for eight, in the Music Hall, but it being filled before seven, Mr. Moody began at that hour. Prayer was led by Mr. Walter, of Free Trinity Church, Mr. Moody speaking on the subject of the prodigal son. There was much power. The chief hymns were, "Jesus of Nazareth," "Come Home," and "Almost Persuaded." There were many inquirers. The crowd outside was very great, and Free West Trinity and the Baptist Chapel, Crown street, had to be opened, and were more or less filled; while several ministers conducted an open-air service in one of the squares. "We have never at any time, I may say, seen the city so moved as it was this day."

The next day, Monday, the meeting was in the South Parish Church, and a prayer-meeting at 3 P. M. Amongst the audience there were between twenty and thirty ministers of various denominations. Pending the arrival of the evangelists, various hymns were sung by a choir which has been organized to assist Mr. Sankey in singing.

Two hours before the time announced for commencing the evening meeting in the South Parish Church, a crowd had gathered at the door, and no sooner was admission gained than every seat and corner of the large church began to be rapidly filled. The people seemed contented to wait any length of time for an opportunity of hearing the singing of Mr. Sankey and the preaching of Mr. Moody. It was soon seen that the numbers waiting outside could not gain admission into the church, and provision was immediately made for having an open-air meeting in the quadrangle of Marischal College.

After devotional exercises, interspersed with hymns and Scripture expositions of a brief and pointed character, Mr. Moody preached from Luke ii. 10: "Behold, I bring you good tidings of great joy, which shall be to all people, for unto you is born this day a Saviour." "His love for the Gospel," he said, "had taken out of his way four of his bitterest enemies. Before he was converted, death to him was a horrible monster, but now he had no fear of it. He had received several letters from people who were probably out of their mind, threatening to take his life, but fear of them never gave him a thought, for he went through the world crying, 'O Death, where is thy sting?' and he heard a voice rolling down from Calvary's cross, saying, 'Buried in the bosom of the Saviour.' He had attended the wounded at the American War, and had seen death under many phases. In illustration he told an anecdote of the war, so graphically, and with so much pathos, that a considerable portion of the audience was deeply affected. The other enemies which the knowledge of the Gospel had removed from his path were the grave, sin, and the judgment, all of which were bitter enemies to his peace of mind previous to his conversion."

Later in the evening, another and yet larger congregation, including a greater number of careless persons, heard another sermon on "the Gospel."

He expressed himself greatly pleased with the character of the meeting; he liked open-air meetings on week days, because all kinds of people could come to them, while, no doubt, a good many came all eyes and mouths open for curiosity's sake. The text he had chosen was an open-air one, and commanded them to preach the Gospel to every creature, and in a few sentences he pointed out how comprehensive was this injunction of the Saviour's. Throughout both his evening discourses, Mr. Moody showed a wonderful power of seizing the circumstances around him to illustrate his meaning, thereby giving a kind of personal interest to what he was saying. Then followed a prayer-meeting in the Free High Church for about half an hour, those who desired private conversation retiring to the hall below the church, the prayer-meeting being continued in the church by several clergymen until after ten o'clock. The inquirers' meeting lasted still longer.

Among the side-meetings held in this neighborhood, was one of special interest for soldiers and sailors, in the Aberdeen School of Song. It is a new hall; and this was the first meeting held in it. The meeting was arranged through the exertions of Sir Francis Outram and Dr. Thomas Farquhar. The wives and friends of the soldiers and marines were also present; and the company was a large one, numbering many hundreds. Mr. Sankey and his choir attended. Sir Francis Outram presided, and the Rev. Mr. Greig engaged in prayer. Mr. Sankey gave a short and effective address, and sang the hymn "Hold the Fort," the audience joining in the chorus. Major Ross then addressed the meeting. The Rev. Mr. Sloan spoke on the text, "Endure hardness as a good soldier of

Jesus Christ." Mr. Sankey followed with the hymn "The Life-boat." After prayer, he again sang, with great power, the hymn "Ninety and Nine." The meeting lasted for an hour, and was intensely interesting. We trust much good was done through it. Several of the officers were present.

At Peterhead two meetings were held, one at five P.M., a second on the Links—an open-air gathering continued in the church, of which one of the ministers writes thus:

"The large church was quite filled in the after-meeting, some standing in the passages. Mr. Moody addressed the anxious. In closing, he asked those that knew they were unsaved but wished to be prayed for to stand up. This being a new thing for Peterhead, it was some time ere any had the courage. At length one, then another, and another, then twos and threes, rose, till between thirty and forty stood before that vast audience to be prayed for. It was a solemn moment. They soon got company, however, for no sooner had God's servant requested the children of God who felt the desire for greater spiritual blessing to rise, than up stood a throng. The front area seats were then cleared for the anxious. Many men on one side, and young women and boys and girls, came forward, and, after the assembly was dismissed, were spoken to personally. I believe great good was done by that short visit,—an impression made on the town that will not soon leave it; many convictions planted in breasts, and former impressions deepened, and not a few led to Jesus. The children of God, too, have received a blessing indeed. The constantly expressed desire is, 'If we could only have had him a week just;' others, 'Well, it is clear we can't have him, and why do we not bestir ourselves and be blessed still more?'"

The impression produced by the "Bible-readings" is thus described in a letter to *The Christian* from Aberdeen:

"We cannot over-estimate the benefit and enjoyment which the privilege of being present at these lectures occasioned to many. We can only hope that the method of studying the Scriptures so attractively illustrated by these lectures may be largely imitated by private Christians, along with the steady consecutive reading and study of books and portions of the sacred word."

After a week's labor in the city, the following results are reported, all the more remarkable because the time had now come when both ministers and people began to leave for summer holidays.

"In Free Trinity Church, as usual, an overflow meeting was held during the earlier part of the evening; and at nine o'clock the meeting for the men began. The audience having been consulted as to whether this meeting should be continued for another week at least, all present, apparently, expressed their desire that it should be so. About the same number of anxious inquirers remained in both places of meeting each night. The average each night throughout the week may be reckoned roughly at one hundred and fifty. This is truly 'great things' done for us and among us by the Lord; and many of God's people are filled with joy at His mighty doings.

"In addition to these results, there are blessings received which come not always to view. There are the reviving and quickening of God's people; the enriching of the experience of the large staff of Christian workers; the tightening of the cords of Christian love and unity; the increase of the spirit of prayer and hopefulness; and largely a new view of the sacred function of praise in the service of Christ, and as a means of winning souls to Him, of comforting the downcast, and of warring against the assaults of the wicked one."

Among the incidents in the inquiry-room was that of a young lady, who, in speaking with Mr. Moody, said, "You made it so plain last night, that I now know the way and the scheme of salvation thoroughly, and there remains but the surrender of the will."

The brethren commenced their second and last week's labors in Aberdeen, June 21, 1874. Mere curiosity had had time to be gratified, but still large audiences flocked to hear them. "Many," says a writer in *The Christian*, " who, with Scotch caution, were inclined to stand aloof from the movement for a short time, have come round to recognize that there is good being done, and that the men are not mere butterflies, fluttering in a breeze of religious excitement. Their influence has gone beyond the gatherings that they themselves bring together. There has been created a renewed interest in evangelistic work, which is bearing fruit in numerous well-attended meetings being held throughout the town, conducted by clergymen and laymen. At the same time there is an absence of that emotional excitement which was greatly in vogue in some previous revivals, and which, in a measure, is to blame for the indifference of not a few good church-going people to evangelistic preaching.

A vigorous lecture on Daniel in the morning, a sermon in the cathedral, Old Aberdeen, which was densely crowded, a closing meeting on the Links—the Scottish " Common"—an evening meeting in the Music Hall, and separate meetings with the men and women who had received a blessing—these were the farewell services on June 28, 1874, in Aberdeen.

" Perhaps in no place which he has as yet visited," says the Rev. John M. Sloan, " have his ministrations been attended by greater or more interested crowds. The Music Hall, larger, we believe, than the City Hall, Glasgow, and capable, when crowded, of accommodating close on three thousand five hundred—was full every night during the fortnight of the evangelists' stay among us. Not only so, but the overflow sufficed to fill at times more than one of the adjacent churches. The Bible lectures, which were held in the South Parish Church, were attended by close on two thousand; while the daily prayer-meeting in Belmont Street Chapel was attended by one thousand or more."

Of the manner in which young men influenced one

another, no better illustration could be given than from the closing meeting in Aberdeen, though similar facts had occurred elsewhere.

"During the evening, a young gentleman rose and said, 'Mr. Moody, if you can tell me how my soul can be saved, you will be the greatest benefactor of my life.' Another immediately rose, and said, 'That gentleman has exactly expressed what I feel.' Another young man rose, and spoke to this effect: 'Some few evenings ago I was in Free Trinity Church at the men's meeting. At one point in the proceedings I was taken aback by the person next to me in the pew rising up and saying, "I want to let this large company of young men, many of them my friends and acquaintances, know that I am a Christian, and that by God's grace I mean to stand on the Lord's side. It will save trouble my telling you all this at once." When he sat down, the young man sitting in the same pew, but on the other side of me, rose and made a statement to the same effect. I felt somewhat uncomfortable sitting between two making such a declaration, in the full view of all the congregation. The place was unpleasantly hot for me. But God blessed the testimonies of that evening to the awakening of my soul, and ultimately to my conversion; and now I am here before this audience to tell them that I too am on the Lord's side, and mean by His grace to live for Him." '

Huntly received a visit—reawakening memories of the efforts made by the excellent Duchess of Gordon. Montrose, where the earnest and zealous Mr. Nixon has lived and labored for a generation, welcomed even a day's work, and Rev. G. S. Sutherland reported that though the visit was " painfully brief, it had left behind lasting fruit:" and Brechin, once the scene of Rev. Dr. McCosh's labors, had its crowded meetings.

Forfar and Arbroath were visited. It may illustrate the observant discrimination with which Scottish Christians followed the steps of the American evangelists, that a most appreciative writer in the *Times of Blessing*, a journal originated for the diffusion of revival intelligence, thus describes Mr. Moody's address in the latter place:

" The first meeting was held in the Old Church (Established); and though the hour—three o'clock, afternoon—was one at which none of the working classes could attend, the large building, capable of holding two thousand people, was well-nigh full. The meeting was opened with the One Hundredth Psalm, led by Mr. Sankey and the organ; and Mr. Irvine, the pastor of the church, engaged in prayer. 'Nothing but Leaves,' and 'Whiter than Snow' followed, divided by the reading of Rom. iii. In this section was found the theme of Mr. Moody's address, 'There is no Difference,'—words which he held up as testifying that all men everywhere stand on the same platform as sinners in relation to the law of God. The audience listened with rapt attention, the illustrations being specially telling. The writer of this notice heard the same address in Glasgow; but on the present occasion Mr. Moody seemed to take a firmer grasp of his subject, and preserved more unity of structure in the address itself. He seems also to be more careful in his way of explaining what faith in Christ is than before, showing by this that if he have given benefit to Scottish ministers by the exhibition of his method, he has also been reaping some benefit from their well-weighed style of expression."

That this kindly criticism accompanied the most cordial and enthusiastic estimate of the man, will appear from another paragraph—almost the only eulogistic description we have thought it good to insert, for, "he that glorieth let him glory in the Lord."

"Mr. Moody's voice has suffered a good deal by his exposure on a wet Sunday on the Links at Aberdeen; when he addressed an enormous audience under umbrellas. It was very husky to commence with, and only got back its old power and sharpness, as he worked it clear. When a man gets a bad cold, and goes on with such colossal work, without intermission, one comes to ask: 'Is he made of iron only in a figure, or is he really so?' The more one sees Mr. Moody, the more one is amazed at the nervous power and the unwearied spiritual and mental activity. Did he only do what he does as an inspirer and organizer of young men's associations, or of work among the young, he would be doing a splendid life-labor; but he is doing the work of three or four evangelists into the bargain, and that with the force of a locomotive engine. One would almost fear him as an embodiment of half a dozen agencies condensed into one person, did one not see unmistakably, every here and there, traces which tell that the masculine nature has the humility of a child and the tenderness of a woman."

Blairgowrie had been praying, and when, early in

July, the evangelists appeared, seven thousand eager hearers met them, and the Rev. Mr. Baxter reports:

"After devotional exercises had been engaged in, Mr. Moody spoke. The discourse abounded in rich utterances of a free gospel. The glad tidings of mercy through Christ were clearly enunciated. The offer of immediate salvation was pressed on every one with great seriousness and solemnity. By means of evangelical truth luminously stated, anecdotes pointed and most graphically given, illustrations fresh and felicitous, attention was arrested and sustained, and many a countenance betrayed in its expression the interest which was being felt and the deep emotion which was being awakened. A wave of divine influence seemed to pass over the immense audience, and so stirred were the hearts of many, that they were ready to say, 'Surely the Lord is in this place.' It was a marvelous, and will be a memorable, meeting. The vast congregation, the glorious proclamation of God's grace, the eagerness with which the truth was listened to, the widespread concern about everlasting interests, will be long remembered with no ordinary degree of pleasure and profit."

At Inverness, the next field, from the beginning of

the year a prayer-meeting had been held daily at noon in the large hall of the beautiful building erected a few years ago by the Young Men's Christian Association, and the people were expectant of a blessing. We shall allow the Rev. G. Robson to describe the closing meeting only taking the liberty to abbreviate:

"The closing meeting, Free High Church, at 8 P. M.; densely packed; the Hundredth Psalm sung, and prayer. Mr. Sankey sang the hymn, 'We shall Part, but not forever,' the choir joining in the chorus. Mr. Moody delivered a most arresting and solemn address. The close of his appeal, when he deplored his inability to speak for Christ with the earnestness he desired, and with tears entreated the unsaved to close with the Saviour, was listened to amid a silence broken only by the irrepressible signs of deep emotion on the part of his audience. There were not many dry eyes in the vast congregation, and many heads were bowed. At the close of the address, the Rev. Dr. Black engaged in prayer, and then Mr. Sankey sang a farewell hymn, beginning, 'And now, dear Friends, we must bid you adieu,' in which he addressed the different classes present. He sang it with even more than his usual distinctness, and the singular appropriateness of these farewell utterances lent to them additional effect. While the Twenty-third Psalm was being sung the meeting separated, the men being invited to an after-meeting in the Congregational Church, and the women to remain in the Free High Church. It is impossible to give any idea, by words, of the deep solemnity and holy emotion which characterized this closing meeting. 'The Lord has been in the midst of us to-night,' said Mr. Moody, as the meeting was separating. 'Ah, yes; glory to His name!' was the reply. The after-meeting was the most solemn I ever witnessed. Pew after pew was cleared for those who professed to be seeking Christ, and still they pressed forward. There were upwards of a hundred of them; and their earnest attention while Mr. Moody, in simple, tender words, pointed out to them the way of salvation—the perfect stillness which prevailed, as, with their heads bowed upon the book-board, they engaged in silent prayer—the manifest anxiety, reverence, and sincerity which animated their behavior during the subsequent solemn exercises—the spirit of prayer manifestly pervading the Christian ladies who filled the pews on either side of the church—all testified to the presence of the Holy Ghost in that hallowed hour, never to be forgotten. The men's meeting in the Congregational Church, conducted by Mr. Sankey, was also greatly blessed of God, and a very large number of inquirers were conversed with. It was late at night before Messrs. Moody and Sankey slipped away from the scene of labors which have been owned of God for the conversion of many souls and the quickening of many believers."

In Nairn and Elgin the same scenes were repeated. At the latter place Mr. Moody urged faith and effort on the Christian people; he read a portion of the ninth chapter of Mark, in reference to the case of the father whose son was possessed of a devil. From it he entreated Christians, like the man in the chapter, to bring their friends to Jesus, to whom no case was too hopeless. "Now," Mr. Moody continued, "if there is going to be a blessing in Elgin, we must have faith. All know Christ can do it, and what we want is to get the 'if' in the right place. 'If' we can believe, that moment we get the 'if' in the right place. Unbelief was the greatest obstacle that Christ encountered, both on that and this side the cross." Mr.

Moody then very earnestly appealed to God's people to have faith, to come as empty vessels, devoid of self-conceit and everything selfish, so that they might be filled.

To Nairn the visit was made on the 21st July (1874), the Rev. Dr. Cunningham, of Philadelphia, giving some aid in the meetings. "An inquiry meeting was held at the close, and about sixty or more were conversed with, while many retired to their homes with an arrow in their hearts. Some professed to close with Jesus, and some left undecided for the Lord. Mr. Moody and his fellow-laborer left the town next morning, while the services were carried on by the ministers in town and an evangelist. The inquiry meeting on Wednesday evening was full of interest, many professing to close with Jesus. The whole town was moved."

The ancient town of Elgin received a two days' visit. An open-air meeting was held on Ladyhill. The *Elgin Courier* thus describes the scene: "The sun, as he sank to rest in the west shed his dying glory over the most picturesque scene on the hillside. It was estimated by some that there were between five and six thousand persons present, it being the largest gathering of the kind we ever remember having seen in Elgin. Tempted by the fine evening all classes of the people turned out, many arriving from all parts of the surrounding districts. At the foot of the hill a platform was erected, which was occupied by the choir and speakers. The whole hillside, for a great distance up and round about was covered with the dense multitude, that presented, with their varied dresses, a most imposing spectacle."

The Rev. R. S. Macphail gives his ideas of the moral and spiritual results as indicated by the adjourned meeting: "In the parish church the scene was unprecedented. Much as we had prayed for seven months and expected, we were not prepared for the results our God gave. Not only did the numbers exceed our most sanguine expectations, but persons remained seeking salvation whose presence filled our hearts with thanksgiving and rejoicing. This has been so at all these meetings, but on Sabbath night most strikingly. On the Thursday previous about two hundred and fifty inquirers were dealt with. How many there were on Sabbath night I do not venture to indicate, as there were fewer means of computing the great gathering. Such a Sabbath

Elgin never saw; and the results of that day's work will, I believe, remain, not only in the lives of very many in Elgin and for miles around, but in the tone and religious character of our city. The power of the word originated influences which, by God's blessing, will tell very powerfully in our midst. We found our way to our homes that night at a late hour 'like men that dreamed.' Truly we might, as we did, say, 'The Lord hath done great things for us.'"

Of a second visit made to Elgin one of the Young Men's deputies from Edinburgh writes in cordial appreciation of the zeal and fervor of the Highlanders: "How the Elgin people pounced upon Mr. Moody when they heard, three days after he had left them, that he had one more free day in the midst of his busy life! Of course they never dreamed of *him* taking a rest; and there was great joy on Wednesday afternoon when it was flashed through the country side that on the following evening there was to be another great open-air gathering. I cannot tell you who were there, or how many, or what a good choir there was, or what Mr. Sankey sung, or which dignitary prayed. I cannot tell you how beautifully the sun was setting, or how fresh the background of woods looked, or how azure the sky was. But these old men penitent, these drunkards petrified, these strong men's tears, these drooping heads of women, these groups of gutter children with their wondering eyes! Oh, that multitude of thirsty ones—what a sight it was! What could the preacher do but preach his best? And, long after the usual time for stopping, was it a marvel to hear the persuasive voice still pleading on with these Christless thousands?

"It is useless to attempt to give even an approximate idea of the extent of the blessing which fell upon Elgin on Thursday night. The whole of Morayshire has shared it, and a powerful hold has been gained in nearly every farmhouse and village throughout the country side; a hold which, it is earnestly hoped, the members of the new Young Men's Christian Association will take immediate steps to develop, and which, with the prayers of the Christian friends of this corner of the vineyard, may yet be fertile of great and enduring blessing."

They could not well pass by Banff, for "a memorial signed by two thousand two hundred ministers, elders, members, and adherents of the various churches in Banff and Macduff had been forwarded to them. An unusual interest was consequently manifested on their arrival. The railway station was quite crowded with people who were waiting to give them a warm welcome."

Open-air meetings, Bible-readings, sermons, inquiry-meetings, for men exclusively, filled up the greater part of a week. The Rev. J. W. Geddie says of the results : " Mr. Moody's words seemed to pierce like arrows, much emotion was manifested in the congregation, and the number of inquirers was greater than before. The meeting for men was also more largely attended, and not a few of the anxious seemed to decide for Christ.

"Thursday, 6th Aug. (1874), was Mr. Moody's last day in Banff. At twelve o'clock he appeared in the prayer-meeting, to the evident delight and satisfaction of all present. He gave what he calls the key-note of the meeting in a few earnest and encouraging words, chiefly in the question, 'Is there anything too hard for the Lord?' Several brethren then prayed with great power and unction. It was felt that surely the Lord would very specially bless the word in the evening.

"And so it was. Thursday evening will be long

remembered by many in Banff. The discourse was pointed, powerful, and pathetic. At the close he thrilled the audience, as he bade them farewell, and with tears urged the unconverted to close with Christ at once.

"We are truly grateful for the visit of these honored brethren. They have been instrumental in giving an impulse to Christian life and work here, which, we trust, will lead to still greater results. We bid them God-speed."

At Craig Castle, the residence of J. S. Gordon, Esq., a series of evangelistic meetings has been held for many summers. The Sabbath evening meeting, 9th August, must have been of unusual interest.

"Every valley and hamlet within a radius of ten miles sent its company in gig, cart, or afoot. The gathering resembled somewhat one of the Covenanter hill-side meetings, save that, while the bibles were still present, the broadswords were altogether absent; and the rendezvous, instead of being a wild, rocky pass, was a hospitable castle with its fairy dell and leaping linn, celebrated in song, and known as one of the loveliest spots in Scotland. The beauty of the scene seemed specially to move Mr. Moody, who referred to it again and again in his discourse, which was one of peculiar beauty, power, and pathos. Standing in an open carriage placed near a towering tree, the preacher spoke for nearly an hour from the parable of the Marriage Feast. A very marked impression was produced, and many retired at the close of the service for conversation with the preacher and other ministers and friends. The Craig gathering of August, 1874, will, we believe, be ever memorable to not a few as 'the beginning of days' to them."

In one of the intervals between engagements, a hurried run was made to Aberdeen, but other towns, like Wick and Thurso, awaited the coming of the evangelists. In that region, the navigation is often uncertain.

Midnight on Monday (10th August), found Mr. Moody steaming slowly out of Aberdeen harbor, after a hard day's work, in which he held four large and successful public meetings. Tuesday morning found him close in shore, opposite Wick, with a contrary wind, and most violent contrary currents, making things on board the *St. Nicholas* about as disagreeable as possible. On the shore, a large party awaited his arrival, but it was soon apparent that the heavy sea

JOHN O'GROAT'S HOUSE. 201

which was running in the bay would make any attempt to land quite out of the question.

But the good people of Wick were no losers by the misfortunes of the first day, for Mr. Moody soon intimated his intention to devote two extra days to Wick, and one of these a Sabbath.

On Wednesday, of course, the whole country-side poured into Wick to hear Mr. Moody, and by six o'clock, the commodious Established Church was crowded to the door. The aid of Mr. Somerville, of Glasgow, was enjoyed here. A monster meeting for the fishermen was held on the Saturday. They were there in thousands, just then, from all parts of Scotland. The fishermen do not, of course, go to sea on Saturday night. The meetings on Sabbath were most successful, one hundred and fifty men professing decision.

John O'Groat's House is famous as the most northern point of Scotland. On Thursday, the 13th, Mr. Moody, with a party of friends, visited John O'Groat's and Duncansbay Head. The news of his presence spread rapidly amongst the inhabitants of the neighborhood, and a considerable gathering of men and women, attired in their Sabbath dress, with Bibles in their hands, intercepted him as he stood upon the site of John O'Groat's House, and urgently requested that he might address a few words to them. Mr. Moody made passing allusion to the circumstances of his visit, to the probability of his never meeting his audience again in this world, to the scenery, the situation, and the tradition of the place. The speaker, standing as he did on the northmost mainland of Britain, with the blue waters of the broad Atlantic rolling between him and his home, seemed as a link binding the two nations together in that unity and brotherly love which are the main characteristics of his doctrine. This was, probably, the first sermon ever preached on John O'Groat's House.

A scene in Wick, whither he returned, is thus described by Rev. George Renny:

"He requested those who were yet unsaved and anxious, to cross the platform where the pulpit stands, and retire to the hall below. Slowly one, and another, and another rose, and, in the face of the audience, moved to the place appointed. It soon became full of inquirers, so much so that there was not standing-room. Mr. Moody then intimated that the church would be cleared for them to return, but that if there were others before him still anxious, they should, in the meantime, move below. The minister's vestry was thrown open and was filled. Thereafter, the back stair, which leads to the pulpit, was also crowded. It was found that not fewer than two hundred men— a few of them with silvery locks, and a few young in years, but the vast majority in the full vigor of manhood, and occupying various positions in the social scale—confessed themselves unconverted, and anxious for salvation. Christians accustomed to speak to the anxious were requested to occupy a certain place in the church; other Christians were asked to adjourn to the Baptist Chapel, and pray for direction, and the revelation of Christ to those who remained, and the promiscuous assembly separated. The inquirers then returned, and took their seats in front of the pulpit. The way of salvation was explained by Mr. Moody, in a very simple and forcible manner, and the texts of Scripture which had been most blessed in the way of delivering and assuring his own soul, were dwelt upon. The gospel was brought home with such simplicity that one felt how true it is. The wayfaring men, though fools, need not err therein. Regret was expressed that the souls before him could not be spoken with individually. He then requested that all would engage in silent prayer, and that as many as were enabled to trust in Jesus should in these solemn moments receive Him as their Saviour. This done, he then asked that those who had now committed their souls to Christ for salvation, should rise up; when slowly, one by one, there rose one hundred and fifty, or thereby—every countenance bearing the imprint of seriousness, every eye bedimmed with a tear, but no excitement and no outburst of feeling. It was a sight for angels to witness. Mr. Moody after this requested them to repeat audibly the words of a dedication prayer, so full of directness and simplicity, that as every lip, quivering with emotion, slowly echoed the words, we seemed carried back to the days of the Covenant. This concluded, there burst from the heart of the audience a prayer from a young man who has been much identified with this work of grace, such as told of the tremulous joy which was present to the minds of all of us, and the earnest desire that all who had witnessed the good confession might by grace be found faithful to the end.

"In a brief time, the newly-professed converts retired, and those who had kept their seats and were still anxious were conversed with, some of whom seemed to find their way to the light. Never, never will that night be forgotten. Many, doubtless, will watch for the halting of these men. Let us continue instant in prayer that they may be kept steadfast and unmovable, always abounding in the work of the Lord."

"It is now," says Rev. W. R. Taylor, of Glasgow, who was at Wick and in the neighborhood with Mr. Moody, "fifteen years since Thurso was visited with a marked blessing, and of that happy period I retain a record, which tells of upwards of four hundred inquirers, and of one-half of these becoming members of the church within a few months thereafter. May God grant like and even greater things in this year of grace." This hope was amply realized.

The encouraging state of things on Monday and Tuesday evenings, combined with the urgent request of friends, led Mr. Moody to decide on remaining here till the end of the week, instead of giving only two days, as first arranged. On the following (Thursday) evening, Mr. Moody preached on Faith. When ministers and other workers dealt at the close of the service with inquirers, they found that the way had been paved for them to an unusual degree, and that many who had been previously seeking hope among their own feelings, were now prepared to close, in the strength of grace, with the offered and offering Saviour. For example, as one man was being conversed with, after the Christian friend speaking to him had said a few words, he suddenly bowed his head on the bookboard, and poured forth from an overcharged heart a fervent prayer, expressive of immediate acceptance of the Lord Jesus as his Saviour, and of thanksgiving for the light received. To speak to inquirers under such circumstances was a work as easy as it was blessed.

A most useful Convention was held in Inverness in the end of August. Of the last week in Scotland, we should be glad to give more ample details did our space admit. The following is a concise account of the meetings:

After the Convention at Inverness, Mr. Moody, with a company of local friends, went down the Caledonian Canal to Oban, and there, on Friday the 28th, gave an address with much apparent blessing in the United Presbyterian Church. There had been much preparatory work in the town, not only in the open-air meetings, but also in other special services; and in the two preceding months the Rev. H. Bonar and the Rev. A. Bonar, had ministered the Word in the Free Church. From Oban Mr. Moody went to Campbeltown, by way of Tarbert, on Loch Fyne, and remained from the 29th to the 3d of September, when he left for Rothesay, taking the Tarbert route, and staying on his way at the house of the Rev. W. Mackinnon at Ballinakill, where many were gathered from various parts of Kintyre to meet him. His work at Campbeltown was deeply interesting, and was crowned with remarkable blessing. He commenced on Sunday the 30th by three services; speaking first to workers, then on the Blood, and lastly on the grand command, " Go ye into all the world and preach the gospel to every creature." The result after that last address was most striking. Upwards of fifty stood up to ask to be prayed for, and to declare their desire to be Christians. The meeting had been overcrowded, and some went to the Drill-hall, where the gospel was preached by willing helpers; but in the great after-meeting in the church, all were united, and it was felt to be a time of wonderful enlargement and power. On the three following days the interest was deepened at successive meetings; till at the last, on Wednesday night, when Mr. Moody had preached on God's invitation and man's excuses, a very large number were gathered into a hall, either as converts or inquirers; and it was manifest that much fruit had been gathered to life eternal. There is the joy of seeing many now rejoicing in Jesus, who were wont to walk in the shadow of death, and believers are learning to work when God is calling in the harvest, as it is written, "He is a wise son who gathereth in summer."

It is well known that the Highlanders are intensely strong in their religious convictions and prepossessions; hence many who knew the Highlands were afraid that Mr. Moody's preaching would not suit the Celtic mind; while Mr. Sankey's songs, it was feared, would stir up a perfect storm of opposition in the minds of the people. Happily, neither of these predictions was verified. Mr. Moody's addresses melted the hearts of thousands, while Mr. Sankey's hymns have become as great favorites in the Highlands as they are in the South of Scotland. In the remote Highland glen you may hear the sound of hymn-singing; shepherds on the steep hill-sides sing Mr. Sankey's hymns while tending their sheep; errand boys whistle the tunes as they walk along the streets of the Highland towns; while in not a few of the lordly castles of the north they express genuine feeling.

A clergyman of the Church of England heard a Scotch minister speak of the work in Scotland at the Mildmay Conference. He was just on the eve of starting for Norway, where he intended to spend his holidays. He decided to come to Scotland instead; it was his first visit to the North, and he enjoyed the magnificent mountain scenery very much. But he enjoyed the spiritual work still more. "Never," said he, "have I enjoyed a holiday like this—such breathings of the Spirit, such holy joy, such delightful meetings as I have seen during my visit to Scotland. Truly this has been a memorable year for Scotland. Let the readers of *Times of Blessing* pray that Messrs. Moody and Sankey's labors may be abundantly blessed in their visit to Ireland, and that the winter of toil in our great centers of population, to which they are looking forward, may be productive of even more glorious results than have followed their labors in Scotland."

The farewell to Scotland we must give in the words of an eye-witness. It was at the close of the Inverness

Convention. " Mr. Moody referred with very much feeling to the work in Scotland. His sentences were interrupted by bursts of tears; he bent over the pulpit sobbing, and buried his face in his hands. Among the audience the flood of emotion was overpowering; the whole meeting was bathed in tears. It was a moment of inexpressible tenderness; the thoughts and feelings of past months came rushing back in a torrent. Mr. Moody said if he had given offense to any one since he came to Scotland, he now asked to be forgiven. He would leave Scotland with a sigh, and he hoped that he and his dear friend Mr. Sankey would be remembered affectionately in prayer at many a Scottish hearth, as they went further in their work. The last nine months had been the dearest in his life. He was leaving friends who would be ever dear to him, and whose kindness he could never forget. Some had departed, especially the honored friend (Principal Fairbairn) who had opened the Glasgow Convention, and had there delivered a speech that stirred every heart, and was said to be the speech of his life. In conclusion, he wished to do what he had not done before—to thank briefly those who had furthered his work. First, he had to thank the ministers. From them he had received nothing but kindness; all denominations had cordially worked with him. "As a layman, I did not expect it. And Mr. Sankey and I have received far warmer welcome than we deserved. Secondly, we owe our gratitude to the Press. Little has been written we could object to. Wherever we have gone, the Press has given us a helping hand, and aided in the success of our work. Thirdly, I have to thank the young men of Scotland, who, wherever I have gone, have rallied round me in such a remarkable way. To officers of the church, to parents, and all others who have aided us, I return my thanks. There has not been one word of strife or discord among the fellow-laborers all these months; and even in the open meetings, which some supposed would open the door to animosities and stupidity, there has been nothing objectionable. God has wonderfully kept us. And now, will you let God's Spirit go on working? Very much more may be done. Dear friends, farewell! May God bless you, and by and by may we meet on the eternal shore!"

Of the spirit in which the work had been prosecuted, and in which he now looked toward Ireland, a hint was given in his Bible-reading, when he said that in considering what should be the subject for the Bible-reading, he thought what was it he wanted most himself. When nine months ago he came to Scotland a perfect stranger, he felt utterly powerless, and could only have been sustained by the Holy Spirit's help; now when he was going to Ireland he felt just the same; and if he attempted to go there resting upon the grace given for Scotland he should fail. He needed a fresh anointing for this new service.

In this spirit of entire reliance upon the Lord, Mr. Moody contemplated the Irish field. God honors those who honor Him. We shall see how much this confidence in the Lord was justified by the results of effort in Ireland.

CHAPTER V.

THE NORTH OF IRELAND.

BELFAST is the capital of Ulster, the northernmost of the four provinces of Ireland. It is also the capital of the Presbyterianism which has become a prominent feature of Ulster, and of which the United States contain so many representatives, the emigration to the Western world having proceeded for a century and a half. Belfast has, probably, a population of over one hundred and fifty thousand persons; it is marked by much enterprize and activity. It is not only nearest to Scotland, but it is more like Scotland in habits and feeling than any other town in Ireland.

As far back as the month of January, the people of Belfast were promised a visit from Messrs. Moody and Sankey in May. But other duties interfered. They reached Belfast on Saturday the 5th of September (1874). A local committee had made arrangements for their services.

On the first Sabbath an early meeting at eight A. M. was announced for Donegal Square Wesleyan Church, of Christian workers, chiefly Sabbath-school teachers and office-bearers in churches. By the time the hour for opening arrived, the aisles were occupied as well as the pews. Ministers of all the evangelical denominations were present. The One Hundredth Psalm—so often employed in Scotland; Mr. Sankey's hymns; prayers by Rev. W. Park; an address by Mr. Moody, on the things God employed, *base, weak, foolish;* a sermon in one of the largest Presbyterian churches at noon; the building over-crowded; the service begun before the time, and a similar service in St. Enochs', the very largest church-edifice in the place—these gave to at least five thousand persons the opportunity to hear the truth, many of them neglectors of the sanctuary.

Next day, a noon prayer-meeting was begun, and Mr. W. A. Breakey thus describes the progress of the evangelists' labors. The Donegal Place Wesleyan Church was the place.

"The building was crowded long before the hour of commencing. There were present Rev. J. W. M'Kay, Rev. Dr. Applebe, Rev. Henry Osborne, Rev.

George Shaw, Rev. J. B. Wylie, Rev. William Johnston, Rev. William Park, Rev. H. M. Williamson, and many ministers from the country districts around. It was felt that it would be necessary in future to move to the largest of our central churches; and it was temporarily arranged that the noon meeting should be held in the May Street Presbyterian Church till further notice. Mr. Sankey sang as usual, both in leading the congregation and solos, accompanied by the organ. The address by Mr. Moody on prayer was well-timed and earnest. Mr. Johnston, Mr. Williamson, Mr. Osborne, Mr. Sankey, and others led in prayer. The evening meeting was announced for Rosemary Street Presbyterian Church at eight P. M. This church is capable of accommodating about two thousand persons, and at seven it was quite full; and those who arrived afterward could barely get inside the porch, just to hear that there was no possibility of their getting into the church. Messrs. Moody and Sankey having arrived at half-past seven, commenced the service immediately, it having been announced by the Rev. Mr. Park that two more churches would be opened, viz., Donegal Street Independent Church, and Donegal Square

Wesleyan Church. Thither many went; but notwithstanding the crowd remained. Mr. Sankey sang two of his solos, and led the congregation in two other pieces. Mr. Moody addressed the people from the text, 'There is no difference.' The manner in which he applied the numerous anecdotes he tells made the message most powerful, and a great many remained to be spoken to on the all-important question. There was also an after-meeting for inquirers in the Independent Church, to which Mr. Sankey went just before Mr. Moody commenced his address. Rev. Mr. Johnston, Rev. John White, Rev. James Robertson, Presbyterian, Independent, and Wesleyan respectively, addressed and took part in that meeting."

A meeting for women only was tried in Fisherwick Place Church; Rev. H. M. Williamson, pastor, presided. The large church was crowded. Mr. Moody addressed the assembly. An evening meeting, for men only, was tried in Rosemary Street Presbyterian Church. About fifty inquirers remained for an after conversational meeting. Both were continued.

On Wednesday, 9th September, the noon meeting was held in May Street Church, which was crowded, as was the meeting for women assembled in

Fisherwick Place Church. At eight P.M. another crowded meeting for men was held in Rosemary Street Church. The Donegal Street Independent Church was opened for a general meeting of men and women, and it too was largely attended. Mr. Sankey and others addressed it. Many in both places remained for the after-meetings. This being the usual evening for prayer-meetings in the various Presbyterian churches, it was remarked that the attendance at them was if anything larger than usual. There is an evident stirring among God's people to keep pleading with Him. While Mr. Moody preached, many prayed.

The committee of arrangements announced a week in advance the chairman and the subjects for the noonday prayer-meeting. At the evening meeting for men only (the division became necessary from want of a larger building,) the attendance was very large. Mr. Moody, after prayer, asked the body of the house to be cleared, and requested those who wanted to be Christians, and those who had professed to become Christians the night before, to come into the place reserved for them. During the singing of the hymn, "I Hear Thy welcome Voice," he asked those who really were anxious not to be afraid to show it. Almost the first who came forward were two soldiers,—one a color-sergeant of the Thirteenth Regiment, stationed here. This had a good effect, and gave courage to several more timid ones. There were, say, forty at least who thus came forward, and several ministers and Christian friends conversed with them—sometimes individually, sometimes in groups of twos and threes. It was very solemn to watch them anxiously stooping forward, listening to the old, old story of the way of life. It was noticeable how easy speaking was to the class ef young men who are in Sabbath-schools—how useful their stock of scriptural information is in such circumstances; an intelligent faith is the simplest mode of description which can be given of their grasp of the truth. It was felt that this was indeed a blessed night to many. Some went away still anxious; others with beaming countenances, in which might almost be read that they had found peace.

So the meetings proceeded from day to day. The little boys who used to be seen selling newspapers on the streets, supplied themselves with a stock of Sankey's melodies, and plied the passers-by with, "Hymn-books with songs sung at Moody and Sankey's meetings!" Large numbers of these were put in circulation.

On Saturday a children's meeting was held in May Street Church at noon—Mr. Sankey presiding. The church was crowded, the day being fine. Perhaps a little better than one-half were children, a great many of their parents being present with them. Rev. Messrs. Shaw, Park, Robertson, Dr. Watts, Woods, etc., and Charles Finlay, Esq., J.P., were present. Rev. John White and others led in prayer. Rev. Mr. Robertson (Wesleyan), gave an excellent address. Mr. Sankey was there, sang "When He cometh," and addressed the children suitably. Mr. Charles Finlay prayed. Among the requests for prayer read, was one which Dr. Watts stated was for a young man who had recently adopted materialistic views.

At the end of the first week the Rev. Wm. Park writes:

"The meetings have been immense. With the exception of the first two evening meetings, when the crowd was overwhelming, they have been calm, quiet, earnest, almost beyond description. The women's meeting at 2 o'clock has been most popular. But the deepest impression seems to have been made on young men. Fifty or sixty would be a very moderate average of those who have attended from night to night the inquirers' meeting, and on last evening the number seemed larger than ever. It was most interesting last night to go from seat to seat, and, in answer to questions asked, to hear such replies as these: 'Yes, sir, I think I found Christ here on Monday night;' 'I gave Christ my heart on Wednesday night;' 'I should so wish to trust in Christ, but I cannot come.' It is hard to move young men in a busy town like Belfast; and the presence of so many in the inquiry rooms, and the tears which so many were shedding freely, proved plainly how deeply they are moved now. We do not know, of course, how this movement may proceed, and we must be very cautious in counting up results, but we thank God for what He is doing."

On Sabbath, the 13th September, Mr. Moody held a second meeting for Christian workers, at the early hour of eight, and the place was crowded, so that the overflow filled an adjoining room. The address was touching entire consecration to God, and more wholehearted activity in his service. An open-air meeting was held at half-past two o'clock in an open space, in the midst of the mill-workers of our town. The attendance was estimated variously at from ten to twenty thousand! The weather was exceedingly favorable. Mr. Moody's address was founded upon Mark xvi. 15, " Go ye into all the world, and preach the gospel to every creature." Mr. Sankey sang " Jesus of Nazareth passeth by," and the glistening eye, and the deep sighs of many, showed that it was even so.

In the evening, Mr. Moody held a meeting exclusively for inquirers; none else were admitted: the attendance was upwards of three hundred.

At the meeting for women, on Monday, in Fisherwick Place, there were present about fifteen hundred. An evening meeting for women was held, to give to workers in mills and warehouses opportunity to attend. More than an hour before the time of meeting, the streets around were packed with a dense mass of women; and when the gates were opened, the place was filled almost in a moment; and after that, with the overflow, three large churches. In all these meetings, the anxious, willing to be spoken to, were more than could be overtaken.

Strangers from long distances visited Belfast to attend the meetings, and in this way the work was widely extended.

The most marked features were desire to hear the Word of God, willingness to be spoken to upon the state of the soul, frank confession on the part of many that they do not savingly know Jesus; and most blessed of all, the equally frank confession on the part of many that they have "found Him of whom Moses, in the law and the prophets, did write, Jesus of Nazareth."

On Thursday, 17th September, the number waiting to be spoken to was so great, that an attempt to speak to each individually was scarcely made. Two or three addresses were given with the view of pointing them to the Lamb of God.

The Friday mid-day meeting was for professing Christians—the subject "Assurance."

The work began, meantime, to spread to the adjacent towns. Meetings were held for some four nights in Bangor, ten miles from Belfast, by H. Moorhouse, Rev. H. M. Williamson, and some others, and considering the size of the town, the attendance there was equally remarkable.

An intelligent observer, from the center of Ireland, thus described his impressions of the meeting on the second Sabbath. It may stand for the description of many similar occasions:

"The opening prayer, by the Moderator of the General Assembly, could be heard everywhere, and distinctly too, by all that vast multitude. It was really in the Holy Ghost. All were brought unto God's presence for a blessing. To be in the open air, it was extraordinary; the people must have felt themselves being lifted up right into the presence of God.

"Mr. Sankey then sang, alone, 'Jesus of Nazareth passeth by.' It was not difficult to hear him everywhere, as there was scarce a stir, and God was really arresting the people, who were eagerly drinking in every utterance of that sweet hymn, so full and so fragrant of 'Jesus only.'

"During the address, it seemed as if some mighty spell was binding the people, and riveting their attention. Mr. Moody preached from 'Go ye into all the world, and preach the gospel to every creature.' I never heard the gospel outside preached with such power before; all could hear; all might take. As I stood listening, I could not help saying to myself, 'Oh, if I was a sinner unsaved, I could be saved here to-day a thousand times over,' as the Lord Jesus was set forth in such a variety of ways. But I am certain as the faithful word was proclaimed with burning heart and lip, that not a few were taken out of themselves and put right into 'the arms of Jesus.' God's dear children, too, were surely quickened and blessed. I could hear the 'Amen,' and 'praise,' and 'thank God,' as the word came down in the power of the Holy Ghost upon that great audience, going up from the hearts of many of them.

"Mr. Moody said, 'God has put it into the hearts of these ministers to call this meeting to-day. Now, I have a full and free salvation for every one of you, for the worst of you, and the best of you. The gospel is for the very dregs of sin and sorrow; the apostles might reason concerning this man and that man, and this people and that people; and say, 'Oh, there's no use in my going there.' But, in the face of the command, all must vanish, for they had a gospel for all, 'for every creature.' Those who will not take eternal life, their damnation is sure."

Some idea may be formed of the interest felt in the meetings from the circumstance that for the second daily meeting for women, in Rosemary Street Church, an immense congregation assembled an hour before the time for commencing, when it was found necessary to close the gates. By this time a disappointed crowd

A PROTRACTED MEETING.

had assembled, and, after some delay, it was announced that May Street Presbyterian Church, Donegal Place Primitive Wesleyan Church, and Donegal Square Wesleyan Church would be opened for the "overflow." To these both men and women were admitted.

After the Friday evening meeting, when the Rev. T. Y. Killen had closed with prayer, Mr. Moody asked those in the assembly who had not accepted Christ, and yet wished to do so, to stand up. Mr. Moody said, truly, "Thank God, I can't count them, there are so many!" He then invited those in the gallery down, and directed the spectators and others present to leave, and clear a space in the body of the church, in order that the inquirers might be conversed with. A large number came forward, far more than at any preceding meeting, and it was with difficulty the church could be cleared at a reasonable hour, owing to the groups in conversation with troubled ones scattered through the church. Rev. Hugh Hanna dismissed the meeting, after prayer.

The Saturday (19th September) meeting, in May Street, was for the young, and was conducted by Mr. Sankey. The attendance was so great, that after the aisles were filled, the doors had to be locked, and many turned away. Mr. Sankey was followed by Revs. Dr. Knox, Hugh Hanna, and George Shaw. Several hymns and the Twenty-third psalm were sung. It was a delightful meeting, and the children seemed to enjoy it heartily.

The Rev. William Park, the faithful chronicler of the work (successor to Rev. John MacNaughton), writes. at the close of the second week: "The after meetings are, in their own way, as crowded as the regular services. The lecture-room and two class-rooms of Rosemary Street were filled each evening with men and women waiting to be spoken to personally; and, on two occasions, personal dealing with individual souls could not be carried out on account of the vast numbers to be dealt with, and general statements of the plan of salvation, by one after another, had to be resorted to instead. Many will come out, under the influence of feeling no doubt—especially in an assembly of women. But the private conversations we have had with many, both men and women, show how wide-spread, and, in a multitude of instances, how deep is this religious earnestness, this longing after Christ. 'I have been teaching a Sabbath-school class for years,' said one young lady, 'and the awful thought laid hold of me the other evening here, that I have been teaching what I knew nothing about; but I have really given myself to my Saviour now.' 'Pray for me,' writes a mother, 'that my unfaithfulness to my own sons, none of whom are converted, may be forgiven, and that my mouth may be opened to speak to them about salvation.' 'I believe I found Christ here two nights ago,' said a young man one evening, 'and I have brought two of my companions here, to be talked to to-night.' 'I knew the truth,' writes another, 'But I never seemed to feel it before. I trust I can now say and feel that Christ has found me, even me, cold-hearted and dead as I was.' Need I tell you there are difficulties and hindrances? And yet the Lord has been pleased, so far, wondrously to open the door for His servants; and, as far as I am aware, at no time has there been so deep a religious feeling abroad in our town and province since 1859, as there is at this moment. Ministers, elders, Christian men and women, are coming from far and near to hear the good news, to see the good work. We have several ministers and friends from Scotland here at present. May they carry home with them good tidings; may they be stirred up themselves, and be used by the Holy Spirit as the means of stirring up others."

In the *Witness*, a weekly religious paper which has done good service in diffusing information, the catholicity of the movement is emphasized:

"Not the least gratifying feature of the movement is the happy bringing together of all evangelical denominations to which it has given rise. In all the meetings, Presbyterians, Episcopalians, and Methodists are mixed and mingled without distinction. On Monday night, in Rosemary Street Church, the Rev. Mr. Dickson, incumbent of the Mariners' Episcopal Church, was one of the busiest among the inquirers; and on Tuesday evening, the Rev. I. H. Deacon, incumbent of Trinity Episcopal Church, occupied the pulpit of Eglinton Street Presbyterian Church. If the present stirring do nothing more than help to banish the bitterness of sectarianism, and lead Christian men to live and work in accordance with the truth that we are all one body in Christ, it will have wrought unquestionably a work for which none can be too thankful."

On the third Sabbath the "overflow" from the 8 o'clock morning meeting filled two other large buildings. A second open-air meeting was held, as before; and, at a meeting of anxious inquirers in the Ulster Hall, the largest building in town, at 7, the area of that building was as full as it could comfortably be for the purposes of the meeting about half-past 6. Rev. Mr. Park, Rev. Dr. Murphy, and subsequently several other ministers in town, and many Christian workers, were in attendance to converse with them. Many professed to have had their doubts removed. Mr. Moody and Mr. Sankey left the meeting in charge of the ministers, and at 9 o'clock went to May Street Church, to a large meeting of men assembled there, which Mr. Moody stated he had specially convened in order to enlist young men in active Christian work.

Four crowded meetings were held on Monday (21st Sept.), and the Tuesday evening meeting was announced for St. Enoch's at 8 o'clock, but as early as half-past 5 there were persons waiting for the gates to be opened. The meeting was commenced by the Rev. Mr. Hanna, pastor of the church, at a quarter-past 7. Rev. Mr. Ballard, Rev. Dr. Knox, Mr. Sankey, and others took part in the meeting. About one-half of the assembly waited for an after meeting. This was taken charge of by the Rev.

Messrs. Hanna, Henry, Carlisle, and Shaw. Mr. Moody asked the anxious to retire to Ekenhead Church, which was speedily almost filled. There cannot have been less than a couple of hundred who came over here to be talked to by ministers and Christian workers, and among them were many interesting cases. Eglinton Presbyterian Church was opened about half-past 7 o'clock for the "overflow" from St. Enoch's, and the Rev. Mr. Deacon, Episcopal Church, took the chair there. Rev. Mr. Macintosh and others spoke. The Frederick Street Wesleyan Church was also opened for the "overflow."

On the 23d, a new feature was introduced to Belfast, namely, a Bible-reading by Mr. Moody at 2 o'clock in Fisherwick Place Church. He urged upon all the necessity of systematic and regular Bible-reading, recommending the plan of reading and comparing the various passages on a particular subject, and exhausting it before proceeding to another. In the evening, more than an hour before the time appointed, St. Enoch's Church was crowded, so that the meeting practically commenced at a quarter-past 7. Rev. Messrs. Hanna and Robertson took part in the service, and Mr. Sankey led the singing. Inquirers, as before, were directed to retire to Ekenhead Church, while the young men were sent to the men's meeting in May Street. About one-half of the assembly in St. Enoch's remained for an after meeting, conducted by Rev. Messrs. Simpson, Spence, Black, and Hanna. Ekenhead Church was filled with inquirers.

On Saturday, 26th September, the noonday meeting for children was held in May Street Church. The attendance was so large that it was necessary to close the gates, and many left disappointed.

The Rev. W. Park says, after the third week's labors: "St. Enoch's, Mr. Moody says, is one of the largest churches, if not the largest, he has preached in, in Europe, and it is full every night an hour before the time. A separate church has now been taken for the inquirers, and they pass to it from St. Enoch's as soon as Mr. Moody's address is concluded. Ministers and Christian workers make their way to it about the same time, and no one else is admitted. Thus perfect quiet is insured. The 2 o'clock meeting is no longer set apart for women. It is a Bible-reading, and all are admitted. And every evening there are now five meetings in five different churches, including the inquiry-meeting and the young men's meeting.

"There are one or two things which may be noticed with regard to the week's work. Christians are being deeply moved and roused to diligence and duty. Last Sabbath morning the meeting for Christian workers, which had been removed to May Street Church on account of its size, filled every corner of the building ten minutes before 8 o'clock, and its overflowings filled two other places of meeting besides. Many are now offering themselves, Christian women as well as men, to engage in the work of directing inquirers, and they now find their own souls stirred, and their faith strengthened in their efforts to guide and comfort others. I believe that in no other town which Mr. Moody has visited has there been such a number of anxious inquirers from the very outset as in Belfast. There seems to have been a mighty movement at work unseen for months past among young men and women—an anxious longing after Christ, which made itself felt and seen at once when these special services began. The meeting in the Ulster Hall on last Sabbath evening was one of the most precious and happy services I have ever attended. It was held at 7 o'clock, to prevent ordinary church-going people coming to fill up the space which was required for others. No one was admitted at the door but those who wished to be talked with about salvation, and those who had tickets from the committee as workers. The immense hall was not too large for the numbers who came. Two hours were spent in earnest private conversation. Then all gathered into the floor of the hall, and every one who had a text to repeat was asked to rise and give it. Many of the most precious promises of God's word were thus brought out, accompanied sometimes with a single sentence of explanation or illustration. One or two hymns were sung, and some prayers offered up; but even after Mr. Moody left many remained, unwilling to leave till they could find rest in Christ. I do believe that many in that meeting were enabled by the Holy Spirit to receive and rest on the Lord Jesus Christ as He was freely offered to them in the gospel. If, from this circle of seekers and believers, we pass to the outer circle of mere spectators, their feelings and words are of the most varied kind. Some hate this revival work with a bitter hatred. Some mock it and caricature the workers and their work. But not a few feel solemnized as they see God's hand so plainly in this movement. They are willing to be spoken to about religion, and willing to think about what is said. Not a few young men who seemed given over to the world and sin, are now asking the way to heaven; and it is touching to see these youths, to many of whom we should scarcely have ventured to speak about religion before, with tears in their eyes, waiting so earnestly to be talked to by any Christian about the way of life. Here is one of the requests for prayer handed in last Friday: 'Pray for a young man who has been in deep darkness and strong temptation, so that he has had thoughts of drowning himself, but has now found his way to the inquiry-meetings.' Here is another: 'A young man who is deeply anxious about his state desires the prayers of this meeting, that he may be able to see Jesus as a personal Saviour.' Last Sabbath morning in my own Sabbath-schools, three young men presented themselves as teachers. They had been brought to Christ at these meetings, and wished to work for Him.

"Nor is the blessing confined to those who hear the word which is sung or spoken by those friends who are now in the midst of us. In the General Hospital at present a young man is lying, suffering from a severe accident. He had not been at any of these meetings. A medical man, who is earnest in God's service, went to see him, and talked to him about his soul and his sin. On Thursday last he put into my hand a letter which he had received from him in which he says:—'This morning a terror seized me, and I am in awful anguish of soul. I see how great a sinner I have been, and there is a great weight upon my soul. I would like to see you soon.' From places at a distance we receive letters, saying that the first drops of the blessing have been felt, and are being anxiously waited for."

When men are in earnest in inviting attention to God's word, they become ingenious in making fresh presentations of its truth; so, when the Rev. William Fleming Stevenson of Rathgar, Dublin, presided at a noon-day meeting in May Street, he addressed the meeting on the subject of "The Searches of the Lord," viz., the search after the lost referred to in Luke xv., and the search into the heart referred to in Psalm cxxxix. Mr. Moody followed up this by a practical address on the necessity of Christians searching their hearts, whether they were as actively engaged in Christian work as they might be.

At the Bible-reading in Fisherwick Place Church Mr. Moody's subject was the seven "Beholds," beginning with Job's confession, "Behold, I am vile," and ending with the statement as to Saul of Tarsus, "Behold, he prayeth."

A new feature in Belfast was a boys' meeting, commenced in the Linen-hall Church Schools, and addressed by Christian gentlemen.

The correspondent, of whose judicious and discriminating reports we have already availed ourselves, says, after the fourth week's labor:

"On two occasions this week we have tried the plan of admitting by ticket to the evening service in St. Enoch's Church, and have found it to work admirably. These tickets are given out in some central place, and the only condition necessary for receiving them is, that the persons who apply have not yet been able to hear Mr. Moody and Mr. Sankey. In this way these ticketed meetings bring in a new class, and enable our brethren to reach three thousand on each occasion who have not been reached before."

At a special meeting for converted young men, to which admission was by ticket, nearly four hundred appeared.

On Monday Fisherwick Place Church was thrown open to inquirers from 2 till 10 o'clock at night. These eight hours were divided into three parts, and a separate set of ministers arranged to be present at each. Other Christian workers came in large numbers; and, though the inquirers were many, there was not one but was personally dealt with about salvation. Those who took part in it felt it to be one of the most profitable evenings since this good work began. In more than one case young men from a distance—in one or two cases from Scotland—have come to Belfast on business, or to attend these meetings, and have found the pearl of great price. To-day, at the noon prayer-meeting, thanks were returned on behalf of a mother in Edinburgh for the conversion of her son in Belfast. This request for prayer was presented yesterday: "A young man who came into town to attend these meetings is afraid of returning home without Jesus. In the inquiry-meeting last night he was pointed to Christ, but has not yet found peace."

There have been instances of Roman Catholics and Unitarians convinced of sin at these services, and brought to the feet of Jesus. There does not seem, speaking generally, to be the same deep and awful sense of sin among those who are awakened as there was in 1859, but there is a true feeling of the need of Christ as our Sacrifice and our Saviour.

A young man in one of our large business establishments found Christ about a fortnight ago at an evening in Rosemary Street Church. Next day he gathered some of the men who are employed in the warehouse round him, and spoke to them about the meetings. One of them said lightly to him, "What sort of meeting had you last night?" "I thought a moment," he said, "what reply to make, and then I answered, 'That meeting has changed me for life, at any rate.'" Less than a week after that man came back to tell him that those words had been ringing in his ears ever since, and that now he too had become a changed man for life.

The blessing spreads. In Bangor and Carrickfergus very interesting meetings have been going on, and, in the former place especially, there are many anxious inquirers.

At the noon meeting on October 4th, Mr. Moody said, "When Mr. Sankey and he were about to leave Edinburgh, one thousand four hundred persons professed to have been converted since their arrival.

People who did not believe in the work, however, asserted—with what truth he did not know—that one thousand one hundred of these were women, obviously hinting that this kind of thing could only make progress among females and weak-minded men. When he and his friend went to Glasgow, therefore, they made it a special prayer that they might be able to refute this notion by being honored in the conversion of young men, and this wish was so far gratified, that when they were about to leave that city, they held a meeting of those who believed that they had been brought to Christ since their coming; and out of the three thousand two hundred who attended, one thousand six hundred and thirty were men. Foiled in this point, the enemies of the work now found a new cause of fault-finding. They could not deny that many men had been blessed, but they affirmed that these were not of the class which most needed to be wrought among, the abandoned class of the community. When coming to Belfast, therefore, Mr. Moody prayed that he might be specially owned in doing good to this class; and his prayer had so far been answered, that on the preceding Sabbath evening, at the meeting of converts held in the Assembly's

Hall, May street, the first three who rose to tell that they had become changed men were men who had been drunkards, one of them acknowledging that he had been twice drunk on the previous Sabbath. He had also heard of another case where a mother, whose heart had been broken by a son who almost nightly was brought to her door drunk, now had the comfort of seeing him in his right mind. Nowhere, in all Europe, had he met with more encouraging results than in Belfast."

At the mid-day prayer-meeting on Friday, a young man, well known some time ago as one of the finest scholars in Queen's College, Belfast, who carried off with ease every honor for which he competed, stood up before the crowded assembly, and with deep feeling, said, "Many here know how careless and prayerless I was, yet some of my Christian friends never gave me up, but continued to pray for me. Blessed be God, He has heard their prayers, and last Sabbath, having sent the arrow of conviction into my soul, He enabled me to rejoice in my Saviour. It pleased our God and Father to enable me to be much in prayer since then; and thanks be to God, though it is not one short week, it seems as if I had lived almost a hundred years of Christian life." Nor is this the only literary man of repute that has come under the influence of the present movement in Belfast.

Whatever attracts notice in Belfast, especially in religious matters, interests the entire province of Ulster. Many had heard of, many had seen the work. It was no longer confined to Belfast. In Bangor, Donaghadee, Carrickfergus, and Randalstown meetings were held nightly, and deep religious earnestness appeared. The want of a sufficiently large building was felt, and a great open-air meeting to supply this want was held on October 8th. The Rev. H. M. Williamson, successor to the late venerable Dr. Morgan, writes of it, and also of Mr. Moody's last work in the town:

"The joy of last week has almost been forgotten, by reason of the greatness of the blessing bestowed upon us this week by the God of all grace. It has been to us as the waters of the sanctuary in Ezekiel's vision, ever increasing in depth until now, when the waters are risen, 'they are waters to swim in.' It is a most glorious sight to witness the fishers standing upon it from one end of the city to the other, and the fish, according to their kinds, exceeding many (Ezek. xlvii. 1–10).

"Sabbath morning dawned upon us very wet and windy. We had fears that it would be impossible for the masses of the people to meet in the open air; but a little while before the hour of meeting the rain ceased, the sun shone out, and the weather became most auspicious. Here let me say it has been most noteworthy that, during the last weeks, while we have had most inclement weather, every Sabbath-day, and at the hour of our great gatherings, it has been all that could be desired. To-day, while I write (October 8th), the day of our great meeting in the Botanic Gardens, the sun is shining brightly, and the weather more than we asked or expected. Doubtless some will say, 'A happy conjunction of circumstances;' the children of the heavenly Father know Him 'who hath gathered the wind in his fists.'

"Mr. Moody held his usual meeting on Sabbath evening for those in deep distress about salvation, and for those who had found eternal life during the past weeks through faith in Jesus. The meeting was exclusively for men, and admission solely by ticket. The hall in which it was held was completely filled. Mr. Moody stated in the noon-day prayer-meeting on Monday that, in his judgment, it was the most remarkable meeting he has had yet in Europe. To God be all the praise! One after another of these young men—and they comprise the very flower of our youth—rose, and, with clearness and wonderful felicity of expression, in burning words, declared what God had done for their souls. At length, at nine o'clock, the meeting was closed.

"Meanwhile another meeting of men was assembling in my church. It was already very nearly filled when we heard the tread of a large company approaching. It was a phalanx of these redeemed youths. They sang the new song. In a spontaneous burst of praise they were telling forth the wonders of redeeming love. No language can describe the scene. The heavenly echoes of that burst of praise, I think, will never be forgotten by any who heard it. The meeting that followed, consisting of some two thousand men, I need not say, was one of profound interest—Jesus was felt to be in the midst.

"During each day of this week and at every gathering, more and more of the presence of the God of salvation has been manifested. Let me in a sentence or two, describe one, which, in sober language, was most wonderful. Mr. Moody addressed on Monday evening in Fisherwick place Church, a meeting of men. At the close of his address, all who had recently been found by the Good Shepherd, and also all who were seeking Him, were requested to retire to the adjoining lecture-room. Some six hundred men did so. Mr. Moody again sifted them, by requesting that those only who were deeply anxious to be saved should adjourn to another room. Probably nearly three hundred did so. In breathless stillness Mr. Moody addressed them, very briefly stating that he could do no more for them—that they had heard the gospel, and that it was for themselves to decide. He called upon them to kneel and pray for themselves. They bowed as one man, and now here and there might be heard the short cry for mercy—a few earnest words of supplication, probably about thirty or forty so cried to God one after the other. Surely the Lord is in this place! was the thought which rose in holy fear in the hearts of all.

"After a short prayer by Mr. Moody, he addressed them very faithfully. He again held forth Christ, and invited all to rise who felt that they could there and then accept Jesus. All of that large company, save twenty or thirty, stood up, and solemnly avouched the Lord to be their God. This wonderful sight cannot be described. The glory of it cannot be realized even by those best acquainted with divine things. 'Unto Him that loved us and washed us from our sins in his own blood, and hath made us kings and priests unto God and his Father, to Him be glory and dominion for ever. Amen' (Rev. i. 5).

"Thursday, October 8th, was the gathering of the masses in the open-air. The weather was splendid; everything as regards order and decorum, all that any of us could wish. It was the largest open-air meeting I ever attended. I cannot pretend to fix a limit to the numbers. He who counts the stars knew the history of each present, and what were the dealings of his heart with Christ and the free offers of his salvation. The only regret that seems to be expressed by any was, that the services were so short.

"Mr. Moody addressed the vast multitude from the words, 'I pray thee have me excused.' With graphic felicity, great clearness, and soul-piercing power, he exposed the miserable pretenses by which sinners impose upon themselves in refusing a present offer of present blessedness. The address seemed to strike with convicting power many consciences, and, from many instances coming under my own observation, at the inquiry-meeting in Fisherwick-place Church, I have reason to believe in salvation power."

One of the wisest, purest, most experienced and also most cautious clergymen in Ireland is the Rev. Dr. Kirkpatrick, the senior minister of Rutland Square, Dublin. In a letter to the Irish papers, he said: "It is understood that the American evangelists, Messrs. Moody and Sankey, whose labors in Scotland and in the North of England have been followed, it is believed, by great spiritual benefit to hundreds and thousands of persons, are about to visit Dublin, and that the Exhibition Building has been engaged for their reception. In prospect of this visit, it may interest many of your readers to be furnished with some brief account of the services which they have been conducting for the last few weeks, in the North of Ireland. Having had occasion to be recently in Belfast, I went to attend one of the evening meetings, at which Mr. Moody was to give an address. On reaching St. Enoch's, the place of meeting, half an hour before the time of service, I found the gates locked, the house having been filled for near an hour previously. On obtaining admission through the gate, by special favor, I was still unable to enter the church, the doors having been secured to prevent the entrance of a crowd of people who had scrambled over the railings. After some time I was admitted, and I observed that every available spot was occupied in a church which Mr. Moody says is larger than any church in which he has ever preached in Europe or America. He had proceeded towards the conclusion of his address. His words were not eloquent in the ordinary acceptation of the term; they were homely, vigorous, pungent, setting forth the 'old, old story' of the cross, and bringing it to bear with directness of appeal and intense earnestness of manner on the consciences of his hearers. The immense audience was held in fixed attention, nor was there the slightest appearance of levity, inattention, or disorder in any part of the house, that came under my observation. Immediately after this service I attended a meeting of persons—most of them young—who waited to converse with Mr. Moody, and with others whom he employed to assist him— most of them being ministers—in giving instruction to these inquirers. The object proposed by these private conferences was to answer questions, to remove difficulties and doubts, to confirm purposes of good, and to lead to decision in the service of Christ. These meetings are uniformly held after Mr. Moody's addresses, and there are often fifty or a hundred, and sometimes two or even three hundred, who remain for these conferences.

"On the next day I was present at the mid-day prayer-meeting, at which there were from one thousand two hundred to one thousand five hundred persons in attendance for an hour every day in the week. One of the local clergy presided, and others besides Messrs. Moody and Sankey led the assembly in prayer. These evangelists always recognize the ordained ministry, and avail themselves of clerical aid in every place which they visit. I observed many of the clergy mingled with the general audience.

"At two o'clock, an hour after the close of the prayer-meeting, Mr. Moody held what he calls his Bible-reading service. On this occasion he read a chapter of the Old Testament, illustrating and enforcing its lessons with characteristic energy. Immediately at the close of his address, Mr. Sankey folowed with an appropriate hymn, which was sung with the most touching pathos, and was well calculated to deepen the impression made by the appeal of Mr. Moody. There are many other special services held by Messrs. Moody and Sankey, but I confine my statement to what I have myself seen.

"In reference to this great movement, I remark :—

"1. The amount of solid good accomplished, time will tell; but it is surely a matter of vast moment that multitudes of people should be roused from their ordinary state of spiritual insensibility to inquire about the interests of eternity.

"2. There are none of those doubtful physical accompaniments which characterized the awakening of 1859. There is no other excitement than that which is produced by the truth of God, brought home to the hearts of a listening multitude of awakening sinners.

"3. The great object of these evangelists seems to be to turn sinners from the error of their ways, and to bind in loving union believers of every Christian denomination.

"4. The ministers of religion and many of the most intelligent and sober-minded Christians recognize these men as faithful and honored servants of the Divine Master.

"5. Messrs. Moody and Sankey go from place to place, expecting that God will bless His own truth proclaimed by their lips, and they desire and hope that a similar spirit of prayerful expectancy may take hold of the people of Dublin."

Next to Belfast, Londonderry is the most important city in Ulster. It retains the old walls, which its siege made memorable, and while a large Roman Catholic population finds employment in its manufactures and trade, the spirit of the place is strongly Protestant. The place has long enjoyed very faithful ministrations in its pulpits. It was visited in the early part of October.

With much cordiality the ministers of all denominations joined in the original invitation to Messrs. Moody and Sankey, and also assisted in the furtherance of the work. Presbyterian, Wesleyan, and Independent seemed to have but one object and one desire—to make the work of revival among the people as general and wide-spread as possible. The First Presbyterian Church was selected for holding the meetings, as it was the largest and therefore best able to accommodate the numbers likely to be present.

Messrs. Moody and Sankey arrived in Derry from

Belfast on Saturday evening, and commenced their labors on Sunday the 11th Oct., with the same spirit of energy and enthusiasm which carried them through so much in Belfast. There were in Mr. Moody's discourses the same fertility of illustration and pointed application, the same earnestness and simplicity, the same zeal and enthusiasm, and the same intense desire to win souls for his Master. Three services on the Sabbath, and the same number on each of the following three days of the week, with inquiry-meetings each evening, made up his programme, and he never seemed to fail either in body or mind. He appeared conscious of the shortness of his visit, and seemed to grow more earnest in consequence.

While Mr. Moody faithfully presented the gospel Mr. Sankey was no less faithful in his lessons in song. He was so admirably assisted by a local choir as to draw a special eulogium from Mr. Moody at one of the noon meetings. He said he had heard a great many choirs assist at these meetings, but he had never yet heard one which sang so sweetly and so well as the one which had been organized to assist in singing the praises of God in Londonderry. On the same occasion he referred to the importance of the

Church paying greater attention to the subject of praise. Some were only for singing the psalms, but he thought they should also sing "new songs." A new hymn was just as good as a sermon. They could sing the gospel into many a man's heart. He hoped the Church would feel alive to its duty in this matter of praise, and not be hindered by prejudice, which is the twin sister of unbelief.

The opening meeting was intended for Christian workers, and Mr. Moody dwelt especially on the subject of Christian work, and gave some earnest and practical counsel. On the same day two meetings were held in the First Presbyterian Church, one at four and the other at eight o'clock. The ordinary congregational services were conducted in the church at twelve o'clock, without, of course, any instrumental accompaniment in the praise. At both special services the church was crowded to overflowing, and the gates had to be closed half an hour before the commencement of the service. Indeed, at the evening-meeting, the church was filled at seven o'clock, the people crowding in such numbers to the service. Overflow-meetings were held in the Wesleyan Chapel, and were well attended, though better in the evening than in the afternoon.

On Monday, Tuesday, and Wednesday, three services were held each day, including one children's service. Owing to the heavy downpour of rain on Monday, the church was not so well filled as on the other days, when the congregations were very large; but on each evening fully two thousand found accommodation in the church, filling it from floor to ceiling, while the hundreds unable to gain admission went to the Wesleyan Chapel, where they were suitably addressed. The concluding meeting on Wednesday evening was especially large, and the services particularly solemn. On each occasion the meeting was conducted after the style of the meetings in Belfast,—already familiar to our readers.

The audiences were thoroughly representative. Young and old of all classes, not only of the inhabitants of Derry, but of the surrounding districts, for miles around, attended. Excursion-trains on the Irish North-western Railway and Northern Counties Railway brought many into the town, while hundreds walked and drove many miles, in order to be present at the meetings. The attendances steadily increased to the close, and as the last of the services approached, there seemed to be a general expression of regret.

A noticeable feature of the meetings was the large number of clergymen present at them.

The prevailing characteristic of all the meetings was intense solemnity, but without any undue excitement. The services seemed to awaken the liveliest interest in the public mind, and to produce a marked impression. The inquiry-meetings after the first night were well attended, large numbers of both sexes remaining for conversation and prayer with Mr. Moody and the Christian workers who were admitted (by ticket) to converse with the anxious. In this respect every precaution was taken that none but duly qualified persons should be admitted. The time occupied at these meetings was brief, but the addresses and conversations earnest and impressive. The upper room was set apart for female inquirers, and the lower schoolroom for males.

The Rev. A. C. Murphy, one of the ministers of Londonderry, gives his impressions of the men and their aptitudes in such a way as indicates that ministers have something to learn from them.

"Better sappers and miners of spiritual indifference, and the infidelity that is born of sinful living, could not be found. In addition to his astonishing vigor and versatility of thought, and his keen sympathy with all the familiar movements of the human heart, the speaker's organizing faculty and instructive wisdom give him an all but absolute sway over large assemblies; while the 'sweet singer' who accompanies him always manages to hit the mood of the moment by some appropriate cadence of joy or tenderness. The audience are never allowed to weary, and wish one part of the service ended before the next part has begun. Even the least affected go away rather regretting than relieved that the exercises are over. It would do a world of good if those who are in the habit of conducting public prayers would learn from Mr. Moody the triple virtue of brevity, of point, and of confining themselves more or less closely to the matter in hand. Ministers, as a rule, have little idea what damage is done by long, vague, expository prayers. The Bible lecture, again, is, in its way, an excellent mode of instruction, substituting as it does for the logical treatment of a subject the more popular treatment by association of ideas. It is, besides, peculiarly appropriate in Mr. Moody's mouth, as his two principal studies are the word of God and the book of the human heart."

After this four days' visit to Londonderry, the evangelists returned to Belfast. The Rev. Mr. Park thus describes two further meetings:

"Admission was to be by ticket, and for four days we were busily engaged giving out these tickets. Great care was exercised that none but anxious inquirers should receive them for the one evening, and none but those who made a credible profession of having been brought to Christ during the past few weeks for the other. The name and address of the applicants were taken down, and the name of the congregation with which they professed to be connected, so that every minister may obtain a correct list of his own people who have been moved and blessed. As far as we can judge, we gave out somewhere about two thousand two hundred tickets for the first meeting, and about two thousand for the second. That is to say, more than four thousand persons *profess* to have been brought under serious concern about salvation, or to have accepted Christ, during the past few weeks. We cannot pronounce on all, or indeed on any of these cases; we must wait to see the fruit of the new birth in the life and conduct. But the mere fact that such a vast number have professed to be anxious or to be converted shows how wide-spread and mighty this movement must have been.

"Among those who came to get tickets, there were many cases of the deepest interest. One man had attended some of the services at the beginning. He had then fallen ill of fever, and as he lay in the hospital, he thought over what he had heard, and came out of it, he believed, a new man. By far the greatest number who told us about themselves were able to point to some text or texts of Scripture which had been to their souls a window through which they saw the truth. John iii. 16 and John vi. 37, seem to have been useful to hundreds; John i. 12 and 1 John i. 7, were very precious to many: John iii. 14 and 15 had enabled others to see the simplicity of the way of salvation. Matt. xi. 28 and John xiv. 1 seem to be not only full of comfort for Christians, but full of guidance and comfort also for the anxious and inquiring. Isa. liii. was often quoted as the passage on which the soul was resting, and sometimes 1 Pet. ii. 24. Rev. iii. 20 was mentioned by others who had opened the door to the Saviour who knocked so long. It is well that those who have to instruct inquirers should know these passages, which have been useful to so many.

"How can I describe these two great meetings? On Thursday night? After those who had inquirers' tickets and those who had workers' tickets were admitted, five or six hundred of the general public were accommodated in the galleries. Amid breathless silence, Mr. Moody preached to an audience of nearly three thousand persons, taking up text after text, trying to make the way of salvation plain and easy, and pressing home the truth upon every heart. Earnestly did he urge the duty of immediate decision. When he had finished, Mr. Sankey sang 'The farewell hymn,' and the assembly was at once dismissed, to go home, and think, and pray. Great numbers were in tears. Many were unwilling to leave the church. At length all seemed to have gone away, and the lights were put out, when the minister of the church (Mr. Hanna), passing down the aisle, thought he saw dimly some figures in a pew. He found two women waiting with a companion, who was in deep anxiety about her soul. He took them into the vestry; he talked to her and prayed with her. He asked her companions to pray for her also, which they did; and before she left the room the darkness had passed, and the brightness of pardon and peace was shining in her face."

From Belfast, the brethren proceeded to Dublin. It was a hopeful sign that a well-attended noon prayer-meeting was in operation, that a great body of the ministers had agreed together as to the mode of operations. At a prayer-meeting during the week before the arrival of the evangelists, the Rev. Dr. Marrable, Rector of St. Andrews, read the opening of Ezekiel xxxvii., which, by a happy coincidence, formed part of the Scripture for reading in the Episcopal service, on the Sabbath when the evangelists were to commence. The preparations had been very thorough.

A central building, called the Metropolitan Hall, was secured on the north side of the city for the daily noon prayer-meeting. It has capacity to seat almost two thousand people. On the south side £500 had been paid for a month's occupancy of the Exhibition Palace, also central, where were held the daily evening meeting, and the afternoon service on the Lord's day. This is a huge glass building, capable of seating in its center aisle and transept about twelve thousand persons, and affording numerous rooms for after and inquiry meetings. Part of it had been screened off, sufficient to accommodate five or six thousand people, and seats had been made for four thousand, to be added to as the demand for accommodation increased.

There was a thorough working committee, composed of ministers and laymen of all the evangelical churches, and the unity prevailing was an excellent beginning and foretaste of the blessing we expect.

We infer from the reports that concerning no town yet visited had there been such deep anxiety. It was the first where the Protestants are few and the Roman Catholics many; it is the capital of the country, and especially of the Roman Catholic population of the country.

"For the first time," says the Rev. James S. Fletcher, Incumbent of St. Barnabas, Dublin, "and in connection with this movement, have we seen the clergy of all the evangelical churches working cordially together, without the least shade of envy or party spirit—all feeling that they are workers in the same holy cause, children of the same Father, servants of the same gracious Master.

"On Sunday last the Christians of Dublin witnessed a sight to gladden their hearts. It has been estimated that at the first service at 4 o'clock from *twelve to fifteen thousand* persons were in the palace. Never before was it put to so blessed a use. I am persuaded that in future years many a dear child of God will remember it with deepest gratitude, and will say, 'I was born there.'

"The weather being beautifully fine, the attendance increased each succeeding evening. On Monday evening, and again on Tuesday evening, Mr. Moody spoke of Jesus coming 'to seek and to save that which was lost,' interspersing his discourse with many forcible illustrations. The following evening his subject was the powerlessness of the Law to save, and then he set forth Jesus as the only and all-sufficient Saviour. Thursday and Friday evenings were devoted to showing the necessity of Spiritual Regeneration. On all these occasions the Lord Jesus was lifted up, and every eye and every heart directed to Him. Will He not fulfill His gracious promise—'I, if I be lifted up, will draw all men unto Me?' Blessed be His name, already we can tell of many having been so drawn."

The Rev. Hamilton Magee writes:

"The noon-day prayer-meeting in the Metropolitan Hall continues to grow in numbers, interest, and power. At the meeting to-day Mr. Moody presided; and the hall, which accommodates more than two thousand three hundred persons, was filled in every part. The eagerness of the people to be present is something wonderful, and there are abundant and increasing tokens of the presence of the ever-blessed Spirit of God.

"Mr. Moody seems jealous lest the attention of the people should be directed too much to *him*. He is ever pointing them to God himself as the Author of blessing and Source of power. Indeed, it is this losing sight of himself in God which seems to me to constitute one of the great secrets of his success.

"In all our meetings hitherto, little or no reference has been made, by name, either to Protestants or to Roman Catholics. This is, in the judgment of most of us, as it should be. Mr. Moody is exceedingly careful in this matter not to give needless offense, or provoke opposition that might be avoided. He addresses sinners as such—telling them the very same 'old, old story' of redeeming love, or, as a good man known to us has put it, he deals with the catholic or universal disease of sin, and the catholic remedy provided in the gospel. The disease has affected us all equally; the remedy is provided for and offered to us all equally. There is here no distinction of persons. His method in this matter constitutes one great secret of Mr. Moody's peculiar adaptation for evangelistic work among the mixed audiences that gather around him in a city like ours."

In *Times of Blessing*, November 12, 1874, the Rev. J. G. Phillips writes:

"To a stranger attending one of the services of these American evangelists, it would seem as if they were addressing a Dublin audience for the first time, the crowds are so great and the interest evinced is so intense. Day after day every meeting is crowded. Neither time, distance, nor weather, appears to have much effect in diminishing the number of those who attend. On Monday morning, the 2d inst., as the rain was coming down very heavily at the hour for the noon gathering, and had been doing so for some time previously, I thought there would be but a very small attendance at the prayer-meeting; but when I got there I was agreeably disappointed to find that the audience was not much smaller than usual. And last night, Friday, the attendance at the Exhibition Hall was larger than I have seen it on any week-night since these meetings began. And not only is the work growing broader, but I believe it is also growing deeper; it is becoming a more personal thing with many. It is not simply what Messrs. Moody and Sankey have to say; but it is, What have Christ and Christianity to do with *me?* To many hearts this question is now brought home, and many, very many, with deep earnestness are asking: 'What must I do to be saved?'

"The inquirers' meeting, which I have already mentioned, held in the Metropolitan Hall at half-past 8 o'clock, was a most interesting one. A large number was present, and many went away rejoicing in Christ.

"The meetings of Sabbath were an index to those of the whole week; for, from the prayer-meeting at noon on Monday, to the children's service in the Exhibition Palace at noon to-day, Saturday, all the meetings were most interesting, solemnizing, and edifying, and were all very largely attended. The interest attaching to these meetings is not confined to the people of Dublin and its immediate neighborhood. Persons are coming from some of the most southern and western counties of our island to be present at these services. I myself was speaking at one of them to a man who had brought his son, a boy about fourteen years of age, a distance of one hundred miles for this sole purpose. And when these persons go back, in many cases they go not unblessed, but carry gracious sheaves with them, and thus their own neighborhood comes in for a share of the blessing which is now falling so richly on Dublin."

The Rev. W. Fleming Stevenson, author of *Praying and Working*, and minister of a large Presbyterian church in Dublin, gives his general impressions after three weeks' observation and hearty co-operation:

"A third week has in no way diminished the attendance. Instead of lesser numbers, additional seats for nearly a thousand have been provided in the Exhibition Palace, and even the passages in the Metropolitan Hall are now thronged. Once or twice the quietness prevailing has been slightly broken; but it is marvelous that when so many must stand, and even then perhaps not hear, the stillness is so deep. There are some who do not miss a meeting; but the evening audience is a very shifting one, and the faces are always changing. The number who have heard the gospel at this time must therefore be enormous. Indeed, there are scarcely any that one meets who either have not been at the meetings, or who are not planning to go. In tram-cars, omnibuses, railway carriages, the services are a subject of universal conversation, and of universal interest. The visitors from the country are always on the increase. The other day some people in a small southern country town organized an excursion-party of thirty, and a second of sixty has been organized since in the same place. Christians come two hundred miles to rejoice and help in what is done. A gentleman came seventy miles, found the Saviour, went back for his family, and now they are all here.

"Some of the abandoned have stolen in, and many drunkards have been brought by their friends. The motley character of the evening crowd is striking: every section of the population is represented, even to the outcast; and surprises are constantly felt as one and another are recognized of the most unlikely to be there. Two Roman Catholic servants noticed, not far from them, faces with which they were curiously familiar. The men were disguised, but it did not need much penetration to discover the two priests who confessed them. The other night a Roman Catholic clergymen, hymn-book in hand, was among the most earnest of the worshipers. Another, who was asked by one of his people if it was wrong to go, is said to have replied that there could be no harm in hearing about Jesus. The reporter of a paper unfriendly to the movement is among those whom that movement has carried toward Christ. There is not an evening that Roman Catholics as well as Protestants have not found their way to the inquiry-room. Probably one reason is that there is no denunciation. Men are not addressed as by their particular Church, but as sinners. Roman Catholics are not even mentioned by name at the evangelistic service; and feeling no hurt, and not having opposition forced upon them, those who go once are pretty sure to return." Having regard to the character of the impressions produced on the multitudes addressed, Mr. Stevenson further says:

"The lack of depth that was noticeable at first, the absence of any great breaking down of men's hearts, seem to be now signs of the past. It is, at last, as if God's word had got a grip of those that came to hear. Those who remain are more deeply concerned, more willing to speak because more sensible of their burden; and their number is rising rapidly. The area of the large concert hall is now occupied with the anxious and those who deal with them, and additional meetings have been held for them in the Metropolitan Hall.

There is not a day but some evidently pass from death unto life, and the crushed and miserable depart to their own house in the joy and peace of believing. An officer of rank in the artillery was in Scotland during Mr. Moody's visit, but did not attend the meetings. He has come in Dublin; there was earnest prayer for him by his friends; and from a very worldly life he has now been brought to Jesus. An open skeptic was constrained to remain, had his doubts swept away as the Lord Jesus drew him to His feet, and on another evening came bringing three more persons with him. Thanks were returned one day for a young minister who had found Christ. A young man had been three months seeking rest. Hearing at a meeting that the gospel is the gift of Christ to sinners, it struck him with so much force that he said quite out, 'That's beautiful.' He apologized afterwards, saying he could not help it just at the moment when he found what he had almost despaired of finding. An ungodly man, whose friends and companions were like himself, came to one of the meetings. It was the only one, for a few days after he died, joyfully confessing to his ungodly acquaintances that Christ had found and saved him at that meeting."

Mr. Stevenson singles out some special features of the work as specially noteworthy:

"Here, as elsewhere, several of the hymns sung by Mr. Sankey alone have been wonderfully blest. An old man of seventy came into the inquiry-room in tears, saying he had found no rest since he heard 'Jesus of Nazareth Passeth by.' A cabman, the other evening, asked that prayer should be offered for himself and his comrades. He had heard the first sermon in the palace, and the same hymn had made him uneasy then, and he had been uneasy ever since.

In a country where party-feeling has always been strong, one notices with pleasure the following:

"The brotherly unity among the ministers is maintained unbroken, and a delightful illustration of the breadth of this unity among all classes was given at a public breakfast this week. Nearly two hundred accepted the invitation to meet Mr. Moody and Mr. Sankey, and among them were over fifty clergymen, some well-known noblemen and military men, and many of the principal citizens of Dublin of all professions. Two hours after breakfast passed only too quickly in brief addresses from representatives of almost every denomination, bearing a united testimony to the singular good that has been done, and expressing a united resolve to carry on the work after the American brethren have left in the same harmony in which it was now begun.

The inquiry was very naturally raised, What results have followed elsewhere? Here is the answer:

"Although the movement was to gather no greater force, it would still be the most remarkable that there has ever been in the city; but there are many who believe that we see only the beginning, that probably even next week will witness far greater things than these, and that spiritual blessings will be showered down on our land. The last tidings from Ulster speak of just such a fullness of blessing there. It is not confined to one or two cities, but the news comes from country towns and hamlets, and lonely prayer-meetings. The presbyteries over the north are stirring, and arranging for special evangelistic work, for the people are everywhere moved. The joy that is thus quickened prompts to but one request for our Irish churches and our Irish people, that prayer be made without ceasing unto God for us."

Mr. Magee gives some illustrations of the force of truth:

"Our Roman Catholic brethren, as a rule, have acted a noble part. They have been respectful, and to a certain extent, sympathizing. In this week's number of the *Nation*—an organ at once of National (as it is called) and Ultramontane principles—an article has appeared, entitled, 'Fair Play!' which is exceedingly creditable, and which indicates the advent of a new day in Ireland. The editor informs his constituents that 'the deadly danger of the age comes upon us from the direction of Huxley and Darwin and Tyndall, rather than from Moody and Sankey. Irish Catholics desire to see Protestants deeply imbued with religious feeling, rather than tinged with rationalism and infidelity; and as long as the religious services of our Protestant neighbors are honestly directed to quickening religious thought in their own body, without offering aggressive or intentional insult to us, it is our duty to pay the homage of our respect to their conscientious convictions; in a word, to *do as we would be done by.*'

"One very marked feature in the movement is the number of men that are influenced. Many people have remarked the large proportion of them that are inquiring.

"A few nights ago an old gentleman, more than seventy years of age, threw himself down on his knees and sobbed like a child. He said, 'I was utterly careless about my soul till last night, but I have been so unhappy since, I could not sleep. I seemed to hear ringing in my ears, "Jesus of Nazareth is Passing by," and if I don't get saved now I never shall be.'

"Already the influence of this work has begun to tell upon the most remote districts of the country. Parties of thirty, fifty, sixty, etc., are being organized from the most distant parts to Dublin. Many of these carry back with them much blessing. We hear of the young converts witnessing for Christ fearlessly in the trains on their way home from their meetings.

"Mr. Dowling, an Episcopal clergyman, one of the best expositors of Scripture we have among us, said he had heard and read much of the work carried on by our brethren, when they were in Edinburgh and elsewhere, and he had thought much of it; now that he had seen it for himself he thought much more of it than ever. He regarded it as the noblest testimony to the power of evangelical truth ever given in this country. He was delighted, he said, with the thoroughly Biblical character of the movement. It put honor upon the Personal Word, and honor upon the Written Word, and honor upon the Holy Spirit, the great mediating Energy between the Personal and the Written Word. Speaking of Mr. Moody's preaching, he said that the Bible seemed a quiver in his hands, and every text a sharp, polished, glittering arrow that God gave him for us to shoot straight into the heart and conscience of his hearers."

A novel feature in Dublin was the public breakfast in the Shelbourne Hotel, with Sir E. Synge Hutchinson in the chair, addresses in admirable spirit from Lord Carrick, Lord James Butler, Dr. Craig, Rev. Charles Dowling, of the Irish Church, and many other clergymen. Two of the largest rooms in the Shelbourne Hotel were completely filled by the company, which numbered about two hundred. The object the gathering evidently had in view was the encouragement of Christian unity, which every speaker in the course of the proceedings warmly advocated, in the belief that it is especially needful at the present time, and essential to the further spread of the gospel in this country. The company was thoroughly representative in its character, both clerical and lay.

Mr. Moody said that was the first meeting of the kind he had ever attended. The question had been asked, "What was to be done to keep up Christian unity?" He would tell them. Keep preaching Christ, and don't talk about their church, creed, or doctrine, and then people would be attracted to them as surely as iron filings to a magnet. By this should all men know that they were Christ's disciples, that they loved one another. He hoped they would preach Christ simply, treating men not as of this denomination or that, but as sinners. He would leave them one word, 'Advance.' When General Grant, after a career of victory in the West, was put in command of the Potomac Army, which had been before invariably defeated, he was asked to retreat. Retreat had been the constant word, and at his council of war all his commanders were in favor of falling back; but he remained silent, and an hour after, the army were astonished to receive from him the command, 'Advance in solid column at daybreak.' This was his counsel to them."

One of the aspects of Mr. Moody's work, which gave special satisfaction to the most judicious Christians in Dublin—and among its fifty or sixty thousand Protestants, are many most earnest and devout believers—was the concert maintained with the ministers. The effects were of the happiest kind.

Rev. Dr. Marrable mentioned that "on their Communion Day the number of those who remained to partake of the Lord's Supper was nearly double what it used to be. This was a good sign and a source of much happiness to him. He felt deeply interested in these meetings, and especially the conversational meetings for anxious inquirers. So eager was he to get into the room that no sooner was the preaching service at the Exhibition Palace concluded with the benediction, than he hastened to the inquiry-room with the avidity of an army surgeon who ran to bind up the wounds of soldiers after a battle. The work of grace that was manifested at these meetings was truly wonderful. Some of those who became converted belonged to Dublin, some came from distant parts of the country—people of all classes—young and old, high and low—are finding the Lord, and rejoicing in Him as their precious Saviour. On the previous night (Sunday) they had a conversational meeting for men—none but men—and there were upwards of fifteen hundred present. The attendance was astonishing. He was diffident about alluding to particular cases; but he could not help referring to the case of a divinity student—he was sure that was not too personal—who came to him and said he was about to enter the ministry, but he did not feel happy about his own soul; but before he left he was brought to rest in peace in Jesus."

Fourteen years ago the Rev. Denham Smith, then a Congregational minister, did a good Evangelistic work in Dublin. He was, like Mr. Brownlow North in Scotland, and Mr. Grattan Guinness in England—able to give some aid in the meetings—pleasing evidence that the fire kindled so long ago had not ceased to burn.

After witnessing five weeks' labor in Dublin the Rev. W. Fleming Stevenson gives the following account of the results:

"No one would question now the magnitude and importance of the spiritual work which has gathered round our American brethren in Dublin. No similar movement has ever produced a like impression. At any previous time of revival, the interest was confined within a narrow circle, but at present it penetrates the entire city; and the country—and not the serious people in the country only—is as much moved as the city. Those who spoke lightly at first —those who thought they could ignore it—those who were persuaded it was only a new sensation, have slowly altered their mind. It is seldom that in a company it is not mentioned with respect. Men who had laughed and sneered at first are now the first to rebuke others if they sneer. The newspapers continue to chronicle the meetings with a fullness never displayed before; special articles are occasionally written, and now and then a thoughtful and favorable editorial draws everbody's attention. Three of the bishops have been at the meetings, and one of them, the Bishop of Kilmore, has warmly commended 'the wonderful work in Dublin' when presiding over his Synod. The eloquent Bishop of Derry, when lately preaching at the re-opening of York Minster, and illustrating the place and power of praise, said that 'in Scotland and Ireland a strong fervor had been awakened, and hundreds and thousands had been made earnest by a single voice as expressed by himself, "singing the gospel of Jesus Christ."' The Rev. Lord Plunket, 'while not personally relishing all the accompaniments of their teaching,' 'blesses God for the good which is being done by our American visitors,' and 'rejoices that Christ is being preached and souls are being saved.' Men of all the church parties attend the halls, and having come once are apt to come again; and one of the most constant workers is Dr. Sydney Smith, the Professor of Biblical Greek in Trinity College, whose daughter wrote the simple and wide-spread hymn, 'Oh for the Robes of Whiteness.' A weekly Roman Catholic journal rebuked the silence of its contemporaries by some abusive articles; and the next week the *Nation*, an able paper in the interests of the same faith, rebuked the rudeness, and bade the movement God-speed.

GROWING IN STRENGTH.

"As for the meetings, there is not only no lessening of interest in them, but a positive increase. It was supposed by many whose sympathies went entirely with them that there would be a falling away, and the supposition was not unnatural. The Protestant population is small—only a fourth of the whole; and nine-tenths of it adhere to the Episcopal Church, in which, more than elsewhere, the ministers shrink from openly identifying themselves with either lay preaching or the inquiry-room. So that while all the ministers of the other denominations came forward round Mr. Moody, probably not more than a third or fourth of those belonging to the dominant communion took the same stand; and some, who are earnest men of God, even took up a hostile position. Yet there has been no slackening of the marvelous attendance, either by day or by night. Every increase of accommodation is met by a fresh inpour of eager men and women. During the last Bible-readings, not only were the passages choked, but a dense throng swarmed round each door, far beyond hearing point, and as many left as would have filled another building. For two Sabbaths it has been necessary to lift the temporary curtain, and allow the people to overflow the entire area of the Palace; and every evening a crowd of two or three hundred, mostly well-dressed persons, patiently waits in the November cold round the outer doors, in the hope that there may be still some place for them when these doors are opened for a few minutes, just before the sermon.

"There are some in this crowd who do not come with the best motives. 'Won't you run in and be converted?' one young man said to another, a few evenings ago, with a laugh. 'Well, I don't mind having a try at it for five minutes,' his companion replied, elbowing his way in. Yet in five minutes after they were seated their faces were riveted on Mr. Moody, a part of that most impressive upturned mass of faces that is fixed on him as long as he speaks; and there is not an evening that men do not acknowledge in the inquiry-room having entered as carelessly as these, and having been arrested and forced to ask, '*What must I do to be saved?*'

"It has to be said, also, that many ministers who do not come prominently forward are ardent friends of the work, and that large as the platform is, the ministers upon it are only a small part of those at the meetings. They come from the most remote districts of the country. And there are very many who at first were doubtful, and who regarded the movement with misgivings, who are now blessing God for what is done in Dublin; and whose prayer is that He may work the same works over the whole island. Even those whose position removes them farthest from sympathy speak now with frank respect both of the service and of the American brethren. Nor can anything be more cordial and delightful than the practical and truly brotherly unity with which the various clergymen work together, rejoicing in the truth, and not seeking their own, but in honor preferring one another; and it is impossible but that this spirit will pass out from them to the other ministers of their respective Churches, or that those who have learned a mutual esteem and acquired a mutual regard in this toil for the Master will shrink back again into their former relation.

The Children.

" Besides the noon prayer-meeting (at which there are now as many brief spontaneous addresses as prayers), the evening evangelistic service, and the Bible Readings, a children's meeting at four, and a men's meeting at nine, have been maintained. The children's day still makes Saturday a festival. When Mr. Moody presided, he turned it for a time, and with the happiest effect, into a huge Sunday-school class, the answers to his questions coming back in overpowering volleys from the thousands of voices, and with so much precision that he once or twice good-naturedly told the children they should be in his place. At all these Saturday meetings there have been little ones led to Jesus; and very happy stories they have to tell, when they come asking for 'a convert's ticket.' 'It was when Mr. Sankey told us about the cleft in the rock, and how, when a little child was put in, it was quite safe; and I just let Jesus put me in,' one will say; and then another; 'It was Mr. Moody that said looking at the brazen serpent meant that we should look at Jesus, and I was very sorry, because I knew I had been naughty; but I did look to Jesus, and I know Jesus loves me, and I'm not afraid to die.'"

Various classes were approached. Thus Sir Arthur Cotton's daughter, Miss Cotton, was induced by Mr. Moody to leave her work at Dorking for a little: and she addressed four very large assemblies of women in Dublin, and three in Belfast. And a concert, for which the Exhibition had been engaged before it was taken for the preaching of the gospel, led to the most characteristic service that has been held, as there could be no public evening service. More than seven hundred soldiers, of every arm of the service, accepted an invitation to tea, presided over by officers' wives and daughters. Mr. Sankey sang for them and with them, and the shout of the chorus to "Hold the Fort" quite overcame many who were present; while Mr. Moody, saying that the sight of the red coats had driven his sermon out of his head, simply told story upon story out of his own experience in the American war till he was overcome with emotion, preaching the gospel with a tenderness and force that were marvelously impressive, and that allowed no surprise when so many of the men remained for the inquiry-meeting, and of those that remained so many declared they had found Jesus. The morning meeting for workers was resumed on the final Sabbath of his stay, and was a re-delivery to men only, of the lecture on Daniel, which he had given at the Bible-reading three days before, with a power which those who heard it previously in Scotland declared he had never approached.

The great building had been engaged for a month, but another week's occupation of it was secured, and a convention for three days was arranged for at the conclusion of the services. We give in substance the account of it, furnished, with many other details, by the Rev. W. Fleming Stevenson, only abbreviating in parts, his graphic report:

"Among the points of interest in Dublin, there is none more singular, and at the same time more solemn than the inquiry-room. Sometimes the large concert-hall has been occupied, sometimes the small, sometimes both. Once or twice the main building has been given over exclusively to women, while the men have been withdrawn to one of the side halls. The numbers who remained for conversation were often very large—many hundreds, now and then approaching a thousand. The band of workers who spoke with them has also been large, and includes, perhaps, fifty ministers. Persons have come of every shade of opinion. A skeptic has written down his feelings in a note-book—an honest doubter, who submits them *seriatim* for answer, and expresses thankfulness as they are met, and his mind is left more open to receive Christ. One has come to scoff, and avows that he only wants to see into the thing ; but a pointed, firm word, spoken in love, has sunk below his shallow scorn, and he finds himself grappling with sin. A gentleman has come from a town many miles away ; he has fallen into sin, and wandered far from Christ. His wife had often borne the burden on her heart to God, and, on returning home from a short absence, finds he has gone hurriedly to the meetings ; now, in the inquiry-room she finds the wanderer restored, full of sorrow, but more full of thanksgiving, and the husband and wife leave the building together, with a joy that is unspeakable. Here are two, a gentleman and his wife that have traveled one hundred and fifty miles from their home. They are greatly moved; the woman sobs, the man cannot check a silent tear that trickles down his cheek; their quest for peace seems only to have brought them into woe; but before the meeting breaks up, the light has broken in, and they rejoice in the Lord. There is a young Swede, who has only recently come from the North, and tells his trouble through very broken English; the next evening he is looking to Jesus. Some are Roman Catholics, probably very ignorant of Bible teaching, but receiving the truth with avidity; coming, perhaps, again and again. Some, with a beaming face and a great but gentle earnestness, are leading in others—sisters with sisters, young men bringing friends. There is a lady who has come up from the country, and has brought in four grown-up daughters. A minister is passing, and stops. He has already long since led that lady to Christ, and he has baptized these four girls; but it is fourteen years since he left their neighborhood for another, very distant. He sits down beside them, and does not leave till the mother rejoices with him over them all.

"In such work as this, the hour passes quickly away. All are busy, too busy to note what happens around them; the sound of prayer and earnest speech rises everywhere; then, as one leaves after another, Mr. Moody stands near the door, and speaks a parting word to each, the lights are put out, and the work of the day is over. For some time past another large meeting has been conducted in another part of the city (in the Metropolitan Hall) at the same hour as the evening inquiry-meeting (for during the day also there are opportunities for inquirers), and yet the attendance at both has daily increased. It is exclusively for young men, and is conducted by Mr. Henry Drummond, who was urgently entreated to leave work of the same kind in Derry, that he might come up to this. At first it seemed harder to deal with them, and less impression was made than elsewhere; but that is all past, and probably there are nowhere more striking instances of the grace of God. Latterly, several of the students have been here, and some have believed; and it is a distinct rallying-point for young men.

"From all this, it is natural to expect that fruit is being gathered every day.

"The son of Christian parents is in a house of business, where one of the young men especially was an undesirable companion, and many prayers had ascended that the lad might be kept from harm. Not only has he been led to Jesus, but four others with him, and among them that very one whose influence was so dreaded. In another house several had scoffed, and were profane and skeptical; but one of the first who decided for Christ there went very simply round the rest, and told them where he stood, that, as he said, there might be no mistake. 'There are four brothers, besides myself,' said a fine, intelligent lad in a printing office, 'and the Lord has found us every one.' Four sisters came together for tickets to the converts' meeting. They had only been a week or two in Dublin, coming to it from a country town, and already they had the joy of believing. A mechanic came in to-day. 'I hurried down from the shop,' he said—it was the fitting shop of one of the great railway stations—'as soon as we knocked off work. There are more than twenty that have been greatly concerned, and there'll be many of them will want a ticket. We have hard times of it among the rest; but I was just like them, and I can't complain. And, Sir, I am just as happy as a king.'

"A gentleman residing in Belfast came up with his family to Dublin; and now, in Dublin, the children have all been brought to the Lord. Two brothers lived in Glasgow while Mr. Moody was holding meetings there. One of them was converted, but he could not induce the other to go to the meetings. Some time after they were separated. The former was obliged to change his residence for London, the latter for Dublin. The heart of the one yearned greatly over the other, and when he learned that Mr. Moody was in Dublin, he pleaded with his brother more than ever. At last he got leave, and hurried across himself to induce him to attend the meetings; in his earnest compulsion, brought him, introduced him to Mr. Moody; and within a week the brothers were rejoicing together.

"An elderly lady introduced herself to a minister, her eyes full of tears. 'Sir, on Monday evening I saw my sins like burning flames. Oh! I did not know before that I was a sinner. I did not know how to escape. It was like fire on every side of me. And they spoke to me of Jesus. I broke out crying quite loud. I couldn't help it. And when I went home, and my son met me, I said: "What will they think of me, acting in that way?" "Mother," said he, "don't be ashamed of the tears of repentance." 'I can't keep from crying now, but they are tears of joy. And Sir, it was my son would give me no rest till I went to the meetings; for he had gone himself, and came back believing in Jesus." Happy mother, happy son!

"A gentleman had not heard a sermon for two years, as he had grown deaf, and his minister's voice was low. He went to Mr. Moody, sat near the front, and heard. His joy was very touching when God had opened not only the ear but the heart, and he came for a ticket to the meeting for converts. An infidel, who was led to come, and was led to faith in the Saviour, afterwards came bringing three like himself.

"I have strung these incidents loosely together; they are examples of what is occurring every day, and what it is hoped will be occurring for many a day to come. There is scarcely a parish or congregation in the city where there has not been blessing, and in some, the blessing has been very full; while numbers who came up from the country have gone back again praising God.

"The town is more full than ever of what is happening. There is comparatively little ridicule, and there is much inquiry. At a well-known meeting of scientific men the other day, the discussion turned largely on Mr. Moody and the meetings, and it appeared that several of those present had been there. One, who does not trouble himself about the Christian faith, said that, he could not find any sufficient natural causes that would quite account for them—causes that would satisfy scientific inquiry—and that he was driven to the persuasion that there must be a supernatural cause.

"At a meeting of one of the principal medical societies, the chairman, in his address, touched earnestly on the opportunity the physician had as a Christian, and the dignity it lent his office ; and though the members are of very opposite religious persuasions, and his course was so novel as to startle many, the remarks met with hearty approval.

"It has been desired to continue at least some of the meetings after the brethren leave, and in the same spirit of unity. There will be the daily noon prayer-meeting in the Metropolitan Hall, except on Saturday, when there will be a meeting for children at two o'clock; and on Sabbath, when there will be an afternoon service at four, in the large concert-hall of the

Exhibition Palace. It is also intended to have a united evangelistic service every Tuesday evening at eight, in the Metropolitan Hall, and to keep up the evening meeting for men."

The Convention of Ministers was a happy inspiration, due to the indefatigable secretary of the General Committee. There were only a few days to prepare, but the details were carried out with an energy that was marvelous. It was like nothing so much as the hearty haste with which the posts went out to 'all the provinces of King Ahasuerus.' Arrangements were made by which return-tickets could be had from any part of Ireland for a single fare, and yet be available for a week; and hospitality was so abundantly offered that every visitor found a kindly welcome. The number of ministers was probably not short of eight hundred, of whom more than half belonged to the Episcopal Church, the Presbyterian and Wesleyan making the bulk of the remainder; but the Independent and Baptist Churches, and the Society of Friends were also well represented. The geographical representation was as complete as the ecclesiastical. From County Kerry to County Donegal, from Connemara on the west, from Cork, and Wexford, and

Waterford on the south, from cities like Belfast and Derry, where the blessing has been rising like a full tide, and from ancient and secluded hamlets, where the news of God's work has been slow to penetrate, from rectories and manses, the streams poured into the capital. The days of the Convention were days of joyful surprise, as friends unexpectedly met from one distant place after another.

Many had already come on Monday evening, and were soon in service, addressing an extemporized meeting that had to be formed of those who could not get access into the building, or speaking with inquirers, and thus came at once in contact with what had been reported to them; for the sermon on that evening, "What shall I do then with Jesus which is called Christ?" (Matt. xxvii. 22), had been with unusual power, and the large halls for inquiry were crowded. It was, however, at the all-day meeting on Tuesday that the Convention assumed its real proportions, and the interest and blessing that had gathered round the previous weeks were carried to their highest point. The ministers formed a compact body, in seats numbered and reserved for them; the crowd stretched beyond, and from one o'clock it was so large that it filled the building from end to end.

"Mr. Moody presided throughout, and members of every evangelical communion joined in the addresses and prayers. The noon hour was devoted, as usual, to the subject for the day; and though the requests for prayer number now sometimes many hundreds, and are simply massed in groups, they were made impressive by the brief supplication of a single sentence with which each group was fittingly followed by the reader, the meeting all the while continuing bowed in silent prayer. The three topics chosen for conference were: Praise and Thanksgiving, How to reach the Masses, and How to fill Ireland with the Gospel. The two former were introduced by Episcopalian clergymen, the latter by a Presbyterian; and besides these longer addresses, there were others of five minutes, which fell to ministers of other communions. Conference, in the strict sense of the word, was precluded by the size of the hall and the audience; but the same subjects were treated on Thursday in a four hours' meeting, when none but the ministers were present, and when, from the smaller numbers, interchange of opinion was easy.

The remaining two hours of the day on Tuesday were occupied by Mr. Moody; the first by the "Question Drawer," and the second by his lecture on "Works." In the former, the answers to which he gave most time were on drunkenness and sectarianism. "God had vouchsafed a blessed unity; woe to the unhappy person who should first break it." Yet it would be broken if there was proselytism. This would be the triumph of sect over Christ. The cry is, "Come out! come out from a sect!" But where? into another sect? Every body of believers is a sect. This spirit that always cries, "Come out!" that proselyting from the Churches, is from Satan. I say, *Stay in.* If you have a minister that preaches Christ—and your town has many—stand by him. You will gain nothing but trouble and pride by leaving him. There are people who consider that denouncing Churches and finding fault with ministers is "bearing testimony." These people will bear testimony for years, and that is all Christ gets from them. I warn you, as a Christian brother, beware of trying to get some of these young people away from the folds where they have been fed. You will heap guilt on your head. The moment we begin to lift up our little party or our Church, then the Spirit of God seems to leave, and there is no more conversion."

The effect produced by these timely words was profound. Those who had come dreading that, after all, this movement would be like some previous, and end in secession and the weakening instead of the strengthening of Christians, were reassured; and throughout this hour and the next, the majority of the ministers who had not heard Mr. Moody speak before learnt something of the power he wields, and were forced into the same unity as those who had been fellow-laborers from the beginning. Indeed, the condition of the meeting was one of the most eager and responsive sympathy. Every chord was true, and vibrated at the lightest touch. Aged ministers bowed their gray hairs, and wept at times with joy. A minister would grasp the hand of another he had never seen before, merely because he sat beside him. One might sit, at first, with a look of wonder and almost contempt, but further on in the day the face would quiver with emotion. Many an eye glistened with quiet tears. Now, for the first time in the meetings, the excitement would not be controlled, but broke out in applause that even the self-recollection of some, and the cry of "Hush!" did not always repress. In truth, the atmosphere was electric, though there was little cloud in the sky; and without any sufficient cause flashes would break out, soft and swift and pervading as summer lightning. At one point during the discussion of Ireland, the central subject of the day, and when Mr. Sankey, seizing the opportunity with his usual tact, sang "Hold the Fort," alone, and the vast multitude, the ministers leading, lifted up the chorus in a mighty shout, the enthusiasm was overpowering and altogether indescribable. Such a scene was never witnessed in Ireland before, for there never had been such a meeting. It was the first time that all these ministers had met on a platform broader than their Churches, gathering close together round their common Saviour; and it is easy to see already that the impression on the country is very deep. Four of the daily papers devoted long reports to the meetings, one of them as much as six columns; and not only is the news thus spread, but even the happy device, by which the committee gave the clergymen of one communion as guests to the members of another, helps the fusing and widens the catholicity. It was a time that will be always memorable in the history of Ireland,—that many hope will be the starting-point of an Ireland where all things will be new.

This concluded practically the labor of the brethren in Ireland. They now turned their faces towards the great cities of England, to which a brief chapter must be given.

CHAPTER VI.

ENGLAND AGAIN.

EARLY in December the American evangelists passed over to Manchester, where much prayer had been offered for a blessing on their visit. The Rev. W. H. Drewett gives a concise view of their opening efforts in that great city. We omit details, the counterpart of which has been fully reported in connection with other places.

"Many thousands of Christian people have been praying for Manchester. The preparatory work, indeed, has been going on all the year, especially since the month of April, when united evangelistic services were held in almost all the Nonconformist places of worship throughout the district. These preparatory meetings were brought to a close last Saturday, with a Communion Service, in which upwards of two thousand Christians of various denominations joined.

" At the meeting for workers on Sunday morning, the attendance was astonishing, numbering nearly, if not quite, two thousand five hundred persons. Most of these had walked distances varying from one to three miles, some far more, though the rain fell in torrents through a thick, cold fog.

"Perhaps the first feeling with many, after curiosity was satisfied, was something like disappointment. But soon the meeting was filled with an influence quite distinct from any of the usual effects of oratory. It seemed as if, as in the olden time, 'the Holy Ghost fell on them that heard the word.' Mr. Moody's theme was 'Christian Courage,' and in dwelling upon it he evidently sought to strike the key-note for all the services to follow. When, at the close of the address, the hymn was sung, 'Hold the Fort,' few eyes were dry.

"The work has been going on since, much as it did during the first week or fortnight in Dublin, and in other places. There is no doubt that Messrs. Moody and Sankey have already made a most favorable impression upon a large portion of the Christian public of our city. The charm of Mr. Sankey's affectionate nature has been felt by many, as well as the power of his gift of song. The gifts which fit Mr. Moody to be the leader of a religious movement like the present are recognized by every one. Men accustomed to authority willingly put themselves under his orders. He inspires confidence. All feel at once his practical good sense and singleness of purpose. Among his natural endowments is a power of pathos which must tell everywhere, but will tell especially upon a Lancashire audience. It seems to lay hold of the men even more than of the women. In his energetic, vigorous nature there is a great depth of tenderness, which now and then breaks forth in his addresses with extraordinary power. Above all, he feels and speaks as though he felt that the excellency of the power is of God, and not of us.

"The crowds which flock to hear our friends, if they do not increase, continue undiminished. Already not a few have found peace in Jesus through their word. Mr. Moody has more than once said in public that nowhere, during the first week of his labors, have such meetings been held as in Manchester. Still, it would be folly to suppose that the work as yet is more than just beginning."

How it proceeded the Rev. C. A. Davis tells us:

"None could withstand the conviction that the Spirit of God was operating in the solemnized assembly as they beheld, under the influence that swayed the meeting during Mr. Moody's appeals, business men, one after another, rising to be prayed for. The address had been growing in earnestness; the speaker seemed to come into contact with the souls of the people before him. He requested any who wished to be prayed for to rise. He quietly repeated the invitation. One was seen to stand in the left-hand gallery and cover his face with his hands; another in the area. Mr. Moody said solemnly, "There is one risen; thank God for that. Another; and another. Christians, keep on praying. Another. Jesus is passing by. You may never have such an opportunity again. You may never again have so many Christians praying for you." Before many minutes people were standin all parts of the hall, amid deep silence, broken only by a hushed response at each new appeal for continued prayer. At the close of the meeting the anxious ones were invited into the inquiry rooms, where Mr. Moody conversed with them individually.

A man with whom the writer conversed, rose from his knees, where he had committed "his whole self" to Christ, and said, "I came from Bolton to-day. I did not think I should find Christ." A brother minister brought up another young convert. It was this man's nephew who had just found peace. The two greeted each other with joyful surprise.

Afternoon meetings for women have been held in the Rev. A. McLaren's chapel, Oxford Road. It is strange to observe them thronging the road on their way to the chapel, and still more strange to see them occupying all the available standing-room in the spacious building. Not less than two thousand women were present on Tuesday afternoon. These meetings, like all the rest, increase in power as they proceed, and on Thursday when Mr. Moody entered the lecture-hall, he found it filled with weeping, kneeling inquirers. Many left with the joy of pardon on their spirits.

The noon prayer-meeting has, with one exception, been held in the Free Trade Hall, with an attendance of from two to three thousand. In these meetings may be found the soul of the movement. It is the daily united cry to God which brings upon the city the power of the Holy Spirit for conviction and conversion. On Thursday, dealing with the objection that this work is not of God, Mr. Moody said, "What do these noon prayer-meetings mean? what do men come here by hundreds, I might say by thousands, to pray for? A genuine work of God. And will He give us a counterfeit? If we ask bread will He give us a stone? The Shunammite fell at the feet of Elisha and said, ' As the Lord thy God liveth I will not leave thee.' She wasn't going to trust in that old staff, nor in the servant. She would trust only in the master; and well it was for her, or she would never have got back her child. And the prayer-meeting clings to the feet of God. We will not have the staff; we will not trust in the servants, but only in the Master Himself; He can and will raise the dead."

Finding one influential class of ministers—whose co-operation was always sought—poorly represented at the meetings, Mr. Moody issued the following circular:

"TO THE CLERGY OF MANCHESTER AND SALFORD.

" Having come to Manchester with my friend, Mr. Sankey, for the month of December, with the one object of preaching Christ, it has been a matter of disappointment that not more clergymen of the Church of England have attended our meetings.

" As God has granted large blessings where unity

has prevailed, we earnestly trust that you will join in seeking a blessing for Manchester.

"*Manchester*, Dec. 4, 1874.   D. L. MOODY."

Not at first, but with increasing knowledge of the work, the Episcopal clergy entered into it in considerable numbers.

The feeling among the men was developed in a wonderful degree at the beginning. In an early meeting, Mr. Moody stated that on Friday a man had found peace, and instantly cried out, "I am coming, mother," when a man rose and cried out in the center of the hall, "That's me," and burst into tears. The incident sent a thrill through the audience. Had there been time for an inquirers' meeting many would have remained, but they were wisely sent home to pray.

The Rev. W. Rigby Murray, who labored with great earnestness in Manchester, thus reports, in the second week of effort here:

"On Saturday evening, the Oxford Hall presented a spectacle which those who witnessed it will not soon forget. In response to Mr. Moody's invitation, some three thousand persons, professedly Christians, and chiefly young men, assembled to hear him counsel them regarding Christian work. The heartiness with which they ever and anon broke forth into song before he made his appearance, and the manliness with which they sang, especially 'Dare to be a Daniel,' indicated that they were ready to receive with gladness the word of command from the lips of the great organizer. He spoke briefly but effectively. He told of the work done by the young converts elsewhere, especially in Glasgow, in connection with the evangelization of the masses. He made particular reference to the noble army of volunteers that rose to their feet in that city when the appeal was made to them, 'Who will work for Jesus?' And then, when he made the same appeal to themselves, calling upon all who were ready to work for the Master to stand up, almost the entire body of young men—a grand and inspiring sight—sprang to their feet. One could not help exclaiming, 'God be thanked! there's hope for our city! Manchester, with such a host, may yet be won for Christ!' By a special arrangement, as it seemed, of Providence, Mr. Reginald Radcliffe was present, and immediately put before them a definite plan for making a great gospel attack, so to speak, upon the city. He suggested that an ordnance map of Manchester should be cut into small squares, each representing a district, and that two or three young persons should undertake to carry the gospel, in the shape of a tract or otherwise, to every house, great and small, within that district, so that no single dwelling should be omitted. The plan appeared to approve itself to the judgment of the meeting, all the more so that he told us how successfully he had carried out a similar one in Edinburgh and Liverpool in years gone by. The Lord grant it abundant success!

"The workers' meeting, yesterday (13th), was the largest since Messrs. Moody and Sankey came to Manchester. The address was most powerful. A forcible appeal was made to Sabbath-school teachers in this city; but one conviction seemed to exist in the minds of the vast audience of five thousand, 'Let us arise and work.'

"Had Mr. Moody come to deliver only this address, his mission had not been in vain. In the afternoon, from fifteen thousand to seventeen thousand struggled for admission. Various meetings had to be held in the Free Trade Hall, Oxford Hall, and Cavendish Chapel; all crowded as they never have been before.

As many more halls of the same size could have been filled. Some twenty to thirty meetings were held in the streets of the neighborhood, where addresses were delivered by ministers and laymen. At every meeting the Lord was present to heal. Anxious inquirers were very numerous. Great numbers professed to find the Saviour. To God alone be praise!

"The meeting for young men, in Oxford Hall, at eight, was also crowded to excess, hundreds being unable to obtain admission. Mr. Moody spoke as if tongues of fire hovered over his head."

The Rev. R. Mitchell said at the second Monday meeting where reports of progress were usually made: "There is no lack of facts to encourage us and strengthen our hands. Last night after the meeting, a gentleman came up to me and said: 'I want to have a talk with you.' So we walked down the street together. He told me he had been a skeptic for years, had heard Messrs. Moody and Sankey in Scotland, but could not understand what it was all about. He was a commercial traveler, having occasion to be from home frequently. When he went home last time, after having been away a month or two, there seemed to be a complete change in the whole house. His wife had been going to the meetings held in Edinburgh, and had been awakened and had found peace in believing, and had been instrumental in leading the whole family to the Lord. This change in his dear ones led him to inquire into the work, and the result was, that the unbelieving skeptic is now a humble believer in the Lord Jesus Christ. On Saturday he came fifty or sixty miles, that he might spend one day in these meetings. He was in this hall yesterday.

"I may mention another case. As I rode home in the omnibus last Friday evening, a medical gentleman, who had been sitting on the opposite seat, came over to my side. 'Mr. Mitchell,' he said, 'a few days ago I was speaking lightly of this revival work. But one of my friends who was living utterly regardless of religion has just been telling me that he has found salvation at the meetings. His very words were, speaking of Christ, "I could die for Him." If that be a specimen of the revival work,' said the medical man, 'it is the work of God.'"

We cannot withhold from our readers a vivid description of two of Mr. Moody's addresses in Manchester, from the correspondent of the (London)

Daily News. They will show the style of address by which Englishmen were instructed and interested:

"He began his discourse this morning without other preface than a half apology for selecting a subject which, it might be supposed, everybody knew everything about. But, for his part, he liked to take out and look upon the photographs of old friends when they were far away, and he hoped that his hearers would not think it waste of time to take another look at the picture of Daniel. There was one peculiarity about Daniel, and that was that there was nothing against his character to be found all through the Bible. Now-a-days, when men write biographies they throw what they call the veil of charity over the dark spots in a career. But when God writes a man's life He puts it all in. So it happened that we find very few, even of the best men in the Bible, without their times of sin. But Daniel came out spotless, and the preacher attributed his exceptionally bright life to the power of saying 'No.'

"After this exordium Mr. Moody proceeded to tell, in his own words, the story of the life of Daniel. Listening to him it was not difficult to comprehend the secret of his great power over the masses. Like Bunyan, he has the great gift of being able to realize things unseen, and to describe his vision in familiar language to those whom he addresses. I am afraid his notion of 'Babylon, that great city,' would barely stand the test of historical research. But that there really was in far-off days a great city called Babylon, in which men bustled about, ate and drank, schemed and plotted, and were finally overruled by the visible hand of God, he made as clear to the listening congregation as if he were talking about Chicago. He filled the lay figures with life, clothed them with garments, and then made them talk to each other in the English language as it is to-day accented in some of the American States.

"The story of Daniel is one peculiarly susceptible of Mr. Moody's usual method of treatment, and for three quarters of an hour he kept the congregation enthralled whilst he told how Daniel's simple faith triumphed over the machinations of the unbeliever. Mr. Moody's style is unlike that of most religious revivalists. He neither shouts nor gesticulates, and mentioned 'hell' only once, and that was in connection with the life the drunkard makes for himself. His manner is reflected by the congregation, in respect of abstention from working themselves up into 'a state.' But this makes all the more impressive the signs of genuine emotion which follow and accompany the preacher's utterance. When he was picturing the scene of Daniel translating the King's dream, rapidly repeating Daniel's account of the dream, and Nebuchadnezzar's quick and delighted ejaculation, 'That's so!' 'That's it!' as he recognized the incidents, I fancy it was not without difficulty some of the people, bending forward and listening with glistening eye and heightened color, refrained from clapping their hands for glee that the faithful Daniel, the unyielding servant of God, had triumphed over tribulation, and had walked out of prison to take his place on the right hand of the king. There was not much exhortation throughout the discourse, and not the slightest reference to any disputed point of doctrine. The discourse was nothing more than a re-telling of the story of Daniel. But whilst Nebuchadnezzar, Daniel, Shadrach, Meshach, Abed-nego, Darius, and even the one hundred and twenty princes, became for the congregation living and moving beings, all the ends of the narrative were, with probably unconscious, certainly unbetrayed, art, gathered together to lead up to the one lesson, that compromise, where truth and religion are concerned, is never worthy of those who profess to believe God's word.

"'I am sick of the shams of the present day,' said Mr. Moody, bringing his discourse to a sudden close. 'I am tired of the way men parley with the world whilst they are holding out their hands to be lifted into heaven. If we are going to be good Christians and God's people, let us be so out-and-out.'

"Last night I heard him deliver an address in one of the densely-populated districts of Salford. Admission to the chapel in which the service was held was exclusively confined to women, and, notwithstanding that it was Saturday night, there were at least a thousand sober-looking and respectably-dressed women present. The subject of the discussion was Christ's conversation with Nicodemus—whose social position Mr. Moody incidentally made recognizable to the congregation by observing that ' if he had lived in these days he would have been a doctor of divinity, Nicodemus, D.D., or perhaps LL.D.' His purpose was to make it clear that men were saved, not by any action of their own, but simply by faith. This he illustrated, among other ways, by introducing a domestic scene from the life of the children of Israel in the wilderness at the time the brazen serpent was lifted up. The *dramatis personæ* were a young convert, a skeptic, and the skeptic's mother. The convert who has been bitten by the serpent, and, having followed Moses' injunction, is cured, 'comes along,' and finds the skeptic lying down 'badly bitten.' He entreats him to look upon the brazen serpent which Moses has lifted up, but the skeptic has no faith in the alleged cure, and refuses. 'Do you think,' he says, 'I'm going to be saved by looking at a brass serpent away off on a pole? No, no.' 'Well, I don't know,' says the young convert, 'but I was saved that way myself. Don't you think you'd better try it?' The skeptic refuses, and his mother 'comes along,' and observes, 'Hadn't you better look at it, my boy?' 'Well, mother, the fact is, that if I could understand the philosophy of it I would look up right off; but I don't see how a brass serpent away off on a pole can cure me.' And so he dies in his unbelief."

The Rev. D. Macgregor reports of the third Monday meeting:

"At noon there was a large gathering. We observed honored brethren from distant towns, who had come to see for themselves, and carry back tidings of the movement. Brethren of the Episcopal Church are becoming numerous. After prayer for the numerous cases brought before us, Mr. Moody made some observations on the subject of 'Praise,' insisting on it as a Christian privilege.

"When the meeting was thrown open, testimony was borne by various ministers and laymen to the progress and permanency of the work in other places. We were especially pleased to have the evidence of a minister from York, who stated that Mr. Moody had begun services in his place of worship some sixteen months before, when the movement was yet but small. About fifty converts had come into connection with his church, and, so far as he knew, they all continued steadfast in the faith, while many of them had become centers of blessed influence. The like testimony has come from other quarters; and when we now hear the oft-put question, 'Will it stand?' we answer, 'It has stood.' What if some do fall away? that is the case also with those who join our churches in the steadiest times."

From the scriptural character of the addresses, and the Bible readings, a new feature appeared in Man-

CORRODING CARES. 315

chester, and is noticed by Mr. Macgregor. It recalls Glasgow, where the book-stores were literally emptied of Bibles during the meetings there :

"We notice that many have learned the habit of bringing their Bibles and turning over the leaves to find the passages. If the Bible readings accomplish nothing else but familiarizing many with the daily use of their Bibles, they will have done much."

It would be delightful, if space permitted, to multiply illustrative incidents. At a meeting, for example, a gentleman said :

"There are many most delightful cases in this hall. I should like to relate one. I was speaking last night to those who were inquiring after Christ, up there in the gallery. I saw one workman sitting there. I felt I did not need to ask how it was with his soul; I could see in his beaming face how happy he was. I went up to him, and said: 'Friend, have you found the Saviour?' 'Yes.' 'How long is it since?' 'Only three nights since I went to the Free Trade Hall, I heard them sing, "Safe in the arms of Jesus;" the first verse I sung carelessly through, but when we came to the second verse—"Safe from corroding cares"—it struck me that the people seemed in earnest—that they meant it—I looked at the verse—I felt it was mockery for me to sing that—I sat down in great trouble. That night I went home in agony. Next morning I went to my work, but I had not got over the trouble. My shopmates saw there was something up with me. They asked, "What was the trouble?" I told them, my soul! my soul! Two nights after I was no better, I went again to the meeting—there I heard, "I must look to Christ and Him alone." Just then I was enabled to look, I went home, rejoicing in the Lord, a new and happy man.' 'Are you waiting for a talk with Mr. Moody?' 'Oh! no, I am just praying and waiting; I brought a dear friend with me to-night, and she's over there; some one's talking to her, and I am praying God may save her.' 'Is it your wife?' 'No, sir, I am not married, but it is a dear friend.' Here he was watching and praying, while she was hearing the way of salvation. I believe his prayers were answered last night."

Mr. Sankey said:

"My heart was moved last night at the Young Men's meeting. I can truly say that during all my wanderings I have never attended a better meeting than the one held last night in Roby Chapel—a more hopeful and prayerful meeting—I am looking for great results from that place. My dear friend, Mr. Drummond, was there, whose father you all know has done so much work in publishing and distributing tracts in Scotland, and, I may say, all over the world. When Mr. Drummond had opened the meeting, he asked all who had been recently converted to rise and tell it. Many stood up and told what the Lord had done for their souls. Old men stood up, young men, and even boys. When we were engaged in silent prayer, Mr. Drummond asked that any who wished prayer for themselves, or for friends, would just stand up and ask it, while the Christians were praying. One by one from all parts of the chapel came the requests, 'pray for me,' 'pray for my soul,' 'pray for my father,' 'for my mother,' 'for brothers,' 'for sisters,' 'for wives.' Mothers! fathers! your sons were there in Roby Chapel last night, praying for you, pleading for you. Won't you join them?"

One man asked prayer for one of his Sunday scholars, who was there in the meeting—before the meeting broke up, that lad had given himself to Christ. A commercial traveler remained to the inquiry-meeting. He had been at one time superintendent of a Sabbath-school. He had, however, fallen into intemperance, and had gone astray. "Now," he said, "I want to get back to my father's house; my dear wife has been praying for me. My eyes are opened once more, and I want to cling to Jesus; He will keep me in His arms safe."

Mr. Beith told of one young man, in a large warehouse in the city, who had been utterly regardless of divine things. "However, he went, as so many had done, to the meeting, to see what was doing. He was almost struck dumb when he heard Mr. Moody speak. Was this the same gospel that he had so often heard preached? Ere long he was melted, went down stairs into the inquiry-room; there he was spoken to by a Christian minister, who pointed him to the only Saviour. He was enabled, by God's grace, to accept the offer of salvation, and went home rejoicing. In his warehouse there was a large number of young men; he was determined to do his duty, so he, in a frank, manly way told of the great change he had experienced. He induced some of his fellows to come to the evening meeting along with him. And before three days there were eleven converted young men in that warehouse. These have now formed themselves into a praying band, for the other young men in that warehouse."

Rev. Dr. Garrett (Episcopal) said, "It does cheer my heart to hear of the work that has been doing here yesterday. I and many other ministers have our own work on Sundays, so that we cannot possibly be present in your meetings. But I wish to tell of the good result I have seen in my own district, a quiet part of Manchester. There has been, I find, a great blessing both in my congregation and in my Sabbath-schools. I wish also to mention one incident which will illustrate the Christian unity springing up amongst ministers of the various denominations, and also the good which is sure to flow from that unity.

THE WINE-MERCHANT AND HIS WIFE.

"At one of your inquiry-meetings I met a minister I had not known previously. I do not even yet know to what denomination he belongs. He was that night talking to a lady who was in terrible distress about her soul; her husband was engaged in the wine trade and had been drawn gradually into the habit of drinking with his customers, so that if he had many bargains to strike in the course of the day, he was sure to come reeling home at night, deluged with this poison. For twelve months, before coming to your meetings, she had never entered a church door. She was, however, here awakened, and led to Jesus. Anxiety was then awakened in her heart for the salvation of her husband, upon whom she wished that minister to call, but as he lived at a great distance from her house, he promised to get some one else to do so. Having observed me at the meeting, and knowing that she was in my district, he wrote to ask me to see her.

"I called on Christmas eve; and spent one of the happiest hours I have ever known in her house. She is now rejoicing in the Saviour, and her husband told me that he has resolved to give up the wine trade, and trust in the Lord to open up to him some other path of life. Yesterday they were both in my church, and I firmly believe that these two have been led to the feet of Jesus."

Mr. C. A. Davis said, "I wish to speak of the mill-girls. Last night three of these girls were led to trust in Christ. One of them said to me, 'Oh, sir, a girl cannot be good in a mill.' It is true, indeed, that it is difficult, there are so many temptations, and so many evil companions. But here is an encouraging letter I have received this morning from a mill-girl who was converted a week since. She says that she has been enabled to tell her co-workers of the change she has experienced, and the result of her faithful witnessing is that ten of her companions in that mill have been impressed, and are coming with her to the meeting to-night. She concludes by asking our prayers that these girls may be converted."

A middle-aged man rose and said: "Last night (Sunday) as you are all aware, was very thick and foggy. I was on my way into Manchester from a neighboring village (I may say that I am a stranger here), and I happened to take the wrong turning in the road, and very soon, without being aware of it, I was on my way to Bolton. After I had walked some distance, I saw a gentleman on the opposite side of the road, and I thought I would just ask him if I was going right. 'Am I on the road to Manchester?' He crossed the road towards me, and said, 'Do you wish to reach Manchester to-night,' I said 'Yes,' 'Well you are going directly from it: your back is turned to the city; but I am going there, and will show you the way.' I was very glad to accompany him. Then all at once he began to ask me questions, which I thought were very impertinent. 'Was I a Christian?' and so on. I said nothing, however, as I did not want to have him leave me. By-and-by I began to like his talk, and by the time we reached the city, we were very friendly. 'Have you ever heard of Mr. Moody?' he said. 'Oh, yes, often, they're building a large wooden hall for them in Liverpool, where I come from.' 'Well, I am going to one of his meetings, will you go?' 'No.' 'Oh, do come in just to hear him.' Well, I didn't like to refuse and went with him; when we got into the hall, Mr. Moody was thundering out the words, 'Whosoever will let him come.' I wondered if this could mean me. However, I came away when the meeting was over. As I walked away with Mr. Bell (that I found was the gentleman's name), I could not resist any longer, and I broke out, 'Can Christ save me—such an one as I am?' 'Oh, yes,' said he, '*Whosoever* believeth in Christ shall not perish, but have everlasting life' (John iii.). We had some more talk, and I bless the Lord that He has now opened my eyes to see that not only is He able and willing, but that He has saved me."

At a public meeting James C. Stuart, Esq., Treasurer of the Committee for Manchester, stated the amount of expenses to be provided for by the friends in the city.

"So far as he could judge, the expenses of the movement would be about £2,000. He wished it to be made public that Messrs. Moody and Sankey received no money from the committee. The sum named was for the rent of halls, printing, and such like expenses."

At a later meeting Mr. Stuart* reported: "At a meeting, held last night, the Young Men's Christian Association decided to purchase the block of buildings adjacent to the Theater Royal for the sum of £30,000. Will you not help us to raise this money before the close of the year? I feel all the more hopeful in this matter, as we have Mr. Moody at our back, and he has promised to assist us, and make an appeal for us. I may add that the building will be used for the men's meeting to-night."

The tide of feeling rose and spread. Salford, and other places in the neighborhood were as it was ex-

---

* Mr. James C. Stuart is the nephew of one of the Editors of this Volume, and a banker in Manchester. His co-operation has been given in Manchester, Liverpool, and London.

pressed, "on fire," and it was greatly regretted when the time of the evangelists expired. The close is thus described:

"The closing week has been the most joyful of all. The tide of blessing, which has been steadily rising, has this week reached its flood; the earnestness of the preacher and the eagerness of the people have seemed alike to intensify, and the unconverted have been called to take refuge in Christ with a vehemence of entreaty which has exerted a mighty influence on the assemblies. During these five weeks God has answered the prayers of many years, and we cannot but feel that what has been going on in the city has made Manchester peculiarly interesting to the dwellers in heaven.

"At nine on Wednesday evening, about two thousand men reassembled in the hall, to hear what Mr. Moody had to say on the subject of the Young Men's Christian Association. Mr. Herbert Spencer occupied the chair, and gave a brief address, intimating that it was in contemplation to buy the Museum for the Young Men's Christian Association for £30,000. Mr. Moody delivered an inspiring harangue, in which he enlarged on the spiritual advantages of the Association, and urged the straining of every effort to reach the young men of Manchester, and to secure the building in question for the Association. A collection towards the object, made at the close, realized £1,800, £1,000 of which was given, I believe, by the chairman. This amount, with former contributions, including £5,000 given last week by Mr. J. Stuart, makes £8,000.*

"On Thursday morning Mr. Moody addressed a crowded meeting in the Higher Broughton Presbyterian Church, and then came on to the noon prayer-meeting in the Oxford Hall, where he read and commented on the earlier part of the 103d Psalm. He said he had to bless the Lord for what He had done for him. It had been the best year of his life. He had been more used by God than in all the seventeen preceding years. He did not know of one sermon he had delivered, that had not been blessed to the conviction or conversion of some souls. It was a delightful meeting. Every word uttered was set to the tune of 'Bless the Lord, O my soul!' When one minister rose to say, 'I have to praise God for the conversion of the brother of dear friends of mine, who have prayed for him twenty-five years; for the

---

* More than the amount has since been raised.

conversion of the sister and of the servant of another friend; for the salvation of three persons in my own congregation; for the dispelling of the doubts of a young man who traveled one hundred and fifty miles to these meetings—all which blessings have been given in the course of the present week;' when another minister rose to say he had never met with so much of scriptural teaching concerning the way of salvation, and the clear direction of inquirers to Jesus, as in Mr. Moody's addresses; and another to say that the last ten days had been the happiest of his life—that he had derived an inspiration, had discovered how to preach Christ, had enjoyed sweeter communion with Jesus, and felt like a man whose chains were broken;—they only uttered what many could have endorsed, as a description of the blessings they themselves had received."

Promising, God willing, to make a visit in January, they left for Sheffield.

Sheffield contains two hundred and fifty thousand inhabitants. It has had among its skilled artizans a considerable number of free-thinkers, and its religious statistics are not favorable.

Three years ago there was a general "mission"

throughout the town, chiefly conducted by clergymen of the Church of England, with the mission preacher, the Rev. R. Aitken (then a veteran in the cause) at their head, with good results. Lay evangelists were called in, among others, Lord Radstock, Mr. Robert Baxter, and Mr. Neville Sherbrooke.

The correspondent of the *Daily Review* (and we are glad to avail ourselves of the side-lights of the secular press) thus describes the state of feeling in Sheffield, during that first week of January, 1875—the week of prayer throughout Protestant Christendom :

"Sheffield is being greatly stirred by the revival services of Messrs. Moody and Sankey. They are at present the subject of conversation in families, offices, workshops, and factories. The merits and demerits of the American evangelists are keenly discussed by excited groups at the corners of streets, and the opponents of the movement attribute its success to vulgar curiosity, sensational advertising, and press exaggeration. Meanwhile the meetings in connection with the movement are on the increase. The numbers seeking admission to them are beyond all precedent in Sheffield. The admission to the mass-meeting last night was by ticket, and it was found necessary to engage an additional hall, capable of accommodating two thousand persons. The average attendance at each of the four meetings held in the Albert Hall yesterday may be stated at two thousand five hundred—total, ten thousand. Thirty requests for the prayers of the noon meeting were read. They were from persons in all stages of life and grades of society. Mr. Moody stated that many more had been received, too late for arrangement, which would have to be deferred till next day. The Vicar of Sheffield made a touching appeal on behalf of a dying man, from whose bedside he had just come. This man, he said, had never heard of Jesus till the previous day. Such a crowd of earnest listeners as attended Mr. Moody's Bible lecture on 'Salvation by Blood' was perhaps never before witnessed in any assembly hall in Sheffield. Mr. Moody proposed at the mass-meeting for men, that similar meetings should be instituted, to be held every night in temperance halls. He asked all approving the proposal to stand up, and nearly the whole assembly responded."

On Thursday the demands for admission became

so numerous, that the committee restricted the admission by tickets, and had the hall-doors closed as soon as the hall was filled. A long list of requests for the prayers of the noon meeting was read previous to the commencement of the service, and it was again intimated that it had been found impossible to arrange nearly all sent in. A new feature was, that many persons desired to return thanks for their conversion through these meetings. Mr. Moody, in a brief address from the words, "Declare His doings among the people," referred to recent accounts of their work in Dublin, Glasgow, and Manchester. These were remarkable for their mention of the great number of young men who had become converts, and devoted themselves to Christian work. He affirmed that none of their public services had been followed by more gratifying assurances than last night's mass-meeting for men. Half an hour before the Bible lecture the hall was filled, the doors shut, and many hundreds left standing around the entrances. It was reported that many of those at the noon meeting had remained in their seats. Mr. Moody illustrated the Bible lecture by some of the most touching anecdotes and appeals; but happily he repressed the distracting exclamations which were frequent among his early audiences here. When he requested a few minutes' silent prayer, a stillness as of death fell on the vast assembly. Many hundreds had to be denied admission to the evening meeting, at which Mr. Moody gave a very impressive address from the words, "Son, remember." Two other meetings—one for men, another for women—were held elsewhere. The total attendance at the meetings that day was about twelve thousand.

On Friday, Mr. Moody having gone to Manchester, the prayer-meeting was presided over by the Rev. Rowley Hill, Vicar of Sheffield, and participated in by other clergymen. Several laymen also took part in the proceedings. Forty requests for prayer were sent in by letters and telegrams. The evening meeting was presided over by the Rev. Robert Stainton, Independent minister, and addresses bearing on religious work were delivered by ministers of all denominations. A meeting for men only took place at a later hour in the Temperance Hall, and was largely attended. The singing was conducted by Mr. Sankey, who rendered, with much effect, some of his most touching solos.

HOW TO ADDRESS CHILDREN. 331

Rain having fallen heavily all forenoon, the children's meeting at midday on Saturday, the 9th, was not quite so largely attended as had been anticipated. About one hundred adults were present. Mr. Sankey presided, and in his opening address gave an interesting account of the children's meetings in Edinburgh. He deprecated lengthy addresses to children. His experience was, that such meetings could be made attractive to children by brief, simple discourses from several speakers, along with the singing of hymns in which the children could intelligently join. Addresses were also given by the Vicar and other speakers, among whom was Mr. Drummond from Edinburgh, a young man already well known in connection with the present revival movement. In closing the meeting, Mr. Sankey made a touching allusion to his approaching departure, that being in all probability the last children's meeting he would ever address in Sheffield. The evening meeting was crowded, and many hundreds were denied admission. Mr. Moody spoke from the words, "He was wounded for our transgressions," etc., and the picture he presented of Christ's death drew tears from hundreds. When he spoke of the resurrection, the enthusiasm became irrepressible; it broke out in every part of the hall. On the conclusion of the service, hundreds went to the inquiry room. A meeting for men was held in the Temperance Hall, which was crowded. This meeting was addressed by Mr. Drummond and others. The excitement and enthusiasm have not been so high in Sheffield before. Mingling in the crowd, one hears Mr. Moody compared to Paul on Mars' Hill. The attendance up to Saturday night reached sixty-eight thousand.

Four meetings were held in the Albert Hall on Sunday the 10th. The first, for Christian workers, at eight o'clock, was well attended. It would probably have been crowded, but a thick drizzling rain, which continued most of the day, kept many at home. A service for those who do not usually attend any church or chapel took place at eleven o'clock. The hall was filled, but not quite by the class for whom the service was intended. Strenuous efforts had been put forth amongst the denizens of the slums to awaken their interest in the movement. Hundreds on hundreds of tickets were given away amongst them, and expectations were entertained that they would attend in large numbers; but a cursory glance was

FINAL MEETINGS. 333

sufficient to convince the practised observer that the audience did not differ in any perceptible degree from former audiences. Many new faces were to be seen, but they were those of decent, orderly working-people, or visitors from the rural districts—not the besotted countenances of the residents of the slums. A meeting for women only was announced for three o'clock, but by half-past two the hall was crammed to suffocation, and the wide street in front was blocked with a crowd of both sexes. Every means of persuasion was tried to induce those who were crushed out to go and listen to other speakers elsewhere, but in vain—they would hear none but Mr. Moody. Finally, Mr. Moody left the Albert Hall, and addressed the people assembled, to the number of many thousands, in the parish churchyard, situated in the center of the town. Similarly the hall was crammed, and thousands denied admission, an hour before the commencement of the evening service.

The interest and the numbers grew as the days of the second week passed, till the sixteenth, when final services, four in number, one of them being for converts to the number of about six hundred, the fruit of the fortnight's labor.

To the value of the work in Sheffield, testimony was borne by the Vicar (the Rev. Rowley Hill, M. A.):

"I rejoice that God has put it into the hearts of those two evangelists to come and visit Sheffield. We wanted a good stirring up from end to end in this town, and there is nothing that more delights my heart than to have people brought under the sound of the Gospel. A great number of people who do not go to church or chapel have been stirred up by these men, and I trust very great blessing will result from it. All I have heard fall from the lips of Mr. Moody, or sung by Mr. Sankey, was really refreshing to one's soul. No doubt we shall always have starchy, stiff kind of people who don't 'like that sort of thing;' but when a man preaches the Gospel, when a man is seen doing the work of God, and when there can be little doubt the Holy Ghost is working with him, it is a solemn thing to do anything as gainsaying that work, or do anything to oppose or hinder it."

From Sheffield the American brethren proceeded to Birmingham—" the toyshop of the world" as it has been called, with a population of four hundred thousand. Of the first week's work there, a writer in the *Signs of the Times* reports:

"The audiences are very much larger than at Manchester; and the city is moved to a much greater extent. The noon-day meetings in the Town Hall are attended by three to four thousand people, and the evening meetings in the Bingley Hall by ten thousand to fifteen thousand.

"One cause that has undoubtedly conduced to this result is the prominence given by the Birmingham newspapers to reports of the meetings. Two or three columns have been given by some of the local papers every day, furnishing accounts of the proceedings, whereas in Manchester the Press took little or no notice of the movement. Another cause is, that many of the local clergymen of the Church of England have taken a leading part in the movement at Birmingham."

Prominent among the ministers who stood by the evangelists in Birmingham, was the Rev. R. W. Dale, successor to the pulpit of the well-known John Angel James, author of the "Anxious Enquirer," and who for a long life-time preached and lived the truth in the city.

We shall allow the *Birmingham Morning News*

to convey the impression the evangelists made on the community. One does not look for the report of the spiritual results in a secular paper:

"Unheralded, and comparatively unknown, Messrs. Moody and Sankey came to England, without any new creed or sectarian formula, and straightway began a work which gathers power and force as it goes on. On a dull, raw, and inclement Sunday morning in January, such is the unseen magic of their names, that they can crowd a large hall in the center of a practical, industrial town with worshipers at an hour which would be considered early even on a week-day. That same evening they attract to a still larger edifice crowds which would be almost unusual in a period of intense national excitement. Again at noon-day, at a time when the bench and the desk chain their workers with the strongest bonds, thousands after thousands throng to meet them at the prayer-meeting until the Town Hall presents the appearance of a gigantic bee-hive, swarming with masses of people, to whom it is evident there must be some strong inducement thus to forsake the ordinary routine of their lives.

"Nor does the story close here. In the evenings

at Bingley Hall is gathered together an assembly which equals the population of many towns, and a degree of enthusiasm manifested which promises to increase the numbers present at every succeeding meeting. A small harmonium, a few simple hymns, and short, stirring addresses on religious topics comprise all that the public see or hear. Yet the influence of Messrs. Moody and Sankey is overwhelming; and although it may be almost too soon to speak definitely of the permanent results of their labors in 'evangelizing the masses,' it is not too much to say that in numberless instances they have evoked a state of anxious inquiry with regard to the future in minds which ordinary religious services failed to arouse."

Then follows a description of the men, not however required by our readers, interested particularly in knowing what manner of work they appeared to do. The *News* proceeds:

"Entering Bingley Hall, between four and five o'clock in the afternoon, the visitor sees a wide wilderness of chairs. Although it is more than three hours to the commencement of the service, groups of intending hearers are scattered about the building, some sitting meditatively quiet, reading hymn-books or

Bibles, others holding subdued discussions upon revival themes. In the galleries are temporary stands, which make the hall a sort of oblong amphitheater, the speakers' platform being on one of the sides. The abundant use of crimson cloth in draping the stands has given a very comfortable aspect to what is, perhaps, in its normal state one of the dreariest-looking public buildings in the Midland Counties. As the hours wear on, small groups of people are, by a wise arrangement, admitted as they assemble at the doors, and thus crowding and crushing at the entrances in a great measure are obviated. Suddenly, from some part of the assembling mass, is heard the beginning of a hymn. As fresh comers enter, the strains are taken up, and the effect in the empty and resonant space is singularly impressive. Rank after rank of the silent sitting crowds take up the melody, until it fairly rolls through the building. The greatest favorite seems the hymn 'Hold the Fort.' Singing this and other hymns, crowds of people continue to pour in until the hall is filled, ten thousand chairs being occupied. Round the galleries, too, is a thick fringe of human faces, and the hall seems to be from one end to the other literally packed with human beings.

"The Gospel addresses delivered every evening to these vast audiences by Mr. Moody have their effect, heightened by the hymns and solos of Mr. Sankey. In his discourses Mr. Moody evidently knows the power of describing home-life, both scriptural and modern, with all its pathetic touches. Relating now some of his own American experiences, or again, incidents of his stay in England or Dublin, he charges home upon his hearers the lessons he wishes learnt. Now and again he moves many persons in the audience to tears by a homely expression so entirely spontaneous and unstilted that it carries every one with it. And when, after the sermon and a period for silent prayer, the preacher exhorts those who 'really would like to be Christians to go right to the Presbyterian Church,' where he would meet them, and between two and three hundred persons obey the call, it cannot but be doubted that Mr. Moody's oratory, whatever its excellence or defects, can produce results which are unusually and significantly powerful."

Of Bingley Hall, a correspondent of the *Christian* shrewdly says (and the hint is worth the consideration of all who desire moral and spiritual results): "It has been provided with nine thousand chairs. They were hired for a fortnight, at a cost of seven pence per chair, including fixing and removal. It may seem incongruous to say that a person is more likely to be converted in a chair than on a seat without a back, but this is really so, for if he be sitting in an uncomfortable position, it is impossible that he should pay the same attention, or yield himself to the influences around him in the same degree, that he would if his attention were not distracted by his physical discomfort.

"Not a sound of footsteps is heard, for the floors of the galleries, as well as of the area, have been laid with sawdust. The noiselessness consequent upon the arrangement is not a mere negative advantage, for the unusual stillness in so vast a throng adds wonderfully to the solemnity of the audience."

The "Convention," as at Inverness, Dublin, and elsewhere, wound up the Birmingham services. The Rev. Newman Hall, from London, the Rev. W. Fleming Stevenson, from Dublin, and many strangers, took part, and made addresses.

It was held in Bingley Hall. Mr. Moody presided all day. It was a great meeting in every sense of the term. The audience numbered from five thousand to six thousand.

The attendance of ministers of all denominations, from all parts, was very large. The results of the services are thus summed up by an intelligent observer:

"Messrs. Moody and Sankey have finished their term here, and retire for a week to rest, before they enter on their engagements in Liverpool. The last three days have certainly been the most impressive we have had. Evidently the Lord has been on the scene. If we don't take that view of the unparalleled movement in the history of Birmingham, we are even at a greater loss to account for it than the world itself. That there will be much that will pass away with the men as they go will prove nothing against those who stand, and will be nothing worse than what happened in our Saviour's time, when 'many went back, and walked no more with Him.' But, separating the chaff from the wheat, we have these *four* great blessings left:

" 1st. Christians have learned to love one another, and work together for one common object—the salvation of souls.

" 2d. A great quickening of the divine life in the souls of believers. We have learned to pray more, to watch more closely, to work more earnestly for God.

"3d. Many souls have been converted of whom there is no doubt. Their works bear witness that they are born of God.

"4th. Vast numbers have heard the word, who, although they have not yet found the Lord, may be led to think, to believe, to praise God for his salvation.

" May our hearts be tuned to sing the praise of our dear Lord Jesus Christ, and yield to Him the full tribute of affectionate service !

"Mr. Moody speaks in high terms of the committee that arranged for him and assisted him here, of the building where he preached, and the orderly character of the congregations."

A visit was made on Friday, February 5th, to say farewell to those who had received spiritual life, as they hoped, during the fortnight's mission. At the service held in Bingley Hall, about fifteen thousand persons were present. Seats were railed off for those who had been converted, and every one of them was filled, admission to that part of the hall being by ticket. Mr. Moody addressed himself chiefly to the converts, and the service was concluded by a hymn of farewell, sung by Mr. Sankey. Great emotion was exhibited by the audience.*

In Liverpool.

These eminent evangelists commenced their labors in Liverpool on Sabbath morning, 7th February, under the most encouraging circumstances. The services were well attended—thousands were excluded from the afternoon and evening meetings from want of accommodation. The people listened with intense earnestness. The meetings were held in the Victoria Hall—the new building specially constructed for the purpose being so named. It is entirely of wood, and has cost about £4,000, a large sum for a building that was only to be used for a month, and taken down at the end of that time.

"It affords accommodation to about 8,000 persons, exclusive of platform seats. It is lighted by eighty-

---

* Up to this point the Editors have enjoyed, and gratefully acknowledge the valuable aid of the Rev. I. S. Woodside, whose earnest labors in Northern India have been greatly blessed of God, and whose season of much-needed rest in this country has been varied by not a few useful labors. May he be permitted to see in his chosen field similar religious awakening !

three windows, and there are no less than twenty doors for exit, all opening outwards. There are five staircases for the gallery. Very complete arrangements have been made for lighting and warming. Interiorly the sides or walls have been covered with canvas and papered with oak paper. Ventilation is provided in the roof by two large trunks with outlets. In rear of the large hall are two 'inquiry' and meeting-rooms, and retiring rooms for ladies and gentlemen. About thirty thousand cubic feet of timber have been used in the construction, and three thousand two hundred superficial feet of glass. The erection has occupied altogether thirty-nine working days."

The first meeting—for Christian workers—was held at eight o'clock in the morning, and though the weather was intensely cold and raw, about five thousand or six thousand were present. Probably so great and so striking a gathering of a similar character has never before been seen in Liverpool. The somber appearance of the building itself was a little relieved by the red baize around the front of the galleries, on which, in large white letters, were the texts, "Believe on the Lord Jesus Christ;" "Be ye reconciled to God;" and "Ye must be born again." At the platform end of the building was exhibited in still larger letters the words, "God is love." A large number of ministers and laymen occupied seats on the platform, where also were stationed the choir of young ladies and gentlemen who have been specially trained to sing at the service.

Precisely at eight o'clock the choir, which seemed to be excellently trained, the voices being bright and well-balanced, and skillfully led, commenced the hymn, "Jesus Loves even Me."

The Rev. Henry Baugh (Episcopalian) having engaged in prayer, Mr. Sankey having sang "Hold the Fort," and some other pieces, Mr. Moody delivered his address to Christian workers, and in the course of his remarks said:—"Now if we are going to see a great work in this town of Liverpool, the children of God must be of good courage. Let us expect great things and not be afraid of public opinion." Before the departure of the congregation he condemned the sale of hymn-books at the doors on Sundays, and continued: "It had been said that they were making money out of the sale of the hymn-books. But this was not so, for they were only connected with the publication of one edition, the proceeds of the sale of which were handed over to Mr. Hugh Matheson of London, for charitable purposes. The enemy were also saying that they were making a great deal out of the sale of organs. They were not selling organs, nor were they hired by any organ society or company to represent them. He saw boys selling an account of his life, with portraits of him. He wished people would not buy them."

Even with the miserable weather, there was an audience of at least ten thousand people at the evening meeting, and it is said about four thousand or five thousand persons were unable to get admission. The great bulk of the audience was composed of the middle and respectable artizan classes, with here and there representatives of the poorer classes in fustian jackets, while no mean proportion of the assembly was made up of youths and girls. On the platform were several ministers, and several gentlemen of prominent positions.

On Monday the first of a series of mid-day prayer-meetings was held at which about three thousand people were present.

The evening meeting was held at half past seven,

and was attended by an immense gathering. Mr. Moody opened with the hymn, "Free from the Law," and Mr. T. Shuldham Henry led in prayer, and was succeeded by the reading of Luke, chapter 15, and a solo from Mr. Sankey. Mr. Moody preached on Christ's mission in the world. At the conclusion of his sermon Mr. Moody asked all who were unconverted to stand up, and a great many stood up. An after-meeting was held for which about two thousand people remained.

On Tuesday's mid-day prayer-meeting no less than five thousand people were present.

At half-past seven on the same day the evening service was conducted, which was likewise well attended. Mr. Moody spoke of Christ's willingness to save sinners, and said there were hundreds of ways in which he sought them out. Referring to eternity, Mr. Moody said he believed in the old-fashioned hell and the old-fashioned heaven; and as he believed no heart could conceive the bliss of heaven, so he believed no heart could conceive the horrors of hell. Several thousands stopped for the inquiry-meeting, held immediately afterwards.

On Wednesday the noon prayer-meeting was

crowded. Mr. Moody opened the service with the hymn, "Sweet Hour of Prayer." A large number of requests were read, and prayer offered on their behalf.

At the evening service Mr. Moody preached from Isaiah, 6th chapter, to a large and attentive audience. An inquiry-meeting was held at the conclusion of this service, and several thousand people remained to be conversed with.

Thus, with little variation from week to week, the services continued in Liverpool. Of the third week it is testified:

"Despite the arctic severity of the weather during the past week, the audiences at Victoria Hall at the afternoon and evening meetings of the American evangelists have been as crowded as ever, and large overflow meetings have been held in the evening in Newsome's Circus. The anxious inquiry-room, which holds between two and three hundred, has been unable to contain all who resorted to it, and some hundreds of anxious inquirers have been addressed and conversed with in the large hall at the close of the evening service."

That Mr. Moody encouraged no "healing slightly"

of wounded hearts, will appear to a thoughtful reader, familiar with a certain style of revival effort, from his words to the Christian workers in Liverpool:

"I don't fear so much evil from attacks of our enemies as from the want of wisdom amongst some of our friends. Only the other night I heard one friend say to the anxious inquirer to whom he was speaking, 'You believe you are saved, and you are saved.' Now, that is not in the Word of God. You cannot find it in the Bible, that we are saved if we believe it. We are told to believe in Christ. Another said, 'Do you *feel* you are saved?' Now, that is the worst possible advice. What we want is to get men out of their feelings. Feeling is the last plank the devil slips beneath the sinner when he is trying to reach the Rock of Ages. When the poor sinner feels his feet on this plank he thinks he's all right. But soon away goes the plank, and he is again cast on a sea of perplexity. Then he cries, 'Dear me, I thought I was converted, I felt so happy!' What we must have is to get them to rest on some text of God's Word, and then they'll stand safe. I could point many other errors, but I wish just to show you the right way of dealing with the anxious.

Have a Bible in your hand, ready to show chapter and verse for every hope. It does them good to see the Word of God. I have no sympathy with that class who tell the inquirer, 'Now you are converted.'

"We don't know that—God alone knows the heart. Let it be a question between the sinner and God himself. It is well to have some useful passages marked in your Bible ready to turn up. I will give you some that I have found of great benefit: Romans x. 10; Isaiah i. 18; John v. 24; John i. 13; 1 Peter ii. 24."

There is no minister in Liverpool enjoying more fully the confidence of the Christian public than the Rev. J. B. Lowe, D.D., of St. Jude's. He writes thus:

"If I were to select one word by which to express my impression of the work of Mr. Moody and Mr. Sankey in this town, I should speak of its *genuineness.* The men themselves are *genuine.* They are not artificial, with anything of the character of an actor; they are true men, their heart in the Lord's work, and their eye single. Some persons are disappointed when they first hear Mr. Moody, and say he does not come up to the expectations they had entertained respecting him. Herein he differs from an artificial got-up man, who would put his best foot foremost, and come prepared to make a great impression, and to take every one by storm.

"But Mr. Moody aims not to produce a mere effect, but to instil vital truths of saving power into the minds of his audience, and the impression made by him grows stronger and stronger as he proceeds. His manifest sincerity and earnestness are prominent features. Some, after hearing Mr. Moody for the first time, are surprised at the fame of these evangelists which has been noised abroad, but on going again have formed a higher estimate of his preaching. His continual increase in power over his hearers, is, in its way, an illustration of the proverb, 'The righteous shall hold on his way, and he that has clean hands shall wax stronger and stronger.'

"As regards the genuineness of the work, as well as of the men, one is struck with the great simplicity of Mr. Moody's speech, and the total absence of carnal excitement in his manner and utterance. Earnestness there is, indeed, and zeal and eloquence (though not oratory), but it is moral and spiritual, not carnal or sensational. His manner is rather behind than at the head of his subject-matter."*

---

* Probably no one has better known or more cordially sustained Mr. D. L. Moody than Mr. J. V. Farwell, of Chicago, equally known as an energetic merchant and Christian worker. "The good thing," said he, "about Brother Moody is, that he keeps on the one line, and the longer he is known the more he is trusted."

CHAPTER VII.

LIVERPOOL TO LONDON.

In this concluding chapter we shall not attempt to enter into the same details as have been given concerning other places, for the religious newspapers of March and April, and even the better class of secular papers have been describing the evangelists' work in Liverpool, Birmingham, and London. We shall endeavor to combine with the facts, the expressed opinion of widely-known Christian men. We shall also seek to answer the very natural question: "What is the state of religious feeling in places visited, say a year ago?"

Rev. R. W. Dale, of Birmingham, the Rev. Mr. James' successor says, in the *Congregationalist:*

"Some people have said that it is easy to get crowds of women to 'hysterical' religious services. But although the morning and afternoon meetings were largely attended by women, I believe that the majority of the evening congregation always consisted of men, and of men of all kinds—rough lads of seventeen or eighteen, working-men, clerks, tradesmen, and manufacturers. I happen to have on my desk a list of persons that came into Carr's Lane Lecture-room one evening, to tell me that they had 'found Christ,' during the fortnight that Mr. Moody and Mr. Sankey were here; out of twenty-one on the list eleven are men. I have another list of persons who came to me the same evening, who had been quickened to earnest religious anxiety, but were not yet at rest; out of thirteen, eight are men. I believe that these lists imperfectly represent the proportion of men to women among those who were impressed by the services; for I generally find that men are slower to express religious decision than women.

"How, I ask, is the great interest of the people in these services to be accounted for? The truest, simplest, and most complete reply to the question which I can give is, that the power of God was manifested in an extraordinary degree in connection with them."

After mentioning concurrent circumstances favorable to impression, such as expectation raised, general concern among church-goers who never decided, and letters of friends, Mr. Dale adds:

"After the first day or two, the services were 'advertised' in a very much more efficient manner than by newspapers or placards: every evening, at the 'after-meeting,' a considerable number of persons received Christ as their 'Prince and Saviour,' and judging from those with whom I conversed, most of them went home with overflowing joy. I have seen occasional instances before of instant transition from religious anxiety to the clear and triumphant consciousness of restoration to God; but what struck me in the gallery of Bingley Hall was the fact that this instant transition took place with nearly every person with whom I talked. They had come up into the gallery anxious, restless, feeling after God in the darkness, and when, after a conversation of a quarter of an hour or twenty minutes, they went away, their faces were filled with light, and they left me not only at peace with God, but filled with joy. I have seen the sunrise from the top of Helvellyn and the top of the Righi, and there is something very glorious in it; but to see the light of heaven suddenly strike on man after man in the course of one evening is very much more thrilling. These people carried their new joy with them to their homes and their workshops. It could not be hid.

" On the Sunday after Mr. Moody and Mr. Sankey

had left us, I invited those members of my own congregation to meet me who had come to Christ during the services of the preceding fortnight. A few who were still out at sea, longing to make their way to quiet water, came with them. Nothing was easier than to tell the difference between the two classes; I think I could have separated them into two divisions without asking a question and with scarcely a mistake. Those who were still 'inquirers,' if they did not look anxious and troubled, looked like other people; the 'converts' were bright with their new joy. It is as yet too early to obtain any general information about the extent of the influence which I have attributed to the converts themselves; but among the names that I have on several lists of persons that I saw myself, I find the names of two clerks who sat side by side at the same desk, three pairs of brothers and sisters, three husbands with their wives; and four brothers —rough working-men—all of whom have been awakened to religious thought by Mr. Moody's addresses.

"The people were of all sorts, young and old, rich and poor, keen tradesmen, manufacturers, and merchants, and young ladies who had just left school, rough boys who knew more about dogs and pigeons than about books, and cultivated women. For a time I could not understand it—I am not sure that I understand it now. At the first meeting, Mr. Moody's address was simple, direct, kindly, and hopeful: it had a touch of humor and a touch of pathos; it was lit up with a story or two that filled most eyes with tears; but there seemed nothing in it very remarkable. Yet it *told*. A prayer-meeting with an address, at eight o'clock, on a damp, cold January morning, was hardly the kind of thing—let me say it frankly—that I should generally regard as attractive; but I enjoyed it heartily; it seemed one of the happiess meetings I had ever attended. There was warmth and there was sunlight in it. At the evening meeting the same day, at Bingley Hall, I was still unable to make out how it was that he had done so much in other parts of the kingdom. I listened with interest; everybody listened with interest; and I was conscious again of a certain warmth and brightness which made the service very pleasant, but I could not see that there was much to impress those that were careless about religious duty. The next morning at the prayer-meeting, the address was more incisive and striking, and at the evening service I began to see that the stranger had a faculty for making the elementary truths of the Gospel intensely clear and vivid. But it still seemed most remarkable that he should have done so much, and on Tuesday I told Mr. Moody that the work was most plainly of God, for I could see no real relation between him and what he had done. He laughed cheerily and said he should be very sorry if it were otherwise. I began to wonder whether what I had supposed to be a law of the Divine Kingdom was perfectly uniform. I thought that there were scores of us who could preach as effectively as Mr. Moody, and who might, therefore, with God's good help, be equally successful.

"In the course of a day or two my mistake was corrected; but to the last there were sensible people who listened to him with a kind of interest and delight with which they never listen to very 'distinguished' and eloquent preachers, and who yet thought that though Mr. Moody was 'very simple and earnest,' he had no particular power as a speaker. I do not intend to suggest any comparison between Mr. Moody and our great English orator, but I have met people who have talked in the same way about Mr. Bright, and who seemed to think that to speak like Mr. Bright was possible to nearly everybody.

"One of the elements of Mr. Moody's power consists in his perfect naturalness. He has something to say, and he says it—says it as simply and directly to thirteen thousand people as to thirteen. He has nothing of the impudence into which some speakers are betrayed when they try to be easy and unconventional; but he talks in a perfectly unconstrained and straightforward way, just as he would talk to half a dozen old friends at his fireside.

"The number of persons who remained for the after-meeting was so large, that a general appeal had to be made again and again to Christian people in the congregation to give their help. Some responded who had more enthusiasm than good sense. But notwithstanding this, the results of the after-meeting were extraordinary. I have already spoken of the number of persons with whom I conversed myself, to whom, while I was conversing with them, the light came which springs from the discovery of God's love and power, and from the acceptance of His will as the law of life. Testimony after testimony has reached me from converts, to whom the same light came while conversing with others. 'I went up into the gallery,' said one young man to me, a day or two ago, ' and Mr. Sankey walked up and down with me, and talked to me as though he had been my own father, and I found Christ.'

"*The preaching without the after-meeting would not have accomplished one-fifth of the results.* It was in the quiet, unexciting talk with individuals that the impressions produced by Mr. Moody's addresses issued in a happy trust in Christ, and a clear decision to live a Christian life. The galleries were a beautiful sight. Mr. Moody's quaint directions were almost universally followed : ' Let the young men talk to the young men, the maidens to the maidens, the elder women to the elder women, and the elder men to the elder men.' Cultivated young ladies were sitting or standing with girls of their own age, sometimes with two or three together, whose eager faces indicated the earnestness of their desire to understand how they were to lay hold of the great blessing which they seemed to be touching, but could not grasp. Young men were talking to lads, some of their own social position, others with black hands and rough clothes, which were suggestive of gunmaking, and rolling-mills, and brass-foundries. Ladies of refinement were trying to make the truth clear to women whose worn faces and poor dress told of the hardships of their daily life. Men of business, local politicians, were at the same work with men of forty and fifty years of age. And there was the brightness of hope and faith in the tone, and manner, and bearing of nearly all of them. Christian people who want to know the real nature of the work of our American brethren, and to catch its spirit, should take care to spend a few hours at the after-meeting. If they go twice, they will find it hard to keep away.

"Separate arrangements were made for those of the young men who preferred an after-meeting of their own. A Presbyterian church in the neighborhood of the hall was thrown open for them, and the attendance was generally very large. Mr. Moody does not approve of the publication of the number of persons who have declared that they have been led to begin a Christian life as the result of these services, and I therefore do not feel at liberty to publish in these pages the information on this point which is in my possession. A week after he had left us, he returned to hold a farewell meeting for converts and inquirers. Ministers sat at the office of the Young Men's Christian Association to receive applications for tickets from both these classes of persons. In every case I believe that there was personal conversation with the applicants. Their names and addresses were registered, and the congregations with which they were already connected, or with which they intended to connect themselves.

"The effect of this work has extended beyond those who were present at the services; and very much of the good that has been effected is never likely to be known. Since I began to write this paper, a son of one of the members of my own church, a lad of seventeen, came to me and said he wished to enter the Church. I talked to him for a few minutes, and took for granted, that Mr. Moody's services had led him to religious decision. He had all the brightness and joyousness which I have come to regard as characteristic of the typical 'Moody convert.' I asked him which of the services had had the greatest effect on him, and he said that his business engagements had prevented him from going to any of them. 'How was it, then,' I asked, 'that you came to trust in Christ?' 'Well sir,' he said, 'I could not go to the meetings, but I heard a great deal of what these two gentlemen were doing, and I came to the conclusion that they could not be doing it themselves, but that God must be doing it; and then I came to see that I could look to God myself and get all the good.'

"Some of the most remarkable results of the visit of our American friends are to be found, perhaps, among those who have long been members of Christian churches. I hardly know how to describe the change which has passed over them. It is like the change which comes upon a landscape when clouds which have been hanging over it for hours suddenly vanish, and the sunlight seems to fill both heaven and earth. There is a joyousness, and an elasticity of spirit, and a hopefulness, which have completely transformed them; and the transformation shows itself in the unostentatious eagerness with which they are taking up Christian work.

"If I thought it worth while, I could speak of some things in this work which are not to my taste, and some things which my judgment disapproves. But, before Mr. Moody and Mr. Sankey came to Birmingham, I had arrived at the conclusion that what was said of the early evangelists of Antioch was the truest account of the work of these American evangelists in Scotland and Ireland—'The hand of the Lord was with them; and a great number believed, and turned unto the Lord.' This conviction has been deepened and confirmed by all that I have seen of them. When Whitefield and Wesley were renewing the religious life of England, there were learned, orthodox, and devout ministers who were distressed by 'The Decay of the Dissenting Interest,' and the low state of religion throughout the country; there were ministers who had written pamphlets on these subjects in the hope of re-awakening in the Christian churches of that time the faith and zeal of earlier and better days, but who regarded Whitefield and Wesley with a distrust like that with which Mr. Moody and Mr. Sankey are now regarded by some excellent people. The very objections which are urged against Mr. Moody and Mr. Sankey were urged against the leaders of the great evangelical revival which saved England from sinking into atheism. The result was inevitable; these ministers and their churches missed the blessing for which they had been longing and praying. When 'the power of God' is with men who preach what we acknowledge to be the great truths of the Gospel, it is surely our clear duty to co-operate with them heartily and frankly. If in their methods, and if in their very conception of Christian truth and the Christian life, there are some things which we cannot accept, these may surely be borne with, and even forgotten. These men especially, who are in the habit of insisting on 'breadth' of sympathy with all in whom there is genuine Christian earnestness, and who are always saying that rigid accuracy in doctrinal definitions is of inferior importance to a living faith in Christ, ought to be able to rise above the kind of objections which seem likely to alienate some of them from this work.

"It is possible that in some places, our American visitors may not achieve the kind of success which has hitherto followed them. Before they came to Birmingham, I felt very doubtful whether they would accomplish here what they had accomplished in Dublin and Belfast. I believe they will accomplish very little in any place where they are not sustained by the hearty sympathy of Christian people, and where Christian churches do not earnestly entreat God to manifest in connection with their work the transcendent greatness of His power and love. There were people among whom our Lord Himself 'could do no mighty works, because of their unbelief.'"

The work in Liverpool is thus described by Rev. W. H. M. Aitken, Christ Church (we necessarily abbreviate), after it had been in progress for some time, and when the noonday service was attended by about six thousand persons:

"There is no diminution in the interest which Messrs. Moody and Sankey's visit is occasioning; on the contrary, the meetings have never been so full as during the first days of the present week. It is a very hopeful sign that, at Sunday morning's meeting (Feb. 21), the hall was completely filled by 8 o'clock; whereas, when Mr. Moody first arrived, and there was all the influence of curiosity to bring together a large audience, the hall was not more than half filled at that hour. The meeting for non-churchgoers was again well attended. Some who were present felt that the tone of the meeting was not quite equal to the wonderful morning meeting of the previous Sunday.

"The meeting for women was again crowded; and so was the supplementary meeting for young men at St. James' Hall, where addresses were delivered by the Rev. Mr. Symington, and Mr. Balfour of Edinburgh. In the evening an immense multitude of men was gathered together, and the circus, as well as the Victoria Hall, was crowded. The number of those who were seeking the salvation of their souls is stated to have been very large, both on this and on the two following nights. The circus has been secured for the next fortnight, and is being utilized every night—first for an overflow-meeting, which lasts from 7 30 to 8 30, and then for a meeting specially for young men from 9 till 10.

"Perhaps Tuesday night last was one of the most remarkable harvest-nights that Mr. Moody has had here. After a considerable number of inquirers had gone into the ante-room, he invited the anxious, and only those, to remain in the body of the hall. It is impossible to say that there may not have been some considerable proportion of real believers mixed up with the multitude of persons who remained behind; but as these numbered something like one thousand, even making allowance for the believers present, the number of those who were really seeking after the Lord must have been very large.

"The special meetings in Victoria Hall have

taken an intense hold on the town. The great building is much too small for the work. Messrs. Moody and Sankey hold eighteen meetings in it weekly, and day by day the hall is packed to overflowing. Mr. Moody gave his lecture on Daniel at 8 o'clock last Sunday morning to an audience of not less than ten thousand, and those who could not find room in the hall were addressed in the circus adjoining by Captain Dutton of the 'Allan Line.' Many thousands had to travel long distances in the bitter weather of last Sunday to reach the hall in time for the meeting. No movement like it has ever been seen in this part of England.

"The finger of God is seen in all departments of the work. The erection of Victoria Hall for the meetings, made the expenses of the visit to Liverpool unusually heavy. Nearly four thousand pounds have been already received, and God will provide the rest. Then, again, the apathy of many in the meetings has been turned into the deepest interest. Opposition to the movement is diminishing. In fact, it may be said there is now no intelligent opposition, and any ignorant opposition that exists is fast melting away. When the critics 'come and see' the work of the Lord, they very soon assume a respectful attitude. Testimony to the blessed results of the meetings is most abundant. Every day large numbers of sincere inquirers testify, by their eager desire to know the way of God more fully by private conversation in the 'inquiry-room,' that the truth has taken a living hold upon them. The testimony, not only of the majority of the clergymen of Liverpool, but of ministers from all parts of Wales and the North of England, who have come to the meetings, is that their own souls have been strengthened, and that they feel God is preparing them for times of refreshing and revival in their several spheres of labor such as they have not seen before. There are few Sunday-schools here where the teachers are not teaching with new fervor and power. Some are filled with amazement at what the Lord is doing in their classes. Take one instance of twenty lads, mostly employed in an iron-work at Birkenhead, where youths, as in other work-shops, too often and too readily learn the blasphemous language and vile ways of the workmen. Their Sunday-school teacher is praising God to-day for the change wrought upon his class within the past weeks. Instead of foul talk they are now heard singing Mr. Sankey's Gospel hymns; and by their conduct to their parents and teacher, and both in their work and out of it, they are showing that they have been with Jesus. Take another case of a similar sort. At a shipbuilding yard not far from Birkenhead, the young lads, since these special meetings commenced in Victoria Hall, have met for prayer and the reading of the Scriptures in the smithy during the dinner hour; until the men began to drop in, and the number so increased, that last Sunday week they applied for accommodation for this dinner-hour prayer-meeting in a neighboring mission house, and, at the gathering last Friday, sixty-four were present, and the presence of God was felt to be with them. No one but God knows where the movement in Victoria Hall will end. The remark which dropped from the lips of one of our leading laymen, at the close of the meeting for Christian workers last Sunday week, accurately describes the universal feeling of all Christian hearts: 'We can never be as we have been.'

"The meetings on Sunday last were overwhelming. Four times Victoria Hall was crowded to its utmost capacity, whilst Newsome's Circus and St. James' Hall were twice filled. There must have been not less than forty-five thousand persons present at the various meetings. There were special trains from St. Helens and Southport for the accommodation of many who desired to attend. The morning meeting for Christian workers, although at the early hour of eight o'clock, was not only crowded, but large numbers were unable to gain admittance."

Of Victoria Hall, the following is a lady's account:

"Victoria Hall is the name given to the wooden structure built for Mr. Moody's meetings. It is most successful for hearing, and for speedy entrance and exit of a crowd. It has twenty doors, and can be emptied of the crowds in six or seven minutes in case of need.

"It is as ugly at first sight as can be, but grand in the thought that it was built at great cost for temporary use only, and for the preaching of the Gospel. But at night, seen from the raised back seat of the platform, it looked beautiful and grand; crowded—literally packed in every corner; earnest, listening faces, and perfect décorum and order. Then there must have been the ten thousand that can get standing-room. On the red cloth covering of the front of the galleries are the texts, in very large white letters; 'Be ye reconciled to God;' 'Ye must be born again;' 'Believe on the Lord Jesus Christ.' Above the platform is, ' God is love.'"

Early in March two "all-day meetings" were held in Liverpool, from the addresses at which we may judge of the work in progress in other places where the evangelists had been, as well as in Liverpool.

Tidings of the Lord's Work from various Parts of the Country.

After the meeting had been opened by Mr. Moody, the Rev. Dr. Knox, from Belfast, gave an account of the results of the work in that town; of the Christian unity amongst the various denominations, such as never existed before; and of the large increase in the number of communicants. A hundred had been added in one congregation, three hundred in another, and ninety-five in another. The work had been specially satisfactory amongst the young men, no less than ninety of whom had offered themselves for missionary work. The results have also been very apparent in the various factories and houses of business. There was scarcely one of these in which conversions were not still taking place from week to week. In one place of business no less than forty young women had recently been brought to the Lord, and in another sixty-seven. He also pointed out the great change which had taken place in the character of the preaching of the ministers of the Gospel. They preached the same truths as before, but with a directness and spirit of expectation such as previously they had been strangers to.

Rev. Dr. Harrison, of Liverpool, spoke of the large number of backsliders who had been reclaimed ; and the deep interest taken by the working classes in the movement. In the course of his daily visits he was continually asked by the poor people whether he was attending the services.

Rev. T. Macpherson, called attention to the Lord's quickening all those who professed to be God's people ; the increase of courage on the part of weak and timorous Christians, so that they were enabled to speak for the Master ; the hundreds of letters from relatives showing the intensest desire for the conversion of their friends ; and the extension of the work to all ranks and classes of society, many of the poorest of the poor having evidently been surprised by the manifestation of deep interest in their spiritual well-being on the part of those in a superior social position. In many cases old memories of forgotten truths had been revived. On several occasions no less than from four hundred to five hundred persons had been spoken to in a single night. And the blessings had not been confined to this hall, but in their various congregations the droppings had been falling fast. He further called attention to the consideration that in this movement we had had a proof of what we might expect God to do when His people were united as one.

Rev. Mr. Robinson, of Manchester, gave some account of the results of the work in that city. He had been eleven years in Manchester, and had never seen anything like the present state of things. Christians were bold to speak for Jesus, and large rooms had been engaged in various parts of the town, and crowded meetings and conversions were still taking place. He mentioned that, during Mr. Moody's visit to Manchester, three clergymen had come from Preston, and had gone back full of a desire to commence similar meetings there. He himself had seen some four thousand people gathered together in the Corn Exchange in that town, and there was a great and general quickening of spiritual vitality there.

Mr. Smithson, of Dublin, gave an account of the deputations from the Young Men's Christian Association in Dublin, which were carrying the fire and the heat generated in connection with the work in Dublin all through the country.

Mr. Smith, of Manchester, stated that, as a result of Mr. Moody's visit to that city, the Young Men's Society there was in a most flourishing condition. Six gentlemen had come forward with princely donations, and had placed a sum of no less than thirty-three thousand pounds at the disposal of the Society for the erection of suitable buildings, while eleven thousand pounds more had been collected by others, many of whom were ladies.

Rev. Dr. Bonar spoke of the free breakfasts in Edinburgh, of the house-to-house visitation in that and other towns, and of the power of prayer as a means of gathering in the multitude. "We must pray them in, and avoid dull preaching."

Sunday, March 7th, was Mr. Moody's last day in Liverpool. Mr. Sankey had, however, left on the previous day for Birmingham. At the Christian workers' meeting in the morning, the addresses consisted entirely of imparting practical advice to Christians as to the studies and duties most adapted for their spiritual growth. At eleven o'clock the meeting was for anxious inquirers, and the subject of the address was "Trust." The three o'clock meetings were solely for women, and not only was Victoria Hall filled but also Newsome's Circus and St. James' Hall, whilst even then large numbers could not be accommodated. The address was from the text, "Come thou and all thy house into the Ark," and the appeal at the close of the address was one of the most impressive yet delivered. A very large inquirers' meeting was held at the conclusion of this service, it being computed that nearly four hundred remained.

It was in view of the facts thus reported, and patent, that anticipating the visit to London, the *Daily Telegraph* contained the following language:

"People in the metropolis will soon judge for themselves how far the provinces have been justified in their emotion at the revivalists from across the Atlantic. It takes a great deal to move Londoners in any such manner, and many here will abruptly dispose of the whole business by the familiar phrase, 'religious hysteria.' This success, however, appears rather too complex, and we may add, socially useful, to be explained so easily by the phrases of mad-doctors, materialists, or cynics. Wherever those people come, they seem to effect at once that which archbishops and rural deans and curates from the Universities cannot do: they 'convince people of sin;' they wake hundreds of thousands of hearts to the consideration of 'righteousness, temperance, and judgment to come.' Unless, then, we are to call all religious feeling hysteria and mania; unless St. Paul preaching on Mars' Hill, and Dr. Vaughan in the Temple, are equally appealing to the excitable nervous systems of automata, we cannot clearly see why the churches should be scandalized at the work done by the two revivalists. It rather seems to us, that when Moody and Sankey come to London, the dignitaries and ministers of all the churches would do well to go and see what amazing things real genius and unselfish ardor can accomplish, even in the present age. They will hear, people say, some 'pieces' spoken about this life and the next, which, delivered with a nasal twang or not, go to the souls of people straighter than any sermon bought in Paternoster Row. They will see—if London reproduces what Dublin and Liverpool have witnessed—congregations stirred with the 'old story,' told newly, as the seas are raised by storm-winds. And, notwithstanding all the easy talk about hysteria, epidemics, magnetism, nervous systems and the like, the philosophers and divines have yet to explain to us why it is a bad thing for these Yankee itinerants to turn people by the thousand to right and virtuous lives, and a good thing when a bishop or a cardinal manages to convert half a dozen."

On the termination of the Liverpool meetings the evangelists proceeded to London, and we are obliged to content ourselves with some notice of their opening meetings. It is with satisfaction we notice the friends who stood by them at the beginning, now that they have been given such a hold on the attention of the people that while we write this statement (April 19th), the most exalted personages in the land are among their hearers.

The first of the series of noonday meetings at Exeter Hall was held on Tuesday, March 9th. Lord Radstock was in the chair, and there were present Lord Cavan, Admiral Fishbourne, Samuel Morley, M.P., Revs. Newman Hall, Donald Fraser, etc. The meeting was opened with prayer by Lord Radstock.

Rev. Mr. Chapman, Episcopal clergyman, read

2 Samuel, chap. v. 22 to the end. He said: "The tidings we have heard from Scotland, Ireland, and many of our largest towns, also the spirit of expectation in London, all lead us to inquire—Is it not true that the Lord has gone before us?"

Lord Radstock said—"It will now be open to any brother to lead us in prayer. But as our time is short, the prayers must be short and very definite. Let us ask for a distinct blessing, and look for a distinct answer. Do not let the requests be clouded by many words. There might be time for ten brethren to lead us in prayer in these seventeen remaining minutes, if they will only pray to the point. Let us pray distinctly, so as to be heard; but let us remember that we are not speaking to the meeting, but speaking to God, and that we are responsible for what we say."

Five or six gentlemen then engaged in prayer, and a hymn having been sung, Lord Radstock offered up an earnest prayer, after which the doxology having been sung, the meeting separated.

The next day Messrs. Moody and Sankey were present, as were also the Earl of Cavan, Admiral Fishbourne, Captain Moreton, R.N., R. Paton, Esq., Rev.

Dr. Cumming, and a number of eminent clergymen and ministers.

The proceedings were opened by singing the hymn, "Sweet Hour of Prayer." The requests for prayer were then read by Rev. Mr. Chapman, Episcopal clergyman of Lock Chapel.

Mr. Moody then said—" I wish to call attention to a verse in the 22d chapter of Jeremiah. This verse we have taken as our watchword in every town we have visited for the last twenty months, 'There is nothing too hard for the Lord.' God would have us remember, as we come day by day, bringing these requests before the Lord, that nothing is too hard for Him. Let us lift our eyes to Him, remembering that all power is given to Him in heaven and on earth. There is nothing too hard for the Lord. He can save the greatest drunkard, or the greatest blasphemer, as easily as I can turn my hand. God is challenging the Christians of London to call upon Him. He delights to do great things. Nothing pleases Him so well as for us to ask for great things. Let us, then, boldly ask for a mighty blessing on London. It is to talk to God that we have met to-day; let us be full of faith in the power of Christ.

We may learn from the story of the Shunammite woman, that we are not to be content with the presence of a servant; we must have the Master himself, 'As the Lord liveth, I will not go without *thee*.' His presence must accompany us, if we are to labor successfully in His service."

The first meeting in the Agricultural Hall is thus described:

"For a week past or more the Agricultural Hall has been in course of preparation for their visit, and it was computed that the arrangements would afford accommodation for about fifteen thousand persons. By the hour appointed for the commencement of proceedings every part of this vast space was densely packed, and a crowd outside were knocking at the doors and clamoring for admission.

"It is said that soon after four in the afternoon applicants for admission were on the spot with little bundles of bread and butter and bottles of cold tea, awaiting the commencement of operations at half-past seven. With the opening of the doors at six o'clock people passed in by hundreds, and the interior of the vast building, with its huge circles of gas-jets, its crimson platform, and the throngs flocking into it, presented a very pretty and animated scene, the placards at the entrance requesting the people to take their seats quietly, and not to engage in conversation, being very generally overlooked or disregarded.

"After the evangelists had arrived, Mr. Moody called upon the audience to rise and join in singing the Old Hundredth Psalm, praising God for what He was going to do in London. The grand old tune was sung accordingly, and a mighty and impressive volume of sound it was. The Rev. R. C. Billings offered up a prayer. Another hymn was sung. And then Mr. Moody requested the audience to engage in silent devotion. A concourse of fourteen or fifteen thousand people bowing the head in silence, broken only by an occasional cough, and all presumably animated by a devotional spirit, is rather a solemnizing spectacle; and there were, perhaps, few present who were incapable of understanding the feelings of the man whose voice, when he next spoke, became, after a few sentences, broken and tremulous. It was only for a moment, however, and he finished his prayer in his characteristic tone of energy and earnestness, and then called on Mr. Sankey for his contribution to the service, which it was quite evident was awaited with intense eagerness."

It will be interesting to note the arrangements for the accommodation of the vast multitude thus meeting daily in the hall. In the body of the hall twelve thousand new chairs have been placed, to reinforce two thousand already belonging to the establishment, in addition to room for two thousand on forms. The platform at the west end is arranged in steps, that will seat twelve hundred persons. In the center of the north side is the platform for the choir organized by Mr. Joseph Proudman, of the Tonic Sol-fa Association, and for Messrs. Moody and Sankey. The accommodation here is for two hundred and twenty. The eastern platform is fitted with nine hundred seats, and in the south gallery are three thousand chairs. The addition gives a total of twenty-one thousand three hundred and twenty, not including the west and east end galleries, each capable of containing six hundred more. The lighting of the hall is effected by means of large gas chandeliers, hanging from the roof, aided by lines of gas-jets along the sides, straight, save at the centers, where they rise in three semi-circular arches. The acoustic properties of the hall are greatly aided by an immense sounding-board over the speakers' platform. Mr. A. O. Charles, of the Home for

Little Boys, is acting as manager at the hall, assisted by a number of stewards, known by their wands.

The perfect order which is maintained throughout the services speaks well for the completeness of the organization, and is very helpful both to the comfort and success of the meetings.

There and in other places—as it is deemed desirable to reach the people—the meetings proceed with undiminished interest and power. May the Lord, who has been with these brethren hitherto, pour out showers of blessings over London!

CHAPTER VIII.

PRESENT CONDITION OF THE CITIES VISITED.

IN bringing to a close this record of one of the most remarkable religious movements of modern times—a movement we are thankful to feel not of the past, but still in progress—never we hope to be at an end, we can readily anticipate the question from our readers: How is it in those places where the charm of Mr. Sankey's singing and the forceful eloquence of Mr. Moody are no longer felt? The question is natural and reasonable. Ireland is commonly supposed to have a mercurial and excitable population. There, if anywhere the decline of interest might be expected to show itself. But it has not. From the *Witness* (issued in Belfast) of February 5, we make the following extract. It will be remembered that the evangelists had quitted Ireland in the end of November. We ought to add further that the places reported on, in Belfast, are towns of from five to ten thousand inhabitants throughout the province of

Ulster, and that they were never visited by the evangelists :

"At the noon prayer-meeting, many very cheering reports were given. The Rev. Hugh Hanna, who presided, said that on last Sabbath the communion was dispensed in his church, when sixty-two came forward for the first time. Seven of these were policemen. He also told of a warehouse in town where fifteen of the young women employed have been converted, and are now laboring for the good of others. He was glad to see on every side tokens of a continuance of God's presence and power. A layman described a cottage meeting in which he was interested, which had now gone on for four weeks, and which was crowded nightly with people who were deeply moved, and largely profited by the services. The Rev. William Park said he was sure the meeting would be glad to hear that the good work was progressing in Monaghan. The First Presbyterian Church was so crowded at the special meetings there, that forms had to be placed in the aisles. Inquiry meetings were also held with good results. A stranger next spoke of what is being done at Dromara. Very large and successful meetings are being held here, with sometimes as many as one hundred inquirers remaining at the close. In Lisburn, also, he said, the good work continues, and has now taken a very practical turn—new efforts being made to bring in the neglected and instruct them. Mr. Mullan said that in Portadown they were now in the eleventh week of special nightly meetings. The usual attendance at these was from three hundred to seven hundred, and it was computed that up to the present time three hundred persons have been turned from the error of their ways since the movement began in the town. Special efforts were also being made to bring in the neglected. The town is now divided into thirty-three districts for the purposes of visitation, and this work is being regularly and systematically prosecuted. Rev. R. C. Johnston said he had recently been in Gilford, and he was glad to say the good work had commenced there. A "mission" had recently been held in the Episcopal church with gratifying results — sometimes one hundred inquirers remaining at the close of a meeting.

"During the past fortnight seven special evangelistic services have been held in the Presbyterian church, Greyabbey. The attendance ranged from three hundred to four hundred and upwards each evening, and included a large number of non-churchgoers in working dress. The Rev. Robert Jeffrey was generously assisted by the Rev. Oliver Goldsmith, incumbent of Greyabbey; Rev. S. Hawthorne, Rev. J. K. Elliott, Rev. M. Macaulay, and Mr. Jones, of Belfast.

"The work of grace in the old primatial city of Armagh* has attained to dimensions that are indeed marvelous. The meetings commenced with the New Year, but during the first week they were separate— one meeting being held in the Lecture-room connected with the First Presbyterian church, and another in the Methodist church. In the second week of January the union meetings commenced, and though the meetings have continued every night during the whole of January, and throughout the present week of February, there is no flagging of interest. On last Saturday night, it was computed that there were nearly one thousand people in the Presbyterian church, and nearly two hundred anxious souls in the Methodist church, afterwards inquiring

---

* One of the editors of this volume having been for nearly six years pastor of the First Presbyterian Church in Armagh, he makes this extract with no common gratitude to God.

the way of salvation. It would be presumptuous to attempt to make an accurate census of the souls that have been brought to Christ through the power of the Word and Spirit of God; but keeping within the limits of sober calculation, it may be affirmed that there are over one hundred souls that have been changed from darkness to light, and from the power of Satan to God. A most intelligent person, who knows the city well, said to the writer of this brief report to-day —" The ministers don't know anything like the extent of this movement, or how many are seeking the way of peace, and how many in this city have found Christ to be precious."

"The united evangelistic services that were commenced in Cookstown, on the first week in January, have been continued with increased interest and attention up to the present time. Latterly, a large number of Christian laymen, of different denominations, have cordially united with the ministers in giving short addresses, and leading in devotional exercises. A large, influential meeting of Christian workers was held, when it was resolved to visit the town, distribute tracts, and invite all to the meetings. This plan has been followed with marked success in bringing out many who attend no place of worship."

From Dublin, at the same date (February 5), it is reported:

"Our daily prayer-meeting has been carried on as usual. The encouraging signs about it, which I mentioned last week, have been still more marked since then. And while none of the spirit of heartiness has departed, the numbers attending are steadily increasing. It is evident that the hour of prayer is a time of much enjoyment to many, and we may reasonably hope of profit.

"The accounts given in on Monday of the progress of the Lord's work during the previous week were truly cheering and encouraging. One minister said that Sabbath evening last was the most blessed season he had had in his congregation since he came to Dublin. Another said that in his church between three and four hundred people waited till half-past 10 o'clock in the inquiry-meeting, which was held after the evening service, and they had had most delightful tokens of God's presence. Another minister said that in one of the Sabbath-schools connected with his congregation, attended by about one hundred scholars, sixty of the pupils have lately professed to have found their Saviour. And many of these are very rough and wild boys and girls. A gentleman present said he had been invited by the principal of one of the large educational establishments in the city to visit her school. He went, and he found that out of seventy young ladies twenty-five have professedly, within the last three months, given themselves to God.

"The reports of the work going on in the suburbs of Dublin, and also in more distant parts of the county, were equally encouraging. At the little village of Lucan, in the neighborhood of the city, where united evangelistic services have been held nightly for the last fortnight, the most blessed indications of the Spirit are seen. The meeting on Sabbath night was the most crowded of any, though it was not known till a short time before the service that any meeting was to be held that night. Not a night has passed since the meetings began there in which souls have not been born again. There, as in other places, the fields are white to the harvest, and the people in the neighborhood are very sorry that the services cannot be continued.

"Very interesting accounts also were given of the progress of the work in other parts of our land. In the County Wicklow many are being brought to God from week to week, while in more remote districts many others are being awakened and converted. In Galway the Protestant community is moved to the very center, and some of a different persuasion have been brought to read the Book of Life. In another western town the effect among our fellow countrymen, who in matters of faith do not see with us, has been so great that their spiritual directors, alarmed, sent for the Redemptorist Fathers to counteract the movement. Special reports from these and other places were read by the Rev. Mr. Mullan from *Plain Words* for this month. A very striking incident was related by a gentleman of a town with which he was acquainted. A committee there having charge of the prayer-meeting and united services, etc., had engaged the court-house to hold their meetings in, but a party of play-actors came and secured the house for themselves by paying more money. Their speculation, however, was not successful, for while the prayer and other meetings were thronged with thousands, the audience who patronized the play on the first evening numbered *six* persons, and on the second evening *two!*"

If it be asked how, after a year's experience, is the

work now regarded in Scotland, the following paragraph affords the reply:

"Monday being the anniversary of the commencement of Messrs. Moody and Sankey's labors in Glasgow, an all-day meeting was held in Ewing Place Church. The meeting was in every respect successful, the church being crowded from the beginning to the close of the proceedings. The subject for the first hour—from twelve to one—was introduced by Dr. A. Thompson, of Edinburgh, who delivered an appropriate address on 'Prayer;' various other gentlemen also took part. Dr. A. Bonar took the chair from one to two, and opened up the subject of 'Praise,' which was afterwards spoken of in an interesting and instructive manner by several ministers and laymen present. In taking up the subject for the third hour, namely: 'What more can be done for the lapsed masses?' the Rev. Wm. Arnot presided. At the close it was unanimously resolved to send a telegram to Messrs. Moody and Sankey, expressive of gratitude for the work they did while in Glasgow, and assuring them of continued and prayerful interest in their welfare. In the evening a fellowship meeting was held, when the church was again crowded."

CHAPTER IX.

THE TRUTHS TAUGHT.

WHAT does Mr. Moody preach? This is a natural question. We shall furnish an answer by allowing him to speak for himself, and giving specimens of his addresses on practical topics, as reported with care and fidelity in such organs as *The British Evangelist*, *Times of Blessing*, etc.

THE QUALIFICATIONS FOR SOUL-WINNING.*
Dan. xii. 3.

If we would be soul-winners, we must—

1. Shake off the vipers that are in the Church, formalism, pride, and self-importance, etc.

2. It is the only happy life to live for the salvation of souls.

3. We must be willing to do little things for Christ.

4. Must be of good courage.

5. Must be cheerful.

God had no children too weak, but a great many

---

* Delivered in Rev. Dr. Bonar's church, Edinburgh, 7th December, 1873.

too strong to make use of. God, he continued, stands in no need of our strength or wisdom, but of our ignorance, of our weakness; let us but give these to Him, and He can make use of us in winning souls.

Now we all want to shine; the mother wishes it for her boy, when she sends him to school, the father for his lad, when he goes off to college; and here God tells us who are to shine—not statesmen, or warriors, or such like, that shine but for a season—but such as will shine for ever and ever; those, namely, who win souls to Christ; the little boy even who persuades one to come to Christ.

Speaking of this, Paul counts up five things that God makes use of—the weak things, the foolish things, the base things, the despised things, and the things which are not, and for this purpose, that no flesh might glory in his sight—all five being just such as we should despise. He can and will use us, just when we are willing to be humble for Christ's sake, and so for six thousand years God has been teaching men; so with an ass's jawbone Samson slew his thousands, so at the blowing of rams' horns the walls of Jericho fell. Let God work in His own way, and with His own instruments; let us all rejoice that He should, and let us too get into the position in which God can use us.

There is much mourning to-day over false "isms," infidelity, and the like, but sum them all up, and I do not fear them one half so much as that dead and cold formalism that has crept into the Church of God. The unbelieving world, and these skeptics holding out their false lights, are watching you and me: when Jacob put away his idols, he could go up to Bethel and get strength and the blessing—so will it be with the Church of God. A viper fixes upon the hand of the shipwrecked Paul; immediately he is judged by the barbarians some criminal unfit to live; but he shakes it off into the fire, and suffers no harm, and now they are ready to worship him, and ready too to hear and receive his message: the Church of God must shake off the vipers that have fastened on hand and heart too, ere men will hear. Where one ungodly man reads this Bible, a hundred read you and me: and if they find nothing in us, they set the whole thing aside as a myth.

Again, a man who has found out what his true work is, winning souls to Christ, and does it, such is the happiest man. Not the richest are this—least of all those who have just got converted for themselves, and into the Church—lost what pleasure the world could give, and found none other. Job's captivity turned away when he began praying for his friends; and so will all who thus work for others shine not in heaven alone and hereafter, but here as well, and now.

But you say "I haven't got the ability." Well, God doesn't call you to do Dr. Bonar's work, or Dr. Duff's work, else He had given you their ability, their talent. The word is, "To every man HIS work." I have a work to do, laid out for me in the secret counsels of eternity; no other can do it. If I neglect it, it is not true that some other will do it; it will remain undone. And if, for the work laid upon us, we feel we have not the ability or talent necessary, then we have a throne of grace; and God never sends, unless that He is willing to give the strength and wisdom. The instruments He often uses may seem all unlikely, yet when did they fail?—when once? and why not? Because He had fitted them out as well. He sent Moses to Egypt to deliver His people —not an eloquent, but a stuttering man. He refuses a while, at last he went; and no man once sent by God ever did break down. So was Elisha a most unlikely man to be a successor to the great prophet Elijah. Men would have chosen some famous man, some professor in the school of the prophets. God took one from the plough; but He gave him what was needed. Elisha had but to *keep by* his master to the end; and he received even a double portion of the Spirit. And if we want to get it, we too must keep by the Lord, nor ever lose sight of Him, should He, as Elijah Elisha, in one way or another try our faith.

And further, we must be ready to *do little things* for God; many are willing to do the great things. I dare say hundreds would have been ready to occupy this pulpit to-day. How many of them would be as willing to teach a dirty class in the ragged school?

I remember, one afternoon I was preaching, observing a young lady from the house I was staying at, in the audience. I had heard she taught in the Sabbath-school, which I knew was at the same hour; and so I asked her, after service, how she came to be there? "Oh," said she, "my class is but five little boys, and I thought it did not matter for them." And yet among these there might have been, who knows, a Luther or a Knox, the beginning of a stream of blessing, that would have gone on widening and ever widening; and besides, one soul is worth all the kingdoms of the earth.

Away in America, a young lady was sent to a boarding-school, and was there led to Christ; not only so, but taught that she ought to work for Him. By-and-by she goes home, and now she seeks, in one way and another, to work for Him, but without finding how. She asks for a class in her church Sunday-school, but the superintendent is obliged to tell her that he has already more than enough of teachers. One day, going along the street, she sees a little boy struck by his companion, and crying bitterly. She goes up and speaks to him; asks him what the trouble is? The boy thinks she is mocking him, and replies sullenly. She speaks kindly, tries to persuade him to school. He does not want to learn. She coaxes him to come and hear her and the rest singing there; and so next Sunday he comes with her. She gets a corner in the school of well-dressed scholars for herself and her charge. He sits and listens, full of wonder. On going home, he tells his mother he has been among the angels. At first at a loss, she becomes angry, when a question or two brings out that he has been to a Protestant Sunday-school; and the father, on coming home, forbids his going back, on pain of flogging. Next Sunday, however, he goes, and is flogged, and so again, and yet again, till one Sunday, he begs to be flogged before going, that he may not be kept thinking of it all the time. The father relents a little, and promises him a holiday every Saturday afternoon, if he will not go to Sunday-school. The lad agrees, sees his teacher, who offers to teach him then. How many wealthy young folks would give up their Saturdays to train one poor ragged urchin in the way of salvation? Some time after, at his work, the lad is on one of the railway cars. The train starts suddenly; he slips through, and the wheels pass over his legs; he asks the doctor if he will live to get home; it is impossible. "Then," says he, "tell father and mother that I am going to heaven, and want to meet them there." Will the work she did seem little now to the young lady? Or is it nothing that even one thus grateful waits her yonder?

Another thing we want is, to be *of good courage.* Three or four times this comes out in the first chapter of Joshua; and I have observed that God never uses a man that is always looking on the dark side of things: what we do for Him let us do cheerfully, not because it is our duty—not that we should sweep away the word but because it is our privilege. What would my wife or children say if I spoke of loving them because it was my *duty* to do so? And my mother —if I go to see her once a year, and were to say— "Mother, I am come all this way to discharge what I feel to be my duty in visiting you;" might she not rightly reply—" My son, if this is all that has brought you, you might have spared coming at all!" and go down in broken-hearted sorrow to the grave?

A London minister, a friend of mine, lately pointed out a family of seven, all of whom he was just receiving into the Church. Their story was this: going to church, he had to pass by a window, looking up at which one day, he saw a baby looking out; he smiled —the baby smiled again. Next time he passes he looks up again, smiles, and the baby smiles back. A third time going by, he looks up, and seeing the baby, throws it a kiss—which the baby returns to him. Time after time he has to pass the window, and now cannot refrain from looking up each time: and each time there are more faces to receive his smiling greeting; till by-and-by he sees the whole family grouped at the window—father, mother, and all.

The father conjectures the happy, smiling stranger must be a minister, and so, next Sunday morning, after they have received at the window the usual greeting, two of the children, ready dressed, are sent out to follow him : they enter his church, hear him preach, and carry back to their parents the report that they never heard such preaching ; and what preaching could equal that of one who had so smiled on them ? Soon the rest come to the church too, and are brought in—all by a smile. Let us not go about, hanging our heads like a bulrush ; if Christ gives joy, let us live it! The whole world is in all matters for the very best thing—you always want to get the best possible thing for your money ; let us show, then, that our religion is the very best thing: men with long, gloomy faces are never wise in the winning of souls.

I was preaching in Jacksonville, and, at the house in which I stayed, my attention was attracted by a little boy, who bore a different name from the household, and yet was in all things and in all respects treated as one of themselves ; to the other children he was "brother," and they were "brothers" and "sisters" to him, and with them he came up to the mother for the same good-night kiss. By-and-by I

asked the lady of the house who it was. She told me
the father of the boy was a missionary out in India;
some years before, father and mother had come home
with their five children to have them educated. After
being home a short time, the father resolved to
return to India, wishing to leave the mother with the
children till their education should be finished. She
wanted to go back with him; he opposed to it, saying
it was hard enough for him to leave them, for her it
must be impossible. Still she wished to go,—she had
received and been some blessing in India,—and she
would give up even all for Christ. Ultimately it was
arranged that the children should be received into
various families,—treated as part of them,—and that
father and mother together should return. So with
the boy the mother came to this friend's and stayed a
few days along with him. The night before she had
to leave, sitting with the lady of the house, she told
her how anxious she was that her boy should receive
the impression that his mother had for Christ's sake
cheerfully left him behind, and that for this end she
wished to leave him without a tear at parting. The
struggle this would cost the lady well knew, especially
as the boy was of a peculiarly amiable disposition.

Next morning, passing the door of the mother's room, the lady overheard a sobbing, struggling prayer for strength to do what was on her heart to do. In a short time the mother came down with smiling, cheerful face; and looking so, she took leave of her boy, to go by rail some miles further on to bid a like farewell to another of her family. She went with her husband to India. A short year after, a still, quiet voice came to her, to come up to meet her Saviour. And would not a welcome await her there, who had so loved Him here, and so cheerfully served Him?

They that be wise shall shine, etc. The Lord help us as humbly, devoutly, and cheerfully to abound in His work!

The Lord's Workers.*

WHAT men want in doing the Lord's work is (1) *Courage*, (2) *Enthusiasm*, (3) *Perseverance*, (4) *Sympathy*.

The man who is afraid, who holds down his head like a bulrush, is not the worker whom God will

---

* Delivered to young men in Edinburgh, 14th Dec., 1873.

bless; but God gives courage to him whom He means to use. I have been all along with young men, and a great portion of my work these fifteen years has been among them, and I find that they generally fail for want of courage. There is any quantity of young men in Edinburgh just now whose lives are a blank to them, and who have not discovered that God sends us to do work for Him. He can qualify them for that work. John Wesley said, " Give me thirty men of faith, and I shall storm the citadel of Satan and win it for Christ;" and he did it too. Talk of Alexander being a great conqueror, he was nothing compared with that little man, Saul of Tarsus. Once I had been fishing long, and caught nothing, and I almost got discouraged. My Sabbath services were barren one day, and I was greatly disheartened. My heart was down, and my head was down. In came a brother. "How does the work go on with you?" I asked of a fellow-worker. "Splendidly," he said. " Great blessing on Sabbath." I told him my state of mind. He said, " Did you ever study the life and character of Noah?" "Yes; I know it by heart." "Well," said he, " study it again." And I did so, and I found in him wonderful courage. For one hundred and twenty years that the ark was building, he labored to get men to believe in God's righteousness. He did not get one, and I said, "What have I to be discouraged about after that?" So I went down to the prayer-meeting, and a man behind me clasped me by the hand, and said, "Pray for me, for I am in great trouble." And I thought what would Noah have given for encouragement like that! And a man rose up, and told that a hundred young men had just come to Christ in a neighboring town. What would old Noah have said to that? One hundred and twenty years, and no fruit at all; and yet he had courage to go on preaching! All at once the clouds were all gone from my mind. If you get discouraged, keep it to yourself; don't tell any one about it; for you will just discourage others if you do. Be strong and very courageous if you would do anything for God.

2. *Enthusiasm.*—We need more enthusiasm. The more we have the better. I have a great admiration for Garibaldi, though I cannot, of course, approve of all his acts. When put in prison he said, "It were better that fifty Garibaldis should perish, than that Rome should not be free." This was the cause get-

ting above the man; that is what we want. We want to forget ourselves. There are one hundred thousand men waiting now to be brought to Christ, to be invited to come to Him, and shall we hang back? Let us have enthusiasm. This formalism that abounds at the present day, is the worst ism of all—it is worse than all the infidelity and skepticism of the land. I remember reading in some history of the ninth century of a young general who with only five hundred men came up against a king with twenty thousand. And the king sent to him to say that it was the height of folly to resist with his handful of men. The general called in one of his men, and said, "Take that sword and drive it to your heart." And the man took the weapon, and drove it to his heart, and fell dead. He said to another, "Leap into yonder chasm," and the man instantly obeyed. Then, turning to the messenger, he said, "Go back and tell your king that we have five hundred such men. We will die but we will never surrender." The messenger returned, and his tale struck terror into the hearts of the king's soldiers, so that they fled like chaff before the wind. God says, "One shall chase a thousand, and two put ten thousand to flight." Let us have confidence in God. When men are in earnest they carry everything before them. The world don't read the Bible, but they read you and me.

3. *Perseverance.*—The men who have been successful are not those who work by fits and starts, but three hundred and sixty-five days in the year. By the grace of God, these eighteen years I have been kept working for God. People complain how cold other people are: that is a sign that they are cold themselves. Keep your own heart warm, as if there were no other but you in the world. Keep working all the time at steady, constant work. For the last eleven years I have not let a day pass without saying something to somebody of Christ. Make it a rule that never a day pass without speaking for Christ. People won't like it. If you are a living witness for Christ it makes people mad against you. You will suffer persecution, and be spoken against, and yet they will send for such a man first when they are in trouble or on their death-bed. The man that is popular with the world is not a friend of Jesus. You cannot serve two masters. The world hates Christ, and if you are a friend of the world you cannot be a friend of His. You may be sure that something

is wrong with you when everybody is your friend. Every man here can win souls for Christ.

The public-houses in America are called "saloons." There is a hall with a bar, and behind, a dining-room, and above, sleeping-apartments, and in these saloons the young men congregate at night, and drink and gamble. There was a terribly wicked man who kept a saloon, whose children I was very anxious to draw to my Sabbath-school. So one day I called on this man and said, "Mr. Bell, I want you to let your children come to the Sabbath-school." He was terribly angry, said he did not believe in the Bible, school or anything else, and ordered me to leave the house.

Soon after I went down again and called on this man, and asked him to go to church, and again he was very angry. He said that he had not been at church for nineteen years, and would never go again, and he would rather see his boy a drunkard and his daughter a harlot than that they should attend the Sabbath-school. A second time I was forced to leave the house.

Two or three days after I called again, and he said, "Well, I guess you are a pretty good-natured sort of man, and different from the rest of Christians, or you would not come back;" so seeing him in a good humor, I asked him what he had to say against Christ, and if he had read His life: and he asked me what I had to say against Paine's "Age of Reason," and if I had read it. I said I had not read it: whereupon he said he would read the New Testament, if I would read the "Age of Reason," to which I at once agreed, though he had the best bargain: and I did so. I did not like it much, and would not advise any person to read it. I asked Mr. Bell to come to church, but he said they were all hypocrites that went to church. This he would do, however: I might come to his house if I liked, and preach. "Here, in this saloon?" "Yes! but look here, you are not to do all the talking;" he said that he and his friends would have their say as well as I. I agreed that they might have the first forty-five minutes, and I the last fifteen of the hour, which he thought fair, and that was settled. The day came, and I went to keep my appointment, but I never in all my life met such a crowd as when on the day appointed I went to that saloon—such a collection of infidels, deists, and reprobates of all kinds I never saw before. Their oaths and language were horrible. Some of them seemed as if they had come on leave of absence from the pit. I never was so near hell before. They began to talk in the most blasphemous way; some thought one thing, some another; some believed there was a God—others not; some thought there was such a man as Jesus Christ—others that there never was; some didn't believe anything. They couldn't agree, contradicted each other, and very nearly came to fighting with one another before their time had expired.

I had brought down a little boy, an orphan with me, and when I saw and heard such blasphemy I thought I had done wrong to bring him there. When their time was up, I said that we Christians always began service with prayer to God. "Hold," said they; "two must be agreed first." "Well, here are two of us." And so I prayed, and then the little boy did so, and I never heard a prayer like that in all my life. It seemed as if God was speaking through that little boy. With tears running down his cheeks he besought God, for Christ's sake, to take pity on all these poor men; and that went to their very hearts. I heard sobs throughout the hall, and one infidel went out at this door and another at that; and Mr. Bell came up to me and said, " You can have my children, Mr. Moody." And the best friend that I have in Chicago to-day is that same Joshua Bell, and his son has come out for Christ and as a worker for Him.

There was a family which for fourteen years I had tried to draw to Christ, but they would not come, and I had almost given them up as hopeless. We have a custom on New Year's Day in America of calling on our friends and acquaintances, and wishing them the compliments of the season. Last New Year's Day I thought I should call on the old doctor, which I did, and I offered up just a short prayer. That week he and his wife came to Christ, and next week his son, and a few days after his daughter, and now the whole family are converted.

"*This one thing I do*," said Paul. He had received thirty-nine stripes, and if he had other thirty-nine stripes to receive, " *This one thing I do ;* " forgetting the things that "are behind, I press towards the mark." A terrible man he was—this man of one thing and one aim, and determined to go on doing it. " To every man *his* work " (Mark xiii. 34). If blessing don't come this week, it will come the next, only persevere. Be of good courage, Christ will strengthen your heart.

4. *Sympathy* to touch the hearts of men is needed too. Some men have courage, perseverance, and zeal, but their hearts are as cold as an icicle. Christ might have been born in a palace had He chosen, but poor men would have said He had not come for them; but He was born in a manger, lower than their own rank of life. The minister who speaks to people as if he were separate from them, that tells them what *they* should do, this and that, will not carry them with him. To speak to men from a higher platform is not the way to do them good. It should be what *we do*,—we poor sinners, and you. The milk of human kindness is a great element in bringing souls to Christ.

We have, in Chicago, a meeting for strangers; and it is most blessed. Every Monday night, seventy-five to a hundred young men newly arrived in the city, assemble to find friends. A young man coming from the country to a situation, or to college in town, feels very lonely. He walks the street, and has no one, of all the crowds, to speak to him, and he is miserable.

That is the time when his heart is softest; then, if any one speaks to him or shows him acts of kindness, he never forgets it. The devil watches for friendless youths like those; and the ensnaring paths of vice seem refuges from loneliness. Such a young man, walking along the street, sees a big brown paper pasted on a boarding, or at a railway station, or somewhere else, having painted on it, "Strangers' Meeting to-night. All strangers invited to attend." So he goes, and meets a kind look and words of friendship, and it is better to him than anything in the world.

During our war, there was a Southern man who came over to a Wisconsin regiment, saying he could not fight to uphold slavery. Some time after, the mail from the north came in, and all the men got letters from their relations, and universal joy prevailed. This Southern man said he wished he were dead; he was most unhappy, for there were no letters for him. His mother was dead, and his father and brothers would have shot him if they could, for going against them. This man's tent-mate was very sorry for his friend, and when he wrote to his mother in Wisconsin, he just told her all about it. His mother sat down and wrote to her son's friend. She called him her son, and spoke to him like a mother. She told him, when the war was over that he must come to her, and that her home would be his. When the letter reached the regiment, the chaplain took it down to where this man was standing, and told him it was for him; but he said it was a mistake, that nobody would write to him; he had no friends, it must be for some one else. He was persuaded to open it, and when he read it, he felt such joy. He went down the lines, saying, "*I've got a mother!*" When afterwards the regiment was disbanded, and the men were returning to their homes, there was none who showed so much anxiety as this man to get to his mother in Wisconsin.

There are hundreds of young men who want mothers, and any kindness done to them will not lose its reward.*

---

* The intensity of the feeling under the burning words of Mr. Moody may be judged of from the effect being such that, at the close, there was a great burst of applause with hands and feet just commencing, when Mr. Moody checked it, by quietly lifting his hand and saying, "We don't want applause : *and mind, it's Sunday!*"

THE BLOOD.*

"Some inquirers come to me over and over again, and never seem to get on, but go round and round like a horse in a mill. They don't rest where God rests—in the blood of Christ. Blood runs throughout the whole Bible. Turn with me to Gen. iii. 21. No sooner had Adam fallen, and death entered, than God interposed, and made coats of skins and clothed them. God then must have been the first to shed blood; God covered sin; God dealt in love with Adam, in justice with Christ, when the blood of those victims slain came between Adam and his sin. Turn again to Gen. iv. 4. Abel brought blood. Cain's offering was more beautiful—the fruit of the ground. You may say blood is repulsive, hateful; some women faint at the sight of blood, but by blood was the way God marked out for coming to Him, from the very first, and Abel came by that way, and was accepted. Any religion that is not founded on 'the *blood*,' comes from the pit of hell. There is no other foundation, any other is not God's way. The world is

---

* Delivered in the Free Church Assembly Hall, Edinburgh, 9th December, 1873.

full of Cainites. All who think they do not need the blood of Christ are Cainites.

"Gen. viii. 20, 21. Sixteen hundred years passed away. God saved Noah by the ark, and when he left it he offered the *blood* of every clean beast and fowl on the altar. The second dispensation was founded on blood; it came between Noah and his sin. The world was set up afresh under Noah, but it began from the blood.

"Gen. xxii. 13. Abraham saw Christ's day, and was glad. God opened his eyes probably on that very Mount Moriah, after the sacrifice of the ram was over; and he saw down the stream of time the great Atonement, likely the identical spot, for Mount Calvary was near Mount Moriah, where Christ was to be offered. God so loved Abraham that He spared him his son; but He so loved you that He gave His for you. John said, 'Behold the Lamb of God that taketh away the sin of the world.' Abraham was glad when he saw the substitutionary offering of Christ. All went in all ages to heaven by the royal highway of the blood.

"Exodus xii. 13. 'When I see the blood I will pass over you.' He does not say, When I see the live lamb tied up to the door-post, I will pass over you. No more does He say, When I see the living Christ in all His moral glory and loveliness, scattering blessings all around His path, I will pass over you; but when I see the blood, 'for without shedding of blood is no remission.' Sinner, Christ has shed His blood for you. You will have peace looking to His blood; you will be safe there, or you will be exposed to the wrath of God without it. When you go to the station, and take a ticket for London, and seat yourself in the train, the guard will come to look at your ticket; and it matters not to him whether you are black or white, rich or poor, so long as you have got a ticket. He looks at that, not you. The blood is God's ticket. God says, Have you got your ticket or 'token?' If you are behind the blood, you are as safe as on the golden pavement of heaven. A little sparrow was as safe in the ark as the great elephant. If you are behind the blood you are safe, though you die to-night.

"Exodus xii. 11. They were to eat the lamb, as well as be sheltered by its blood. You should not be satisfied with being safe. You should eat the lamb. God's elect fed on the lamb. The more you feed on

Him the stronger you will become. Feed on His Word; feed on Himself.

"Exodus xii. 2. 'This shall be the beginning of months to you.' Everything dates from the blood; 1873 counts back to Calvary, and begins from the blood. Even infidels date from the blood. Israel's story, for four hundred years of slavery, is wiped out. You may say you are seventy-five years old, but you didn't live till you came to Christ. I was born twice, once in '37; once again in '55; so I am only eighteen years old. Some there are here also, who are only twenty-four hours old to-night.

"Exodus xxix. 16. I was brought up to think that there was no need for the blood of Jesus, and when I knew better I went back to my native town and preached on the atonement, and after I was finished the minister of the place was very angry, and said to me that there was no more efficacy in the blood of Jesus Christ than in that of a chicken. That is Unitarianism. That doctrine is damnable. If, in prayer, you don't come to God through the Lord Jesus Christ, you may as well talk to a post. Call it prayer! It ain't. If you cut the crimson thread that binds the Bible, it falls to pieces.

"Exodus xxx. 10. The sacrifice of atonement was kept up year after year till Christ came. The work was never done. The priest in Israel never sat down. Christ was offered once, and His sacrifice was forever, thank God. Adam and Eve were in God's favor, but the devil tripped them up, and the precious blood of Jesus reconciles us to God. We are '*justified by His blood.*'

"Lev. viii. 23. The ear sheltered behind the blood heard the voice of God, and the hand behind the blood did what was pleasing to God. The unredeemed may give money and build churches, thinking that they will please God, but it is a delusion. Till they get behind the blood their offerings are an abomination to God. Blood upon the great toe denoted walking with God. God often visited men, as Adam and Abraham and others, but He never dwelt and walked with His people till blood was shed and redemption accomplished, and then the Red Sea fled as He walked with them; angels' food came to them; the rock burst with water which followed them. No man could resist them when God walked with them. And we will always be in trouble about government till Christ comes back again to reign, and then men will have a government that will suit them. He will be back again one day and set up His kingdom, but it will be founded on the blood. Your life hangs on this word. Wake up; for you'll never get to heaven unless you are floated thither on the crimson tide of Christ's precious blood.

"Lev. xvii. 11-14. Some people say they hate this subject of blood. I hated it once. I would have walked out of such a meeting if so much had been said about it as is now said. I used to say that a God who demanded blood is a tyrant. But God could not save without it. This is three times repeated. Why? God is very merciful, but He is just too. If the queen was so kind-hearted as not to punish any one, and insisted on pardoning every murderer, and setting free every prisoner, she would not be queen twenty-four hours. Every woman here would rise up and demand that she should not be queen. If you get God's mercy you get His justice too: they go together. He rides in a chariot with two wheels rolling side by side—justice and mercy. God said to Adam, 'On the day thou eatest thereof thou shalt surely die.' Adam sinned and he died. Jesus was man's substitute, and He died for man, for God's justice demanded man's life, or a substitute for him. If you take out the blood from my Bible you may have all the rest.

"1 Peter ii. 24. Who is a substitute for you? Adam sold out cheap in Eden; don't God say ye shall be redeemed without money (1 Pet. i. 18, 19). If gold could have redeemed the world, God would have created a thousand worlds rather than take the brightest jewel in the diadem of heaven, but God demanded life alone, and gave His Son. Consider that God gave the blood of His Son, and you don't care for it, hate it! If you are behind the blood it cries for pardon and gives peace—if you are not, it cries for damnation! 'Let His blood be on us and on our children,' cried the murderers of Christ. Oh! if they had added '*to save us*,' but no, it was to condemn, for they cried, Crucify Him, Crucify Him, and it has been upon them and their children ever since, for they have had no king and no country, but are a hissing and reproach to the nations, and even the little children in America call the Jews 'Christ-killers.'

"Not long ago one thousand Jews assembled in Paris, and clapped their hands in applause of the sentiment that they had killed the Christians' God.

This was indorsing the fearful wickedness of their fathers. There will be a sad prayer-meeting one day: and those who would not have *the blood* to cover their sins, will have to call on the rocks to fall on them and cover them! Get sheltered now by the blood, if you would escape in the days of His wrath.

"He'll prevail by-and-by. The spear forced by the Roman soldier into the side of Christ was the crowning act of sin, yet blood flowed over the spear and covered it, the crowning 'act of love.' Without shedding of blood is no remission. You may say prayers, and build churches, but without the blood it is all useless. Let us look now at—

"Heb. x. 28. Died without mercy. Listen; no mercy! What will you do with the blood of God's own Son? When Jesus left this earth He took away with Him His flesh and bones, but left His blood drained out for you. What are you to do with it? The key to heaven is not prayer, as the little hymn says, but blood.

"A soldier in America was dying in the time of the war, and he was heard to say, 'Blood, blood, blood.' A clergyman, thinking that the scenes of bloodshed on the battle-field which he had recently witnessed were troubling his mind, went to him to lead his thoughts to brighter themes. 'I wasn't thinking of the battle-field,' said he, 'but of the *blood of Jesus*, which has covered all my sins.' Some make light of that blood, and have no faith in it, the only thing that would be a shelter and safety for them. The dying saint of whom brother Sankey sang, left his wife and child joyfully, and went 'sweeping through the gates into the kingdom, washed in the blood of the Lamb.' That was a victor's shout.

"How different such a departure from the coach-driver in California, who, feeling with his foot said, 'I'm on the down grade, and cannot reach the brake,' and died. Oh! shelter yourselves behind the blood of Christ Jesus, He will save every one who believes in Him."

HEAVEN.*

"I believe that heaven is real, hell is real, the devil real. God is real. If God did not wish us to speak about heaven, he would not have put so much about it in the Bible.

---

* Delivered as a Bible lecture. The report is from the notes of a hearer, and can only be regarded as "notes."

"(1.) Let us first locate heaven. Where is it? It is said in Scripture to be *above*. God went *up* from Abraham. God is a Person, has a throne, a dwelling-place (John iii. 13). The angels asked the disciples, 'Why stand ye gazing *up* into heaven?' Jesus was 'received *up*' when he went to heaven. *Down from* God's *dwelling-place* (2 Chron. vii. 14; 1 Kings viii. 30). It is a great pleasure to think that God has a *home* (Matt. vi. 9).

"(2.) But let us now think of the *company* in heaven. 1. The *Father* of grace and glory is there. We say, 'Our Father, which art in *heaven*.' A great many people are lost by that prayer. It is not the Lord's prayer, but the disciples' prayer. The Lord's prayer is the 17th chapter of St. John. Satan rocks many off in a cradle to sleep on that so-called Lord's prayer. None but a disciple of Christ can use it, and say 'Our Father.' To the unsaved, Christ said, 'Ye are of *your* father the devil.' You pray for forgiveness while your heart is full of enmity. 'Thy kingdom come.' That is praying for your own damnation, if unconverted.

"2. Jesus is now in heaven. In Acts vii. 55, 56, Stephen saw not mansions, but JESUS. Yes! the

Master is there, and the redeemed are there. Stephen saw Him at the right hand of God, and he saw Stephen being stoned on earth, and stood up to receive him. Oh! what a reception! Jesus is there! 'That same Jesus' who died for us, whose Spirit quickened us, whose love saved us; and we shall soon see him there; if not before, crowned with glory and honor.

"Acts iii. 20, 21. It is as much the Christian's duty to watch for the second coming of the Son of God from *heaven* as to work for Christ. It is perfectly safe to obey God and watch for His coming again, for it may be at any moment. The marriage-supper of the Lamb is coming, and we may be caught up for it at any time.

"Matt. xviii. 10. 3. *Angels* are there. The pure and spotless creations of God, who have known nothing of sin and sorrow and travail, who have ever lived their life of bright intelligence and holy service in the sunshine of God's presence—these are in heaven, and we shall meet them, and tell them of something they have never felt—the love of Jesus for sinful men.

"Rev. vii. 9, 10. 4. *Saints* are there, the best of earth—all the pure and holy, from righteous Abel downwards. All the old heroes of God, the warriors and kings, the prophets and the poets, the apostles and the early martyrs, all will be there, and we shall be able to hold sweet communion with them all; and our own loved ones, the fathers and mothers, sisters and brothers, the babes, and the young and the old; they will be amongst the shining band who go to swell the ranks of the redeemed before the throne of God. Oh, what a company is there—Father, Jesus, the Holy Ghost, angels, saints—all who have fallen asleep in Jesus—all waiting for us to come; and I don't mean to lose that appointment; and, if I know myself, would rather be torn limb from limb than do so (John xii. 26, xiv. 3). We have work to do to get ready ourselves, and get friends in. What would have been Noah's feelings if one of his sons had been left out of the ark!

"5. Luke x. 20. That's it! our *names* are in heaven. My name's gone on before me. 'Rejoice,' saith Jesus. There's a terrible day coming. It is going to be dark. May God bring that little Miss up there to Jesus!. There would be joy all over heaven, and her name in half a second would be written in the Lamb's book of life, and never to be blotted out again. Just as a man sends goods before him and he follows after, just so our names have gone on before, and we are journeying after them. We are known by *name* in heaven before we get there. The name of every saint is in the book of life, and cannot be blotted out again. A mother of nine children, dying in Connecticut, said to her husband, 'I charge you to bring all those children home.'

"A soldier in America was dying, and was heard to say '*Here!*' When asked what it was, he said, 'Hush, they are calling the roll in heaven, and I am answering to it;' and he cried, Here, and died.

"(3.) *What do we have in heaven?* Heaven is our *treasure-house* (Matt. vi. 20). Many Christians trouble themselves so much about heaping up treasures down here *to leave* them to their children, which is often their ruin. Lot may have Sodom, but look at the end! He was burnt out. Abraham was on the hill-top with God. If your treasure is in *heaven*, your heart will follow. The only things we have, or can have, as saints, will be found there. All else must be left. Death strips us of everything not laid up in heaven. 'Lay up treasure in heaven.' It will be found there all safe when we want it, for there neither moth nor rust doth corrupt, nor do thieves break through and steal."

"(4.) *How we may get a title to heaven* (John iii. 3). You must be born into the kingdom; there is no other way to get to *heaven*, than to be born an heir to it. Have you that birthright? God was alone in creation and in redemption. He is alone in regeneration. Have you got a home beyond the grave? Are you born of the Spirit? that's the question of the day! None but those who are born again enter there.

"2 Tim. iv. 8. Paul was striving for the crown. He got salvation here. The devil found his match when he encountered Paul. Paul, I have no doubt, thanks God to-day for that Philippian jail. The Philippian jailer was saved by his being a prisoner there, and was the first man converted by him in Europe. John Bunyan thanks God for those twelve years in Bedford jail. I dare say the devil was not fifteen minutes in Eden before he ruined man, and he would conquer me to-night before I had tea were it not that my life is hid with Christ in God. But to sufferers for Christ, he says, 'Great is your *reward in heaven.*' There, every man will receive his own reward for his own work. There will be no mixing up, no confusion, but to each man will be given a full reward, according to his own labor.

"Heb. iv. 9. People think that the Church is a place to rest in; but God commands work; and when a man's work is done, he will be told to 'come up higher.' What are we to do before we get there? Let us ask God.

"Heaven is nearer to us than people think. I have read of a man in this country who got discouraged, and dreamed that he went up to heaven, and saw the glories there; and Jesus took him to the battlements, and told him to look down, and asked what he saw. He saw the earth, and men blindfolded, and a fiend leading them to a deep pit; and Jesus asked him whether he would stay in heaven, and share its joys, or go back to earth, and lead men to see their danger and rescue them, and he said he would return, and never wish to go to heaven until God called him. He awoke, but was never discouraged again. The child of infidel parents, a girl of three years old, who had never heard the name of God but in her father's oaths, was dying, and said, "Duley's coming, God," and died.

"This conference is a foretaste of heaven; there

have been no denominations here, but all are Christians; so will we be in heaven. We will love Jesus, too, the more we know Him. I do not love my wife the less because I have been married twelve years. A lady tract-distributor wished to take a lady friend to see a bed-ridden saint. God has many stones in His temple, some for use, and some for ornament, and this was one for ornament, polished by years of suffering. They went up a stair for five stories, and at the first the friend said, 'It is very dirty here.' 'It will be better higher up,' was the reply. At the next story the friend said it was 'very dark there.' 'It will be better, higher up.' And at the top, they came into a pretty, clean sick-room, with light and flowers. A child was dying, and it said to his father, 'Lift me up,' and the father did so; 'Higher, higher,' said the child, and again, 'Higher, higher,' till it was held at the stretch of its father's arms, and its Heavenly Father reached down and took it. Let our prayer be, 'Higher, higher, higher!' 'Nearer my God to Thee, nearer to Thee!' I will look back on this as one of the happiest days of my life, when we talked about Christ. Napoleon struck a medal after a great battle, on one side of which was the date of the battle, and on the other 'I was There;' and we, looking back on this meeting here to-day, will gladly say in heaven itself, 'I was There.'

"God bless you all. We will never all meet again on earth, but very soon WE WILL MEET IN HEAVEN."

The Christian Conflict.[*]

You must all remember that you have THREE TERRIBLE ENEMIES to face. The first is the FLESH, the second the WORLD, and the third the DEVIL. When the children of Israel got through the Red Sea, they began to sing their song of deliverance, and praise God, as if the whole of their trials were over, never thinking of the journey through the wilderness, with all its perils, temptations, and privations, which was before them. You who have been converted must not imagine that your troubles have ceased with your conversion and Red Sea deliverance. We have all got a wilderness journey and a warfare before us, and

---

[*] Being the farewell address to young converts in Edinburgh, 16th January, 1874. Eleven hundred and fifty were present.

we must not forget them, but brace ourselves up for them.

If you turn to Galatians fifth, and read from the sixteenth to the twenty-second verse, you will learn something of your first enemy, *the flesh*. The warfare goes on continually between flesh and spirit. God did not change the flesh at your conversion. It remains still unchanged and unchangeable. That which is born of the flesh remains flesh until it is dropped in the grave, or at Christ's coming; and in the meantime you must pray against the evil passions mentioned in these verses, and keep the old man in the place of death. You must take care not to feed "the old man which is corrupt" by the follies and pursuits of the unconverted world. Read novels, attend the theater, go to the dance, if you want to feed "the old man."

You cannot serve both God and mammon, and the only way you can serve God is by opposing the flesh, and by the Spirit mortifying the deeds of the body. "In me—that is, in my flesh—dwelleth no good thing," says Paul, and this we must always keep in remembrance. Christ is in us; but there is no good thing in the flesh. If we learn *that* fact in the morning of our Christian life, it will be a happy day for us. For a time after I was converted I thought all the conflict was over; but I found it was not so, and so will you.

When God converted us He gave us a new nature —life in Christ—and the flesh lusteth against the Spirit, and the Spirit against the flesh, and *these are contrary* the one to the other.

The flesh will always continue to lust against the Spirit, and you must maintain the conflict resolutely. Ungodly men say they have not that conflict; but the reason is, they have never known the life of God.

There is a story told of a gentleman in our country who had a servant—a negro—we call such Sambo— and he was a converted man, and his master used to banter him about his religion, and to say, "Sambo, you are always talking of the conflict; I don't have any of your groaning and the conflict you talk of." One day they were out hunting. His master blazed away at some ducks, and did not mind the dead ones, but sent Sambo after the wounded ones. "Massa," said he, when he next spoke to him of his warfare, "as you did not care for the dead ducks—you knew you had them; so Satan leaves you all quiet. You are dead, and he lets you alone; but he is after me, because I am wounded, but alive."

I have found, however, that those who try to serve both God and the world have most trouble, and that those who come out boldly for Christ, and turn their backs completely on the world, and are out and out for God, have little or no trouble.

Remember what is said in Philippians iii. 3—"Have no confidence in *the flesh*." Have all the confidence you can in Christ, but have none in yourselves. The moment you put confidence in "*the flesh*," it will bring you into captivity and darkness. Peter had confidence in himself, and it led to his denying his Master. If you are going to work and speak for the Lord Jesus, take care of one thing—do not speak about yourselves. I am disgusted sometimes when I hear men get up at these meetings and talk about themselves, or if they don't get an opportunity of doing it in a speech, they take the chance which a prayer offers, and tell the audience their whole history, when they are ostensibly addressing God. Shun that above all things. When you say or do anything, speak or do it in the name of Jesus Christ, and keep self entirely in the background.

Then will God bless your efforts. When "the flesh" comes and wants you to submit to it, don't listen; but say, "You're not my master; I serve the Lord Christ." "Not I, but Christ;" "Not in the flesh, but in the Spirit," is our happy state. But you need to watch "the flesh" as an enemy; for depend upon it "the flesh" is not dead, and will never be so, until we are in our coffin, or "changed in a moment." I would say to young men: Never get into argument with skeptics or reasoners on doctrine—it will get you into the flesh, and you will never convince them. When Job argued, he went down! The sore boils—his losses—his wife—and all his trials he could stand; but when he got into argument with his friends, "the flesh" came out in all its offensiveness. Do not exhort much in the meetings, but point out what the grace of God has done for you or others, simply and humbly. Talk about the Master, and not about the servant, and people will be always glad to hear you. Let your theme be "*Jesus only.*"

2. THE WORLD.—John xvii. 15, 16: "I pray not that Thou shouldst take them out of the world, but that Thou shouldst keep them from the evil." Remember that you are out of the old creation and into

the new creation. Daniel was kept witnessing for God in Babylon. You must learn to be like a rock in the stream, past which the current flows rapidly, but it is unmoved. You are still in the world, but you are not of the world. You are citizens of another world, and only strangers and pilgrims here. We belong to America; we are only temporary sojourners with you. While here I am an American; so while in the world I belong to heaven—not to America; I live there, that's my home. We have got our naturalization papers out for heaven, and we belong to it alone. What would we do mixing with the joys of this world? We have something better; and as the world is after the best thing, if they see you happy, they will want it. What retards Christianity so much is the Church getting mixed up with the world. People may think that if they go into the world a little—attend the theater, opera, balls—they can get the world drawn into religious meetings; but it is a delusion. Though we throw a piece of fresh beef into the sea, we don't make it fresh; so, though we go into the world ever so little, we don't change it for the better, but it will change us for the worse. We must come right out, and be separate.

Those who are separate draw many with them to heaven; while one worldly Christian deludes and drags many down to hell.

It was the mixed multitude that came with Israel out of Egypt that made them lust after the things of Egypt, and loathe the manna which is called angels' food. If you mix with the world, it will give you a distaste for divine things, and you will be both useless and unhappy.

Worldly Christians are very unhappy. If you do not leave the world entirely, with its novels, theaters, and operas, it will never leave you, and you will be poor, miserable Christians. But if you leave the world entirely, you will have ten thousand times more enjoyment than you could have ever had in the world's pleasures. For eighteen years I have had something better. I enjoy every year more than the preceding, so true is it that if you give up anything for Christ, He makes it up to you many times. His love smile, His gracious approval, is more than all the world. But are children not to play at all on becoming Christians? These boys must not think that I am saying they may not go and play their cricket and their games of ball, but I say that when they are at play, at these healthy exercises, they must always keep in mind that they are Christians, and they must not stand to hear the name of the Master whom they serve profaned by their companions, but leave them entirely if they do not desist.

3. THE DEVIL.—Now look at 2 Corinthians xi. 14: "And no marvel, for *Satan* himself is transformed into an angel of light." It would be well to take a Concordance and look up all the names of the devil. You would find him called the great red dragon, and you would be frightened for him as such, but not as an angel of light. And mark you, Satan does not, as many think, come in a hideous form, in which he will be known, but sometimes even as an angel of light. You want to be on your guard against him, for in him we have a terrible enemy, and all the more dangerous that he can transform himself into an angel of light.

The devil never got away any one who has been converted; but he may make them lose their happiness and spoil their testimony in the world. Samson was strong; but Satan got hold of him, and ruined his testimony to the world. You will find he is called "the prince of this world" in John xiv. 30.

Christ is not the King of this world just now; they cast Him out, and slew Him. And that is a very good reason why we should break off from this world, and have only to do with that one where Christ is on the throne. Bear in mind your three enemies—the flesh, the world, and the devil—who would fain bring us down to hell, and, if they cannot do that, keep us in disquiet and dispeace. But we have three friends for us who are greater than the enemies against us—God the Father, God the Son, and God the Holy Ghost, and all the hosts of heaven. They are able to keep us, and beat back the doubts and fears and evil thoughts suggested by our enemies. When Elisha's servant's eyes were opened, he saw the mountains full of horses and chariots about them—all the hosts of heaven on their side. There are more for us than all who can be against us. Some young converts are much distressed about evil thoughts. Now, the sin lies not in them coming into your mind, but in your harboring them. As one has said, "We cannot help the birds from flying over our heads, but we can prevent them building their nests in our hair." Ask God's help to beat those evil thoughts off. In ourselves we have no power against those terrible enemies; but we have got Christ, the Lion of the tribe of Judah, in whom is our strength, and through Him we may have constant victory.

Turn to Exodus xvii. 6 : " Behold, I will stand before thee there upon the rock in Horeb; and thou shalt smite the rock, and there shall come water out of it, that the people may drink. And Moses did so in the sight of the elders of Israel." Here we have the Trinity. The rock is Christ; the water the Holy Ghost: and "I" is God the Father. The water is everything. There is refreshment, and it follows us; for 1 Cor. x. 4 reads, " They drank of that spiritual Rock that went with them; and that Rock was Christ." There is a tunnel over the Rocky Mountains, and the bore is so contracted that there is no room for a man to escape if two trains were coming alongside of each other; but they have cut niches in the solid rock, into which a person may go and be safe. Two children were thus caught one day—a sister and her little brother; and after she got her brother into one of these niches, she went to the one on the opposite side, and just as the trains were about to whisk past them she cried to her little brother, " Cling close to the rock." The trains passed, and they were safe in the clefts of the rock. This is all you want, dear young Christians; cling close to the Rock of your salvation—Jesus your Saviour. That Rock which is a place both for spiritual rest and refreshment, "that Rock which followeth you, that Rock which is Christ" (1 Cor. x. 4). Get good footing on that Rock: as the Irishman said, you may tremble on the Rock, but the Rock will never tremble, however much the waves may beat against it.

And never forget where God found you. The Lord's portion is His people; Jacob is the lot of His inheritance. He found him in a desert land, and in the waste, howling wilderness. He led him about, He instructed him, He kept him as the apple of His eye. There are *four* precious things here — God *found you;* He *leads you about, instructs you,* and *keeps you* as the apple of His eye.

A story of thrilling interest was lately recorded in an American weekly illustrated paper.

The Spanish authorities in Cuba had arrested a man who, though born in England, was a naturalized United States citizen. He was charged with conspiracy against the Government, and ordered to be shot. But the consuls of both England and America

SAFETY BY THE BLOOD. 443

believed the man to be innocent, and used all the persuasion and entreaty in their power for his release, but the proud Spaniards haughtily disregarded their petition.

The hour of execution had now arrived, and a company of soldiers were drawn up in line. The condemned English-American marched out before them, calmly awaiting his fate. He stood at the foot of the grave, already dug, his coat off, and his hands pinioned behind him. The officer ordered his men to load, and at the word "present," they brought their rifles to their shoulders, awaiting the word of command to fire.

In the awful suspense, suddenly there sprang forward from the bystanders the two consuls; the one drawing from his breast the Stars and Stripes, wrapped it right round the prisoner, whilst the other threw over him the Union Jack. The consuls now stood on either side, defying the Spaniards, who dared not fire on the flags of two of the mightiest nations under heaven, and the man was released, and proved his innocence to the satisfaction of the authorities.

Well may the Christian exclaim, "Oh, the security and the blessedness of being enveloped in the blood-stained banner of the Cross!" or, in the triumphant words of Paul in Romans viii.: "Who shall lay anything to the charge of God's elect?" His banner over us is love! He that toucheth a child of God touches the apple of His eye. Always keep in mind that it takes the same power to keep you that it took to convert you.

"Let us run with patience the race that is set before us, looking unto Jesus, the author and the finisher of our faith." When I was a boy, I used to try to describe a straight path through the snow in a field by looking down at my feet, but it turned out to be a zigzag, because I was looking down at my feet. The way to make a straight path would be to look at an object beyond; and so in this passage we are directed to have our eye on the mark at the right hand of the Majesty in the heavens, and be "*looking unto Jesus.*"

In Col. ii. 6, there are seven things enjoined. The first thing we have to do is to *receive* Christ, then to *walk* in Him, be *rooted* in Him, and be *built* up in Him. We will then be *complete* in Him, and be *buried* with Him in baptism, and be *raised* with Him.

In our country there are sometimes seen great

trees blown over and torn up by the roots, and the occasion of it was the shallow soil. So it is with many professors—they for a while believe, but in time of temptation they fall away, because they had not been rooted in Christ. Be rooted in Christ, and built up in Him as ye have been taught. This points to the inward and outward growth of the Christian. The only way to keep from falling is to grow.

Turn to 1 John iv. 9, 10, and you will see that Christ was manifested to give us *life*, put away our sins; and herein is love, that we then got *peace*, and God dwells in us; and this is *power*, and we will have boldness in the day of judgment, because as He is, so are we in this world.

You will find in Heb. ii. 18, that Christ is *able to succor* them that are tempted; and in Rom. xiv. 4, that He is "able to make us stand." Daniel, Moses, Elijah, were made able to stand. Remember that word "able." Heb. vii. 25, "Wherefore He is able also to save them to the uttermost that come unto God by Him, seeing He ever liveth to make intercession for them." "He is *able* to make all grace abound toward you" (2 Cor. ix. 8) and able to help you to work for Him; and "He is able to keep that which we have committed to Him against that day" (2 Tim. i. 12). What gives us confidence in the Bank of England? Because it is able to pay every demand made upon it. What gives us confidence in a certain line of steamers? Because they have never lost a single passenger; they have a reputation for safety, and we commit ourselves to them with all confidence; and our life is surely safe when "our life is hid with Christ in God."

Be strong in faith, for what God has promised He is able to perform (Rom. iv. 20). We may have the most perfect confidence in the God who has promised. The three men in Babylon who were threatened with the fiery furnace would not bow down to the idol, but said, with all confident boldness, "Our God, whom we serve, is *able* to deliver us from the burning fiery furnace; and He will deliver us out of thine hand, O king. But if not, be it known unto thee, O king, that we will not serve thy gods, nor worship the golden image thou hast set up" (Dan. iii. 17, 18). They were cast into the furnace; but one like the Son of God walked with them, and they came forth unhurt "from the midst of the fire." And so will we come forth from every trial, for our

God is able to deliver us. He numbers the hairs of our head; no one cares for us so. When Joseph was ill-treated and sold into Egypt, it is said, "God was with him;" and He delivered him marvelously. Trust in God, like Paul, who says, "Who delivered us from so great a death, and doth deliver; in whom we trust that He will yet deliver us" (2 Cor. i. 10).

Bear in mind that God never leaves you, and that if you ever get away from Him it is because you have left Him. And if ever you do leave Jesus to go back to the world, do with Him as you would when going to leave any earthly friend. Go into your closet and say, "Lord Jesus, I am about to leave Thee, and go back to the world. I thank Thee for all Thy kindness, and for the joy I have had since I knew Thee; and now, as I do not mean to come to Thee any more, I have come to say farewell." The bare idea of such a thing is intolerable.

"He is able to do exceeding abundantly above all that we ask or think" (Eph. iii. 20); and "He is able to keep you from falling, and to present you faultless before the presence of His glory with exceeding joy," (Jude 24). He is able to keep these young converts.

The next time you and I all meet, we will be

before Him, and that will be a glorious day, "presented faultless before the presence of His glory." May God grant that that may be your end and mine! We need not fall if we put our trust in Him who is able to keep us from falling. I remember Mr. Sankey reading out of the papers the obituary of one who had been holding up Christ, and it ran thus: "*He was a true herald of the cross; he died with the shout of victory on his lips and the trump of God in his hands.*" Let it be so written of us when we go hence. Live in loving fellowship with Jesus, treating Him as a personal friend, and He will never leave you nor forsake you.

As long as we live we never shall forget these blessed happy days we have spent with you in Edinburgh, and I hope we shall meet you all at the Lamb's right hand in the day when He makes up His jewels; and so shall we ever be with the Lord. Amen.

PRAYER.*

I suppose there has been no word on Christians' lips so frequently at this time as the word "PRAYER," and there is not one in this hall who has not thought

---

* Delivered at the noon prayer-meeting, Edinb., Jan. 6, 1874.

often, during the last forty-eight hours, of the importance of prayer.

During this week of prayer, they are a great many not only thinking about it, but talking about it. When there is a special interest and awakening in the community on the subject of religion, then it is that a great many skeptics and infidels, and a great many mere nominal professors of Christianity—we will not judge them—begin talking against "prayer."

They say, "The author of the world doesn't change His plans because of these prayers. The world goes right on. You cannot move God to change His mind or His doings." You hear this on every side. These young converts hear it. I have no doubt that many are staggered by it, and when you kneel down you say, "Is it a fact that God answers prayer? Is there anything in it?"

I think it would do us good in the week of prayer to take the word "PRAYER," and run through the Bible tracing it out. Read about nothing else. I think you would be perfectly amazed if you took up the word "*prayer*," and counted the cases in the Bible where people are recorded as praying, and God answering their prayers.

A great many think it is only the perfectly righteous and pure that pray. But you remember who it was who prayed in this fashion, " Lord remember me when Thou comest into Thy Kingdom." You remember that Christ answered the dying thief's prayer.

We cannot but notice that every man of God spoken of in the Bible was a man of *prayer*. You have therefore very good authority and encouragement for asking God to hear your prayers, and for praying on behalf of others, as we are daily requested to do. Many are surprised at these requests. But many mothers and fathers are rejoicing that they sent them in. The prayers offered up here have been answered, and their children have been saved.

Last night I was more confirmed in my views regarding the power of *prayer* than ever. "This is all excitement," some say; "it is got up by earnest appeals that work on the feelings of people, and move their impulses, making them uneasy and anxious." Now, for example, there was nothing said last night to speak of, and I never was more disgusted with myself than I was on Sunday night. It seemed as if I could not preach the Gospel, as if my tongue would not speak. But still the number of inquirers was extraordinary.

Last night, when there was no speaking at all, and when I just came in and asked that any inquirers might follow me into the moderator's room, taking a few with me, and expecting to come in and ask out a few more when I had seen these, the number was so great that came out without solicitation that I did not need to return. I saw over a hundred inquirers last night, and there were from fifty to seventy that I had to close the door on, being unable to see them.

A great many who have not been at the meetings at all, have been converted in their own homes. God is working, not we. Oh! that we would keep ourselves down in the dust, and every one of us get out of the way, and let God work. It would be so easy for Him to go into every dwelling in Edinburgh, and convict and convert ten thousand souls.

Look at the 6th verse of the 4th chapter of Philippians. "Be careful for nothing, but in everything"—mark that—"by prayer and supplication, with thanksgiving, let your requests be made known unto God." He doesn't say He will answer all, but He says, "And the peace of God, which passeth all understanding, shall keep your hearts and minds through Jesus Christ."

He tells us to make our wants known ; to make our requests known to Him by prayer and supplication. It is right to come and make our requests known. He has told us to come and pray for the conversion of souls.

It is said by many people that God does not do anything supernatural in answer to prayer; that the God of nature moves right on and never changes His decrees. Read the first six verses of the 20th chapter of 2d Kings, and see—" In those days was Hezekiah sick unto death: and the prophet Isaiah, the son of Amoz, came to him, and said unto him, Thus saith the Lord, Set thine house in order; for thou shalt die, and not live. Then he turned his face to the wall, and prayed unto the Lord, saying, I beseech Thee, O Lord, remember now how I have walked before Thee in truth, and with a perfect heart, and have done that which is good in Thy sight. And Hezekiah wept sore. And it came to pass, afore Isaiah was gone out into the middle court, that the word of the Lord came to him, saying, Turn again, and tell Hezekiah, the captain of my people, Thus saith the Lord, the God of David, thy father, I have heard thy prayer, I have seen thy tears, behold I will heal thee; on the third day thou shalt go up unto the house of the Lord, and I will add unto thy days fifteen years; and I will deliver thee and this city out of the hand of the King of Assyria; and I will defend this city for mine own sake, and for my servant David's sake." Was not that a direct answer to prayer? Hezekiah was only praying for his own life; we are come together to pray for the life of others, and not their temporal but their eternal welfare. He was not praying for Christ's sake as we now do, but we can come to-day and ask God to save the souls of men for Christ's sake, not only for our sake, but for the sake of the beloved Son. He loves to honor that Son, and to see Christ honored. We can come now and ask Him to save souls, that it might bring glory and honor to the Son of His bosom, and glory and honor to the Son He delights to honor. "I will," He says to Hezekiah, "defend the city for mine own sake, and for my servant David's sake." That is only one instance.

Look also at Daniel praying. It was his prayers that took the Jews back to Jerusalem. It was his prayers that turned Nebuchadnezzar to the God of

Israel, and brought Gabriel down from heaven to tell him he was greatly beloved. He had power with God.

See also how God answered Jacob's prayers and Isaac's prayers. All through the Bible we have records of the answers to prayers. It would be terrible to think that God did not delight to answer prayer.

Turn to the 20th chapter of 2d Chronicles. There we read that the Moabites, the Ammonites, and others coming against Jehoshaphat, he was afraid, "and set himself to seek the Lord," and that afterwards Judah "gathered themselves together to ask help of the Lord." That is what we want—to seek the Lord not only here in the public assembly, but alone. If you have got an unconverted friend, and are anxious that he should be saved, go and tell it privately to Jesus, and if a blessing does not come, like Jehoshaphat, spend a few days in fasting, and prayer, and humiliation. "If when evil cometh upon us, as the sword, judgment, pestilence, or famine, we stand before this house, and in Thy presence (for Thy name is in this house), and cry unto Thee in our affliction, then Thou wilt hear and help."

When I go into the streets, and see the terrible wickedness, and blasphemy, and drunkenness that is in them, it seems dark, but I look up and think that God can repel those dark waves of sin and iniquity. Let us pray that God will bless this land of Scotland, bless and save all the people in it. It would be a great thing for us, but very little for God. May God give us faith!

www.ingramcontent.com/pod-product-compliance
Lightning Source LLC
Chambersburg PA
CBHW032010300426
44117CB00008B/975